CISCO SYSTEMS

Cisco Networking Simplified

Paul Della Maggiora

Jim Doherty

Illustrations by Nathan Clement

Cisco Press

800 East 96th Street

Indianapolis, IN 46240 USA

Cisco Networking Simplified

Paul Della Maggiora

Jim Doherty

Copyright© 2003 Cisco Systems, Inc.

Published by:
Cisco Press
800 East 96th Street
Indianapolis, IN 46240 USA

Printed in the United States of America 8 9 0

Eighth Printing July 2004

Library of Congress Cataloging-in-Publication Number: 2002113529

ISBN: 1-58720-074-0

Warning and Disclaimer

This book is designed to provide information about Cisco networking. Every effort has been made to make this book as complete and as accurate as possible, but no warranty or fitness is implied.

The information is provided on an "as is" basis. The author, Cisco Press, and Cisco Systems, Inc. shall have neither liability nor responsibility to any person or entity with respect to any loss or damages arising from the information contained in this book or from the use of the discs or programs that may accompany it.

The opinions expressed in this book belong to the author and are not necessarily those of Cisco Systems, Inc.

Feedback Information

At Cisco Press, our goal is to create in-depth technical books of the highest quality and value. Each book is crafted with care and precision, undergoing rigorous development that involves the unique expertise of members from the professional technical community.

Readers' feedback is a natural continuation of this process. If you have any comments regarding how we could improve the quality of this book, or otherwise alter it to better suit your needs, you can contact us through e-mail at feedback@ciscopress.com. Please make sure to include the book title and ISBN in your message.

We greatly appreciate your assistance.

Publisher
John Wait

Editor-in-Chief
John Kane

Cisco Representative
Anthony Wolfenden

Cisco Press Program Manager
Sonia Torres Chavez

Manager, Marketing Communications, Cisco Systems
Scott Miller

Cisco Marketing Program Manager
Edie Quiroz

Production Manager
Patrick Kanouse

Senior Editor
Sheri Cain

Copy Editor
Kris Simmons

Technical Editors
Mark Gallo
Ron Kovac
Daniel Tulledge

Team Coordinator
Tammi Barnett

Book Designer
Mark Shirar

Cover Designer
Louisa Adair

Indexer
Tim Wright

CISCO SYSTEMS

Corporate Headquarters
Cisco Systems, Inc.
170 West Tasman Drive
San Jose, CA 95134-1706
USA
www.cisco.com
Tel: 408 526-4000
     800 553-NETS (6387)
Fax: 408 526-4100

European Headquarters
Cisco Systems International BV
Haarlerbergpark
Haarlerbergweg 13-19
1101 CH Amsterdam
The Netherlands
www-europe.cisco.com
Tel: 31 0 20 357 1000
Fax: 31 0 20 357 1100

Americas Headquarters
Cisco Systems, Inc.
170 West Tasman Drive
San Jose, CA 95134-1706
USA
www.cisco.com
Tel: 408 526-7660
Fax: 408 527-0883

Asia Pacific Headquarters
Cisco Systems, Inc.
Capital Tower
168 Robinson Road
#22-01 to #29-01
Singapore 068912
www.cisco.com
Tel: +65 6317 7777
Fax: +65 6317 7799

Cisco Systems has more than 200 offices in the following countries and regions.
Addresses, phone numbers, and fax numbers are listed on the
Cisco.com Web site at www.cisco.com/go/offices.

Argentina • Australia • Austria • Belgium • Brazil • Bulgaria • Canada • Chile • China PRC
Colombia • Costa Rica • Croatia • Czech Republic • Denmark • Dubai, UAE • Finland • France
Germany • Greece • Hong Kong SAR • Hungary • India • Indonesia • Ireland • Israel • Italy • Japan
Korea • Luxembourg • Malaysia • Mexico • The Netherlands • New Zealand • Norway • Peru
Philippines • Poland • Portugal • Puerto Rico • Romania • Russia • Saudi Arabia • Scotland
Singapore • Slovakia • Slovenia • South Africa • Spain • Sweden • Switzerland • Taiwan • Thailand
Turkey • Ukraine • United Kingdom • United States • Venezuela • Vietnam • Zimbabwe

Cisco Press offers excellent discounts on this book when ordered in quantity for bulk purchases or special sales. For more information, please contact:

U.S. Corporate and Government Sales
1-800-382-3419
corpsales@pearsontechgroup.com
For sales outside of the U.S., please contact:
International Sales
1-317-581-3793
international@pearsontechgroup.com

Trademark Acknowledgments

All terms mentioned in this book that are known to be trademarks or service marks have been appropriately capitalized. Cisco Press or Cisco Systems, Inc. cannot attest to the accuracy of this information. Use of a term in this book should not be regarded as affecting the validity of any trademark or service mark.

About the Technical Reviewers

Mark Gallo is a technical manager with America Online where he leads a group of engineers responsible for the design and deployment of the domestic corporate intranet. His network certifications include Cisco CCNP and Cisco CCDP. He has led several engineering groups responsible for designing and implementing enterprise LANs and international IP networks. He has a B.S. in electrical engineering from the University of Pittsburgh. Mark resides in northern Virginia with his wife, Betsy, and son, Paul.

Dr. Ron Kovac is currently employed with the Center for Information and Communication Sciences at Ball State University in Muncie, Indiana. The Center prepares graduate students in the field of telecommunications. Previous to this, Dr. Kovac was the telecommunication manager for the State of New York and an executive director for a large computing center located on the east coast. Dr. Kovac's previous studies include electrical engineering and education. Dr. Kovac has numerous publications in both the education and telecommunications field, speaks worldwide on issues related to telecommunications, and holds numerous certifications, including the CCNA, CCAI, and the almost complete CCNP.

Dan Tulledge is an Information Technology industry veteran with more than 20 years of IT experience. Dan is currently a technical marketing engineer with Cisco Systems Enterprise Solutions Engineering (ESE) group in Research Triangle Park, NC. With Cisco ESE, Dan has worked on a variety of solutions including IPCC, 802.1x, SAN, content/data center networking, wireless/mobile networking, video, VPN, and various industry-specific solutions. Prior to Cisco ESE, Dan worked with the Cisco Mobile Wireless Group and the Cisco Interworks Business Division. With MWG, Dan submitted a patent on a device to connect personal-area networks to wireless LANs and WANs. Prior to working with Cisco, Dan worked at AlliedSignal (now Honeywell) as a principle network design and performance engineer for the AlliedSignal global network group and with IBM as a networking and systems programming consultant for large financial, manufacturing, and retail customers.

Dedications

I would like to thank my family and friends for their support and encouragement and for putting up with my limited time and attention during the last six months. I would also like to thank my friend and coauthor Paul Della Maggiora, who poured a great deal of energy into this project with me and still managed to keep it fun. I would like to dedicate this book to my wife, Katie, who has always believed in me, even when there was little reason to do so.

—Jim Doherty

Paul: Everlasting love to Christine, Max, and Adam for putting up with my work on yet another book. Thanks to Barry, Mike, and Doug for their advice and guidance. Thanks to Peter, Dan, and Brad for the same. Shout out to the Smokin' Goats, "crazy like fox." Most of all, thanks to Jim Doherty for his diligence and excitement, which has made this book fun to write and something to be proud of, despite the whole "I have a non-ivy-league MBA" nonsense. Now on to Everquest and more sleepless nights…

—Paul Della Maggiora

Acknowledgments

Jim and Paul would like to thank the following people who offered technical advice and clarity, developed the concepts and phrases, and in some cases offered their original presentation material for inclusion in this book: Connie Varner, Gene Arantowicz, Neil Anderson, Joel King, Brian Cox, Bruce McMurdo, Lou Ronnou, Steve Schubert, Stuart Hamilton, Mauricio Arregoces, James Christopher, Ed Collins, Jonathan Donaldson, Mohammed Darwish, Stefano Giorcelli, Alan Glowacki, Graham Gudgin, May Kongfon, Chris Miller, Todd Truitt, Ian Foo, Ed Lopez, Shannon McFarland, Mark Montenez, Chetan Sharan, Tim Szgeti, Dean Rogers, Shannon McFarland, Ian Foo, and Derrick Southall. There were many others who made contributions and we apologize for being unable to mention everyone by name. If you feel you should have been named here, please call Paul at home and ask for a free copy of this book.

A very special thanks to our technical reviewers, Dan Tulledge, Mark Gallo, and Ron Kovac, who didn't provide any original content but felt comfortable enough with us to trash our work and really hurt our feelings. Kidding aside, their commitment, attention to detail, and honest feedback and critiques were invaluable and greatly appreciated and have made this book better than it would have been without their input. Thank you all.

Endless thanks to our Illustrator, Nathan Clement of Stickman Studios, who was able take the crazy pictures in our minds and actually get them on paper. Nathan's work and artistic vision took this project to a level beyond what we could have achieved without him.

We would also like to thank the good people at Cisco Press. Mark Shirar did a fantastic job with the layout concept and thematic icons used throughout this book. Thanks also to John Kane and Patrick Kanouse, who were behind this project from day one, providing great feedback and suggestions, and pretty much giving us everything we asked for. You guys made us feel like divas.

Finally, we would also like to thank all the men and women of Cisco Systems employees, partners, customers, and Cisco Networking Academy Program students. It is their innovation and hard work that have made the exciting technology presented in this book become a reality.

Table of Contents

Introduction

Welcome and thank you for taking a look at this book! Unlike that vast array of networking books written by geeks for geeks, we have written this book for you and for anyone wanting to understand the computer-networking phenomenon that has taken the world by storm. We understand that the vast majority of people working in this industry are not networking experts and that it is difficult to understand complex technical and business issues before knowing the answers to such questions as, "How does the web work?," "What is a router?," and "What is an IP address?"

Whether you are a home computer user who has just purchased a broadband Internet connection or a company executive who wants to understand what your IT staff is talking about, this book is for you.

If you've decided you want to make a career change or you are in school pursuing a Cisco certification, we believe that this book will serve both as a good primer, introducing the concepts of networking in clear and simple graphical terms, and as a useful reference book as you grow in your career.

Keeping It Simple, Keeping It Real

We, the authors, remember what it was like when first approaching the dizzying array of technologies, concepts, and jargon, and we have worked hard to remove the clutter, demystify the lingo, and organize topics into simple, easy-to-understand concepts. We also wanted to finally explain to our mothers what we do for a living. (They think we're both special, by the way.)

Working at Cisco Systems is a great experience. We are surrounded by the best and brightest in the industry, and we have access to people who have literally changed the way business is conducted—and the way people all over the world interact and communicate. Every year at Cisco is a roller-coaster of new technologies, new customers, and new ideas that are constantly changing. It is difficult sometimes to keep up with it all. It is more difficult still to walk into this industry and get caught up. This book is a result of our efforts to distill the useful concepts from the technological noise and share them with college graduates, Cisco Networking Academy Program students, and our own colleagues.

Upon sharing our early work, we realized we might be on to something. More talks with college interns, Cisco Academy students, and non-technical executives at Cisco customers indicated demand for a show-me-what-it-is type of book. This book provides at-a-glance text and illustrations that explain a particular concept or technology in plain and simple language. The material illustrates how these concepts relate to our everyday lives.

So How Do I Use This Thing?

The book is divided into small bites for each concept or technology. Each section contains some or all of the following: a text write-up, topic at-a-glance pages, and whiteboard illustrations of relevant concepts. The text provides a quick and easy introduction to the topic, so you should generally read it first. Useful for future reference are the topic at-a-glance pages, which illustrate core concepts. And the whiteboard illustrations demonstrate important concepts simply and graphically.

The book is ordered from general and global concepts in the front to more detailed networking topics in the back. You can digest each section in one sitting. You can read the book from front to back or look up a single topic that interests you.

The illustrations and descriptions serve to answer the primary questions, "What is it?" and "Why should I care?" We used large, friendly pictures and avoided the temptation to dive down into nitty-gritty details.

We had a good time writing and illustrating this book and hope you find it useful, entertaining, and, if we really hit the mark, indispensable.

Part I

How the Internet Works

At the beginning of the 1990s, www.something.com would have meant nothing to people. Since then, a whole new communication medium has changed the way people around the world communicate with each other. The Internet has done no less than transform the world into a new "age": the Information Age.

Where computers and networking were previously reserved for geeks and bean counters, everyone has been touched by the Internet revolution. E-mail and the World Wide Web are nearly as prevalent as phones and classified ads. Consumers can research or purchase items 24 hours a day. Industries (such as retail, advertising, and music) have experienced radical shifts in business models. Businesses can conduct transactions with each other with no human interaction.

That's great. But...what is the Internet? How does the Internet know where to send your e-mail? What actually happens when you type http://www.cisco.com/? What is happening when everyone wants to see some late-breaking news event and the website is inaccessible? Could students around the world actually use the Internet to attend the same class?

Part I addresses these questions concerning the Internet and how it enables worldwide communications, both through the technologies in use and the applications that have evolved.

How Computers Communicate

The OSI Model

At some point, everyone involved with networking comes across a reference to the Open System Interconnection (OSI) seven-layer model. What is the seven-layer model, and why is it relevant?

The OSI seven-layer model describes the functions for computers to communicate with each other. The International Organization for Standardization (ISO) published this model in 1984 to describe a layered approach for providing network services using a reference set of protocols called OSI. The basis of the definition is that each of the seven layers has a particular function it must perform, and each layer needs to know how to communicate with only the layers immediately above and below it.

At the time of the definition of the OSI networking model, there was little standardization among network equipment manufacturers. Customers generally had to standardize on a particular vendor's hardware and software to have devices communicate with each other.

As a result of the ISO's and other standardization efforts, networking customers can mix and match hardware when running open standards protocols, such as Internet Protocol (IP).

Open Versus Proprietary Systems

The ISO's efforts are an example of the constant struggle for balancing technical openness with competitive advantage. For an individual network-equipment vendor, it is to his advantage to develop technologies that other companies cannot copy or interact with. Proprietary systems let a vendor claim competitive advantage as well as collect fees from other vendors it might choose to share the technology with.

However, proprietary systems can complicate the network administrator's work by locking him into one vendor, reducing competitiveness and allowing the vendor to charge higher prices. If the vendor goes out of business or abandons the technology, no one is left to support or enhance the technology.

The alternative is an open-systems approach in which standards bodies, such as the Institute of Electrical and Electronic Engineers (IEEE) or ISO, define technologies. Ethernet, Transmission Control Protocol/Internet Protocol (TCP/IP), and spanning tree are examples of technologies that became standards. Any network-equipment vendor can implement an open standard.

The OSI seven-layer model was an attempt to provide a model on how open network standards could interoperate with each other and proprietary technologies.

The Seven Layers

The following list outlines the seven layers of the OSI model:

Layer 7, application—The application layer provides the networking services to a user or application. For example, when sending an e-mail, the application layer begins the process of taking the data from the e-mail program and preparing it to be put onto a network.

Layer 6, presentation—The presentation layer provides formatting services for the application layer.

Layer 5, session—The session layer manages connections between hosts. If the application on one host needs to talk to the application on another, the application layer sets the connection up and ensures resources are available to facilitate the connection. Networking folks tend to refer to Layers 5–7 collectively as the application layers.

Layer 4, transport—The transport layer is responsible for taking the chunk of data from the application and preparing it for shipment onto the network. Prepping data for transport involves chopping the chunk into smaller pieces and adding a header that identifies the sending and receiving application (otherwise known as port numbers). Each piece of data and associated headers is called a packet. Content switches operate at this level.

Layer 3, network—The network layer is responsible for adding another header to the front of the packet, which identifies the unique source and destination address. The process of routing IP packets occurs at this level.

Layer 2, data link—The data link layer is responsible for adding another header, which identifies the particular Layer 3 protocol used and the source and destination hardware addresses (also known as Media Access Control (MAC) addresses). At this point, the packet is complete and ready to go onto the network. Ethernet switching and bridging operate at this level.

Layer 1, physical—The physical layer is responsible for converting the packet into binary signals to be transmitted over the network. The actual physical network can be copper, fiber, or wireless radio frequency. This layer also provides a method for the receiving computer to validate that the data was not corrupted during transmission.

The combination of the seven layers is often called a stack. A transmitting workstation traverses the stack from Layer 7 down to Layer 1, converting the application data into network signals. The receiving workstation traverses the stack in the opposite direction: from Layer 1 to Layer 7. It converts the received transmission back into a chunk of data for the running application.

Although there was an attempt to make OSI a practical and implemented networking protocol, the OSI seven-layer model is mainly a reference for other protocols. Most protocols do not fit the seven layers precisely (such as TCP/IP), but the same principles apply.

At-A-Glance—OSI Model

Why Should I Care About the OSI Model?

The Open Systems Interconnection (OSI) model is a conceptual framework that defines network functions and schemes. The framework simplifies complex network interactions by breaking them into simple modular elements. This open standards approach allows many independent developers to work on separate network functions, which you can then apply in a "plug-and-play" manner.

The OSI model serves as a guideline for creating and implementing network standards, devices, and internetworking schemes. Advantages of using the OSI model include the following:

- Breaking up interrelated aspects of network operation into less complex elements

- Enabling companies and individual engineers to specialize with design and development efforts in modular functions

- Providing standard interfaces for plug-and-play compatibility and multivendor integration

OSI Layers and Definitions

The OSI Model consists of the following layers:

Layer 7: Application
Layer 6: Presentation
Layer 5: Session
Layer 4: Transport
Layer 3: Network
Layer 2: Data Link
Layer 1: Physical

The four lower layers (referred to as the data flow layers) define connection protocols and methods for exchanging data.

The three upper layers (referred to as the application layers) define how the applications within the end stations communicate with each other and with users.

Mnemonics can help you memorize the layers and their order. Here's an example:

Princess Di Never Tried Slapping Prince Albert

What Are the Problems to Solve?

An OSI layer can communicate with only the layers immediately above and below it on the stack and with its peer layer on another device. A process passes information (including data and stack instructions) down the stack, across the network, and back up the stack on the peer device.

Extra Layers?

Discussions among technical purists often lead to philosophic debates that can quickly derail otherwise productive meetings. You might hear these discussions referred to as Layer 8 (Political) and Layer 9 (Technical Religion) debates. Although they are not really part of the OSI model, they are usually the underlying cause of heated technology arguments.

At-A-Glance—OSI Model, Continued

Communicating Between Layers

Each layer of the OSI model uses its own protocol to communicate with its peer layer in the destination device. The OSI model specifies how each layer communicates with the layers above and below it, allowing vendors to focus on specific layers that work with any other vendors' adjacent layers.

Layers exchange information using *protocol data units (PDUs)*. PDUs include control information (in the form of headers and trailers) and user data. PDUs include different types of information as they go up or down the layers (referred to as the stack). To clarify where the PDU is on the stack, it gets a distinct name at each of the lower levels.

In other words, a PDU that is a packet includes network layer control information in addition to the data and control information contained at the transport layer. Similarly, a frame is a PDU that includes data link layer control information in addition to the upper-layer control information and data. The PDUs at the data link and physical layers are referred to as segments and bits, respectively.

Encapsulation

The process of passing data down the stack using PDUs is *data encapsulation*.

Encapsulation works as follows: When a layer receives a PDU, it encapsulates the PDU with a header and trailer and then passes the PDU down to the next layer.

The peer layer on the remote device reads the control information that is added to the PDU.

De-Encapsulation

De-encapsulation, the opposite of encapsulation, is the process of passing information up the stack. When a layer receives a PDU, it does the following:

1. First, it reads the control information provided by the peer source device.

2. The layer strips the control information (header) from the frame.

3. Finally, it processes the data (usually passing it up the stack).

Each subsequent layer performs this same de-encapsulation process.

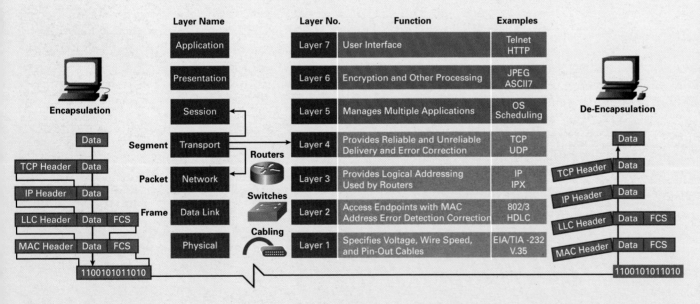

How Websites Deal with Traffic Spikes

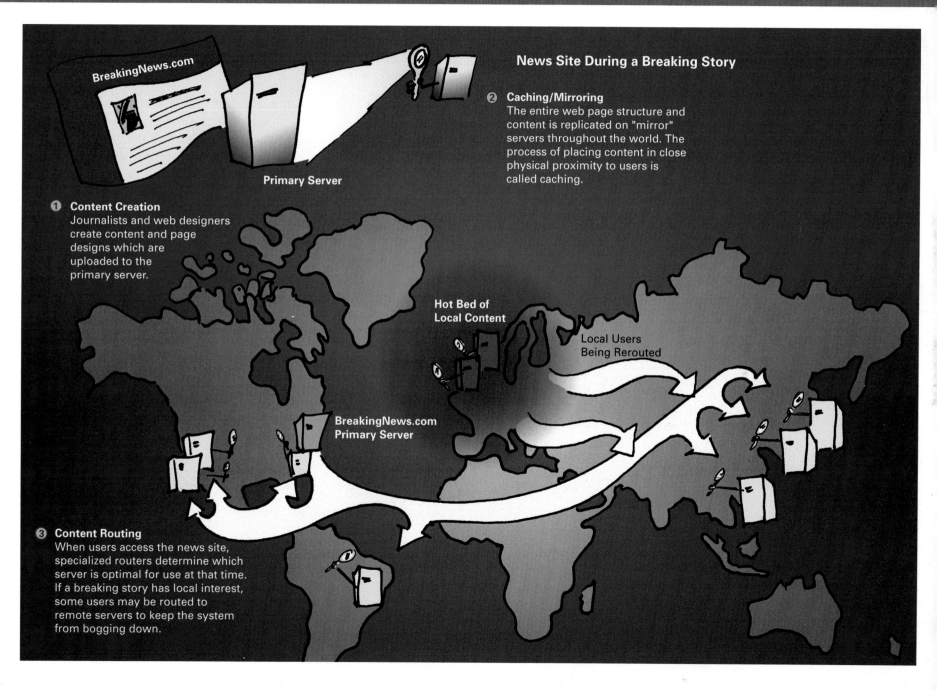

News Site During a Breaking Story

BreakingNews.com

Primary Server

❷ Caching/Mirroring
The entire web page structure and content is replicated on "mirror" servers throughout the world. The process of placing content in close physical proximity to users is called caching.

❶ Content Creation
Journalists and web designers create content and page designs which are uploaded to the primary server.

Hot Bed of Local Content

Local Users Being Rerouted

BreakingNews.com Primary Server

❸ Content Routing
When users access the news site, specialized routers determine which server is optimal for use at that time. If a breaking story has local interest, some users may be routed to remote servers to keep the system from bogging down.

Internet Infrastructure: How It All Connects

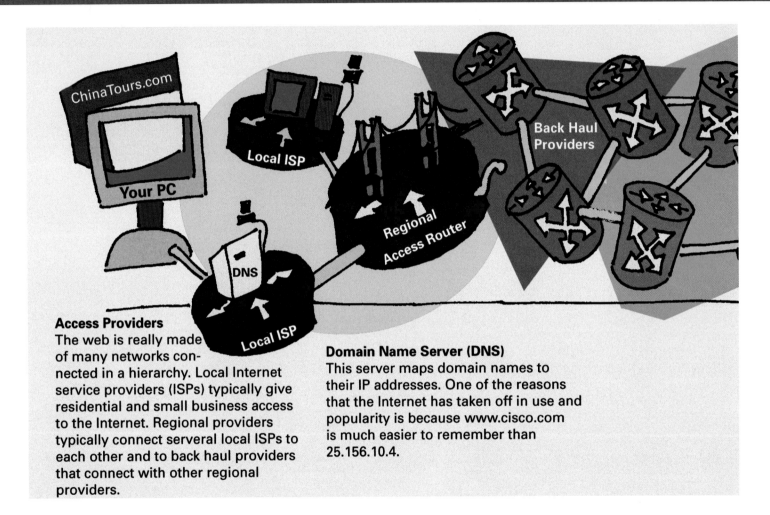

Access Providers
The web is really made of many networks connected in a hierarchy. Local Internet service providers (ISPs) typically give residential and small business access to the Internet. Regional providers typically connect serveral local ISPs to each other and to back haul providers that connect with other regional providers.

Domain Name Server (DNS)
This server maps domain names to their IP addresses. One of the reasons that the Internet has taken off in use and popularity is because www.cisco.com is much easier to remember than 25.156.10.4.

Internet Infrastructure: How It All Connects, Continued

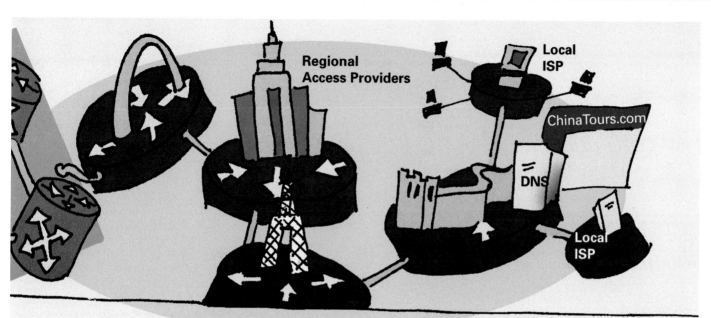

Web Servers
All web pages are stored on computers called web servers. Thousands of these servers can be dedicated servers for companies, hosting servers that house many personal pages, or even single computers housing individual pages.

Back Haul Providers
A few back haul providers comprise the high-speed backbone of the Internet. Only a handful of these providers are capable of handling the massive amounts of Internet traffic that continues to grow. Many parts of the back haul providers overlap with each other, which improves both the speed and reliability of the network.

TCP/IP and IP Addressing

Computers Speaking the Same Language

The Internet protocols compose the most popular, nonproprietary data-networking protocol suite in the world. The Internet protocols are communication protocols used by electronic devices to talk to each other. Initially, computers were the primary consumers of IP protocols, but other types of electronic devices can connect to IP networks, including printers, cellular phones, and MP3 players. In less prolific implementations, people hook devices such as candy vending machines, dishwashers, and cars to IP networks.

The two best-known Internet protocols are the Transmission Control Protocol (TCP) and the Internet Protocol (IP). The Internet protocol suite also comprises application-based protocols, including definitions for the following:

- Electronic mail (Simple Mail Transport Protocol, or SMTP)
- Terminal emulation (Telnet)
- File transfer (File Transfer Protocol, or FTP)

The Defense Advanced Research Projects Agency (DARPA) developed the Internet protocols in the mid 1970s. DARPA funded Stanford University and Bolt, Beranek, and Newman (BBN) to develop a set of protocols that would allow different types of computers at various research locations to communicate over a common packet-switched network. The result of the research produced the Internet protocol suite, which was later distributed for free with the Berkeley Software Distribution UNIX operating system. From there, IP became the primary networking protocol, serving as the basis for the WWW and the Internet in general.

Internet protocols are discussed and adopted in the public domain. Technical bulletins called Requests For Comments (RFCs) document protocols and practices. The documents are published, analyzed, and then accepted by the Internet community.

IP is considered a Layer 3 protocol according to the OSI model. Devices map the IP address to the Layer 2 Media Access Control (MAC) address when transmitting information onto a network.

Because IP addresses are difficult to remember in their dotted notation, the Domain Name System (DNS) maps a readable name to an IP address. For example, when you type http://www.cisco.com/ into a browser, the PC uses the DNS protocol to contact a DNS name server. The name server translates the name http://www.cisco.com/ into the actual IP address for that host.

A network administrator is responsible for assigning which devices receive which IP addresses in a corporate network. The admin assigns a device an IP address in one of two ways: by configuring the device with a specific address or by letting the device automatically learn its address from the network. Dynamic Host Configuration Protocol (DHCP) is the protocol used for automatic IP address assignment. Dynamic addressing saves considerable administrative efforts and conserves IP addressing space.

Generally, devices that don't move around receive static addressing. For example, servers, routers, and switches usually receive static IP addresses. The rest use dynamic addressing.

At-A-Glance—TCP/IP

Why Should I Care About TCP/IP?

Transmission Control Protocol/Internet Protocol (TCP/IP) is the best known and most popular protocol suite used today. Its ease of use and commonality are two of the biggest reasons for the Internet explosion.

TCP/IP offers reliable connection-based packet transfer as well as unreliable, connectionless transfers.

What Are the Problems to Solve?

TCP is a connection-oriented, reliable protocol responsible for breaking messages into segments and reassembling them at the destination station. (It also resends packets not received at the destination.) TCP also provides virtual circuits between applications.

A connection-oriented protocol establishes and maintains a connection during a transmission. The protocol must establish the connection prior to sending data. After the data transfer is complete, the session is torn down.

User Datagram Protocol (UDP) is an unreliable, connectionless protocol. Although "unreliable" might have a negative connotation, in cases where real-time data is exchanged (such as a voice conversation), taking the time to set up a connection and resend dropped packets can cause more harm than good.

End points in TCP/IP are identified by IP addresses. IP addressing is covered later in this chapter.

TCP/IP Datagrams

TCP/IP sends information via datagrams. A single message might break up into a series of datagrams to be reassembled at their destination. The TCP/IP protocol stack has three layers:

- **Application layer**—This layer specifies protocols for e-mail, file transfer, remote login, and other applications. It also supports network management.

- **Transport layer**—This layer lets multiple upper-layer applications use the same data stream. TCP and UDP provide flow control and reliability.

- **Network layer**—Protocols operating at this layer include IP, Internet Control Message Protocol (ICMP), Address Resolution Protocol (ARP), and Reverse Address Resolution Protocol (RARP).

IP provides connectionless, best-effort routing of datagrams.

TCP/IP hosts use ICMP to carry error and control messages with IP datagrams.

ARP allows communication on a multi-access medium such as Ethernet by mapping known IP addresses to Media Access Control (MAC) sublayer addresses.

RARP maps a known MAC address to an IP address.

Dynamic Host Configuration Protocol (DHCP) is a modern implementation of RARP.

How TCP Connections Are Established

End stations exchange control bits called SYN (for synchronize) and Initial Sequence Numbers (ISN) to synchronize while establishing a connection. TCP/IP uses a three-way handshake to establish connections.

To synchronize the connection, each side sends its own ISN and expects to receive a confirmation of it in an acknowledgment (ACK) from the other side. The figure shows an example.

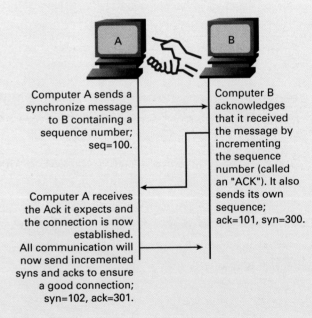

Computer A sends a synchronize message to B containing a sequence number; seq=100.

Computer B acknowledges that it received the message by incrementing the sequence number (called an "ACK"). It also sends its own sequence; ack=101, syn=300.

Computer A receives the Ack it expects and the connection is now established. All communication will now send incremented syns and acks to ensure a good connection; syn=102, ack=301.

At-A-Glance—TCP/IP Functions

TCP Windowing

Windowing is a mechanism that sends the maximum amount of packets without overwhelming an end station with data that it cannot process (thus dropping packets).

The window size from one end station informs the other side of the connection how much it can accept at one time. When a window size is one, each segment must be acknowledged before another segment is sent. This size makes the least efficient use of bandwidth. This figure shows a windowing example.

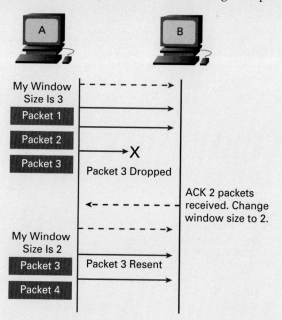

UDP

UDP is a connectionless, unreliable Layer 4 protocol. Unreliable in this sense means that the protocol does not ensure that every packet reaches its destination. UDP is used for applications that provide their own error-recovery process or when retransmission does not make sense. UDP is simple and efficient, trading reliability for speed.

Why not resend? It might not be obvious why you would not resend dropped packets if you had the option to do so. However, receiving old packets out of order disrupts real-time applications such as voice and video. Such applications are usually capable of masking the dropped packets as long as they account for a small percentage of the total.

Port Numbers

Two hosts can have multiple conversations between each other using different upper-layer applications. Port numbers are used to differentiate each conversation (or session) between the hosts. Port numbers (also called socket numbers) keep track of different conversations crossing the network at any given time. The Internet Assigned Numbers Authority (IANA) controls some of the more well-known port numbers. For example, port 23 is always Telnet. Applications that do not use well-known port numbers have them randomly assigned from a specific range.

Port Number Ranges

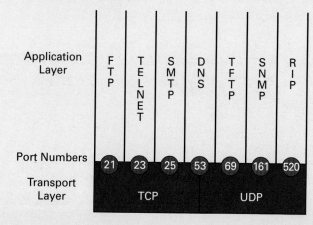

At-A-Glance—TCP/IP Timeline

History of TCP/IP

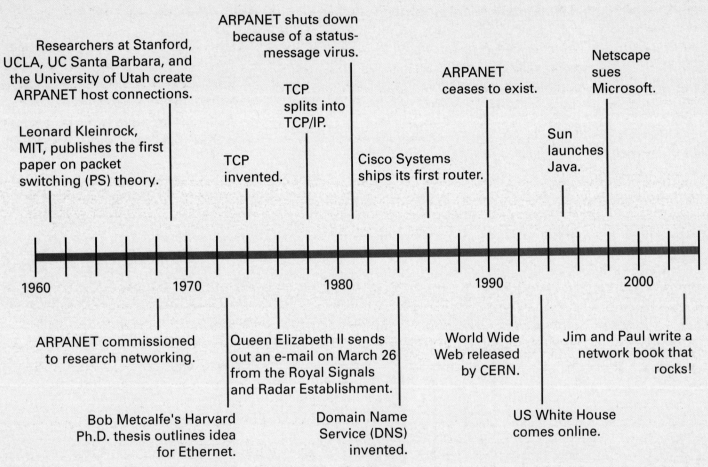

At-A-Glance—IP Addressing

Why Should I Care About IP Addressing?

Behind every URL (website server) and every computer or other device connected to the Internet is a number that uniquely identifies that device. This unique identifier is called an *IP address*. These addresses are the key components of the routing schemes used over the Internet. For example, if you are downloading a data sheet from http://www.cisco.com to your computer, the header of the packets composing the document includes both the host address (in this case, the IP address of the Cisco public server) and the destination address (your PC).

What Are the Problems to Solve?

Each IP address is a 32-bit number, which means address combinations number 4.3 billion. You must allocate these addresses in such a way that balances the need for administrative and routing efficiency and the need to retain as many usable addresses as possible.

The most common notation for describing an IP address is *dotted decimal*. Dotted decimal breaks up a 32-bit binary number into four 8-bit numbers (represented in decimal form). Each section is separated by a period, which aids in the organizational scheme. For example, you can represent the binary address 10101000000010110010001011100 in dotted decimal as 10.128.178.46.

Logical Versus Physical

Media Access Control (MAC) addresses are considered physical addresses because the manufacturer permanently assigns them to pieces of hardware. (They cannot be reassigned.)

A network administrator assigns IP addresses, which only have meaning in a Transmission Control Protocol/Internet Protocol (TCP/IP) network. Used solely for routing purposes, these addresses can be reassigned.

Rather than assign numbers at random to various endpoints (which would be extremely difficult to manage), every company and organization on the Internet has a block of address numbers to use. A two-part addressing scheme identifies a network and a host. This two-part scheme dictates the following:

- All the endpoints within a network share the network number.
- The remaining bits identify each host within that network.

Address Classes

When the IP address scheme was developed, only the first octet identified the network portion of the address. At the time, scientists assumed that 254 networks would be more than enough to cover the research groups and universities using this protocol. As usage grew, however, it became clear that the Internet would need more network designations (each with fewer hosts). This issue led to the development of address classes.

Addresses fit into five classes (A–E). Classes A, B, and C are the most common. Class A addresses have 8 network bits and 24 host bits. Class C addresses have 24 network bits and 8 host bits. This scheme was based on the assumption that the Internet would have more small networks (each with fewer endpoints) than large networks. Class D is used for multicast, and Class E is reserved for research. The following table outlines the three main classes. Note that the Class A address starting with 127 is reserved.

In the following example, the first two octets (128.10) identify a company with an Internet presence. (It's the address of the router that accesses the Internet.) All computers and servers within the company's network share the same network address. The next two octets identify a specific endpoint (computer, server, printer, etc.). In this example, the company has 65,536 addresses it can assign (16 bits or 2^{16}).

128	10	173	46
10000000	00001010	10110010	00101110

Network   Host

Classes	First Octet Range	Network Bits	Possible Networks	Host Bits	No. of Hosts per Network
A	1–126	8	126	24	16,777,216
B	128–191	16	16,384	16	65,536
C	192–223	24	2,097,152	8	256

You can derive the total number of available hosts on a network by using the formula 2^n-2, where *n* is the number of host bits. The −2 accounts for an octet with all 0s (which identifies the network) and all 1s (which is a broadcast address).

At-A-Glance—Subnetting

Subnetting

Subnetting is a method of segmenting hosts within a network and providing additional structure. Without subnets, an organization operates as a flat network. These flat topologies result in short routing tables, but as the network grows, the use of bandwidth becomes inefficient.

In this example, a Class B network is flat with a single broadcast and collision domain. Adding Layer 2 switches to the network creates more collision domains, but it does not control broadcasts. (See the "Ethernet" chapter)

In the following example, the same network has several subnets. You use the third octet (part of the host address space for a Class B network) to segment the network. Note that the outside world sees this network the same as it does the previous example.

Subnet Masks

Routers use a *subnet mask* to determine which parts of the IP address correspond to the network, the subnet, and the host. The mask is a 32-bit number in the same format as the IP address. The mask is a string of consecutive 1s starting from the most significant bits representing the network ID, followed by a string of consecutive 0s representing the host ID.

IP Address	128 10000000	10 00001010	173 10110010	46 00101110
	Network		Host	

Subnet Mask	255 11111111	255 11111111	255 11111111	0 00000000
	Network		Subnet	Host

This subnet mask can also be written as "/24", where 24 represents the number of 1s in the subnet mask.

Each address class has a default subnet mask (A=/8, B=/16, C=/24). The default subnet masks only the network portion of the address; the effect is no subnetting. With each bit of subnetting beyond the default, you can create 2^n-2 subnets. The preceding example has 254 subnets, each with 254 hosts.

Identifying Subnet Addresses

Given an IP address and subnet mask, you can identify the subnet address, broadcast address, and the first and the last usable addresses within a subnet as follows:

- Write the 32-bit address and subnet mask below that (the following figure shows 174.24.4.176/26).

- Draw a vertical line just after the last 1 bit in the subnet mask.

- Copy the portion of the IP address to the left of the line. Place all 0s for the remaining free spaces to the right. This is the subnet number.

- Copy the portion of the IP address to the left of the line. Place all 1s for the remaining free spaces to the right. This is the broadcast address for the subnet.

- You can also find the first and last address by placing ...0001 and ...1110 respectively in the remaining free spaces.

174.24.4.176	10101110001100000000100 10110000	Host
255.255.255.192	11111111111111111111111 11000000	Mask
174.24.4.128	10101110001100000000100 10000000	Subnet
174.24.4.191	10101110001100000000100 10111111	Broadcast

DNS: Matching Domain Names to IP Addresses

At-A-Glance—IPv6

Why Should I Care About IPv6?

The addressing scheme used for the TCP/IP protocols is called *IP version 4 (IPv4)*. This scheme uses a 32-bit binary number to identify networks and end stations. This 32-bit scheme yields about 4 billion addresses, but because of the dotted decimal system (which breaks the number into four sections of 8 bits each) and other considerations, only about 250 million usable addresses exist. When the scheme was originally developed in the 1980s, no one ever thought that address would become scarce. The advent of the Internet, however, along with the trend of making many devices Internet-compatible (which means they need an address), such as cell phones and PDAs, makes running out of IPv4 addresses a certainty. This chart shows the trend of address space.

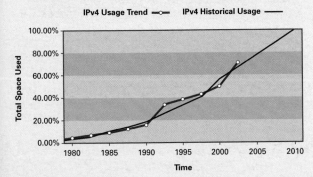

What Are the Problems to Solve?

Network Address Translation (NAT) and Port Address Translation (PAT) were developed as solutions to the diminishing availability of IP addresses. NAT and PAT enable a company or user to share a single (or a few) assigned IP addresses among several private addresses

that are not bound by an address authority. Although these schemes preserve address space and provide anonymity, the benefits come at the cost of individuality, which goes against the very reason for networking in the first place, which is to allow peer-to-peer collaborations through shared applications.

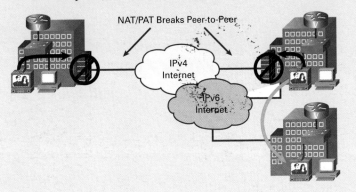

IP addressing scheme version 6 (IPv6) not only provides an answer to the problem of depleting address space, it allows for the restoration of a true end-to-end model, where hosts can connect to each other unobstructed and with greater flexibility. The key elements in IPv6 are to allow for each host to have a unique global IP address, to maintain connectivity even when in motion, and to natively secure host communications.

IPv6 Addresses

The 128-bit address used in IPv6 allows for a greater number of addresses and subnets (enough space for 10^{15} end points—340,282,366,920,938,463,463, 374,607,431,768,211,456 total).

IPv6 was designed to give every user multiple global addresses that can be used for a variety of devices, including cell phones, PDAs, IP-enabled vehicles, and consumer electronics. In addition to providing more address space, IPv6 has the following advantages over IPv4:

- Easier address management and delegation
- Easy address autoconfiguration
- Embedded IPSec (encrypted security)
- Optimized routing
- Duplicate Address Detection (DAD)

IPv6 Notation

This figure demonstrates the notation and shortcuts for IPv6 addresses.

128 bits are expressed as 8
fields of 16 bits in Hex notation:

2031:0000:130F:0000:0000:09C0:876A:130B

As a shorthand, leading zeros
in each field are optional:

2031:0:130F:0:0:9C0:876A:130B

Also, successive fields of 0
can be represented as ::

2031:0:130F::9C0:876A:130B

The :: shorthand can only be
used once per address:

2031::130F::9C0:876A:130B

At-A-Glance—IPv6: Autoconfiguration, Security, and NAT and PAT

An IPv6 address uses the first 64 bits in the address for the network ID and the second 64 bits for the host ID. The network ID is separated into "prefix" chunks. This figure shows the address hierarchy.

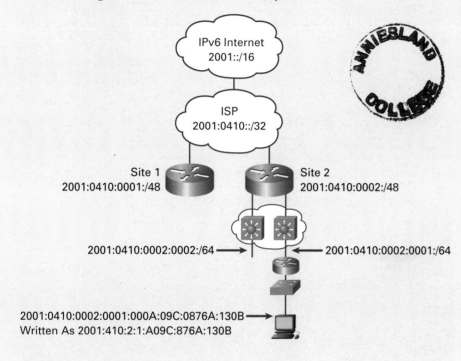

2001:0410:0002:0002:/64 →   ← 2001:0410:0002:0001:/64

2001:0410:0002:0001:000A:09C:0876A:130B →
Written As 2001:410:2:1:A09C:876A:130B

IPv6 Autoconfiguration

IPv4 deployments use one of two methods to assign IP addresses to a host: static assignment (which is management intensive) or DHCP/BOOTP, which automatically assigns IP addresses to hosts upon booting onto the network.

IPv6 provides a feature called *stateless autoconfiguration* that is similar to Dynamic Host Configuration Protocol (DHCP). Using stateless configuration, any router interface that has an IPv6 address assigned to it becomes the "provider" of IP addresses on the network to which it's attached. Safeguards are built into IPv6 that prevent duplicate addresses. This feature is called *Duplicate Address Detection (DAD)*.

IPv6 Security

IPv6 has embedded support for IPSec. The host operating system (OS) can configure an IPSec tunnel between the host and any other host that has IPv6 support.

NAT and PAT

Although Network Address Translation (NAT) causes problems with peer-to-peer collaboration, it is still widely used, particularly in homes and small offices.

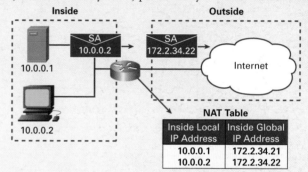

Inside Local IP Address	Inside Global IP Address
10.0.0.1	172.2.34.21
10.0.0.2	172.2.34.22

- Static NAT uses a one-to-one private-to-public address translation.

- Dynamic NAT matches private addresses to a pool of public addresses on an as-needed basis. The address translation is still one to one.

Port Address Translation (PAT) is a form of dynamic address translation that uses a many private addresses to few or one public address. This is referred to as overloading. It is accomplished by assigning port numbers, as shown in this figure.

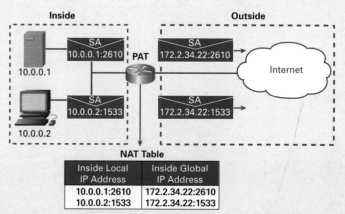

Inside Local IP Address	Inside Global IP Address
10.0.0.1:2610	172.2.34.22:2610
10.0.0.2:1533	172.2.34.22:1533

NAT and PAT

Comparative Features of NAT (Network Address Translation)

Static NAT
- All Addresses Preassigned
- Address Assignments Do Not Change
- 1 Inside = 1 Outside
- Good for Security

Dynamic NAT
- Assigns Outside Address from Pool to Inside Address
- Address Assignments Only Last for a Single Communication Session
- Good for Security
- Preserves Address Space But Can Run Out of Outside Addresses

Comparative Features of PAT (Port Address Translation)
- A Form of Dynamic NAT
- Uses One Outside Address For Many Inside Addresses (Call Overloading)
- Many Inside = 1 Outside
- Port Numbers (Usually Very High) Assigned on a Per-Session Basis
- Fools Packet Instead of Address
- Increases Address Space

NAT Table

Inside Addresses	Outside Addresses
10.0.0.1	172.1.5.1
10.0.0.2	172.1.5.2
10.0.0.3	172.1.5.3
etc.	etc.

PAT Table

Inside Addresses	Outside Addresses
10.0.0.1:1256	17.1.5.1:1256
10.0.0.2:1567	17.1.5.1:1567
10.0.0.3:1683	17.1.5.1:1683
etc.	etc.

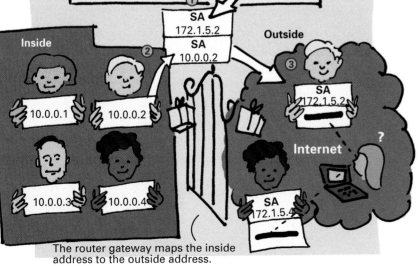

The router gateway maps the inside address to the outside address.

Internet Applications

Going to Class—Virtually

E-learning is Internet-enabled learning. E-learning combines content delivery, management of the learning experience, a networked community of learners, content developers, and experts. In networking terms, an e-learning network takes content in the form of video, audio, and presentations and distributes the content reliably across a converged IP network. Combine this setup with applications that allow users to manage their education plans and track their progress for simplified accountability. Finally, combine this arrangement with applications that include forms of video conferencing to provide live, interactive education across a converged IP network.

E-learning technologies permit students to participate in a class on their own schedule or interact in live classrooms without traveling to the instructor. Users can archive classes and view them on demand at later dates. Applications today synchronize the electronic presentation with the "talking-head" video and audio of the instructor. Thus, a student can view the instructor's video while seeing a clear reproduction of the presentation projection. As an alternative to physically being in a classroom, these tools present an effective facsimile of the actual class.

With usable electronic education such as today's e-learning applications coupled with an Educational Content Delivery Network (ECDN), corporations benefit through significantly reduced travel costs and increased availability of important training.

E-learning has two main areas:

- An ECDN infrastructure that provides services for live and scheduled broadcast, media on demand, and IP videoconferencing
- Applications for collaboration, content creation, and learning-management systems

The first component to consider for an ECDN infrastructure is the concept of a converged voice, video, and data network. This network includes the implementation of quality of service (QoS) marking, scheduling, and provisioning; multicast routing; IP services such as routing; and a network design that addresses high availability. Combined, these services ensure e-learning voice, video, and data traffic reach their destination in the most efficient and reliable way available.

The next component is the applications and devices that facilitate the delivery of live broadcasts, media on demand, and IP videoconferencing.

E-Learning Delivery Mechanisms

Live broadcasts require that audio and video be captured from the source, such as a microphone, audio recording, video camera, or video recording. You convert the captured audio and video into electronic form, which you then broadcast over the IP network. IP multicast protocols facilitate the efficient delivery of the broadcast to all interested locations, whereas QoS mechanisms ensure the network properly prioritizes the broadcast. A live broadcast is like watching television: It is a one-way, noninteractive process.

Media on demand has slightly different requirements. As opposed to a live broadcast scheduled for a particular time, media on demand allows the user to watch or listen to content at any time. This freedom requires that you store the media such that a user can receive it upon request. Media on demand consists of video on demand, audio on demand, and file transfers.

You must first create the media in a similar fashion used for live broadcast: You must record it and convert it to electronic form. However, with media on demand, you store the content on servers and deliver it to users via unicast streams rather than multicast. This setup is similar to requesting a movie on demand in a hotel room. Users can view training at the their convenience, allowing them not only to view the video recording of the trainer but also to watch the associated slides in context with a part of the presentation.

You "push" the content to distributed locations to place the content as close to the user as possible, thereby reducing the consumption of expensive WAN links. This concept is called content distribution and caching. Like a live broadcast, media on demand is a one-way model: There is no interaction with the presenter.

The final delivery mechanism involves IP *videoconferencing (VC)*. As with live broadcasts, the user can view the presenter and associated slides in real time. However, the viewers can also interact with the presenter through the use of IP-based VC. You use standard VC applications and devices for the delivery of interactive video content. These devices enable all participants to interact with each other both with video and audio, as well as collaborate through electronic whiteboard applications and sharing applications.

With the ability to deliver content reliably across an IP network, the final component is a set of applications that facilitate content creation, learning management (the ability to select content and the ability to track progress), and collaboration.

Other Internet Applications

This section and the following pages discuss e-learning in particular. At the end of this chapter, however, you'll see two whiteboard illustrations that explain two other popular Internet applications: e-mail and peer-to-peer sharing.

At-A-Glance—E-Learning

Why Should I Care About E-Learning?

Many businesses count their knowledge workers as the primary company asset. As employees gather and process an ever-increasing amount of information, the ability to deliver information quickly, efficiently, and conveniently can become a competitive advantage. In addition, the pace of technology has reduced the shelf life of information. Individuals, companies, and countries must constantly update their skills or risk falling behind.

E-learning is a collection of solutions that enables the delivery and synchronization of multimedia across the network infrastructure to enable learning, training, and knowledge transfer. In addition to increased knowledge, e-learning provides the following benefits:

• The ability to reach audiences anytime, anywhere

• Centralized information

• Reduced costs

• Improvements in productivity and competitiveness

What Are the Problems to Solve?

Delivering educational information on demand presents several challenges. In addition to moving information, online companies must do the following:

• Deliver content anytime, anywhere

• Manage curriculum and learning plans

• Ensure scalability

• Minimize bandwidth costs

• Eliminate network congestion

Companies must also manage the challenges associated with the solutions that make up e-learning. They must properly design and manage such solutions as media streaming, videoconferencing, video on demand, and interactive multimedia.

Educational Content Delivery Networks

One of the keys to successful e-learning solutions is ensuring that content is available immediately upon request. An Educational Content Delivery Network (ECDN) mitigates network issues, such as network congestion, delay, or poor quality, by setting up a network of intelligent edge nodes that route content requests to the best source for delivery. In other words, ECDN moves high-bandwidth content as close as possible to where it is requested, nullifying any network issues that would negatively affect the prompt delivery of content.

At-A-Glance—E-Learning, Continued

Videoconferencing

Videoconferencing (VC) is a solution unto itself but has several e-learning applications as well.

Corporate training classes and more effective meetings are common VC applications. A less common but more interesting application is consultations. With smaller cameras and the increased computing power of laptops, it is now practical to use VC to troubleshoot technical problems or diagnose patients or systems.

Private WAN or Internet?

You can run all the applications shown over both private WANs and the public Internet. The main differentiation between the two is the availability of quality of service (QoS) over some private WANs, which makes the application less susceptible to delay, loss, and jitter during time of congestion.

Live Media Streaming

Live media streaming makes virtual classrooms fully interactive. Collaboration servers not only enable students to view a live class or demonstration, but also allow them to ask questions and participate in real time.

Interactive Multimedia

Interactive multimedia is the shared use of resources such as whiteboard applications, presentations, and documents by multiple users in separate locations.

Media on Demand and Video on Demand

Media on demand and video on demand are two of the most versatile aspects of e-learning. Media on demand and video on demand allow people to view classes whenever they want.

Live classes and their associated media (such as slides) are stored on a server and delivered to edge nodes via ECDN. Users can then view the classes at any time from virtually any connected location.

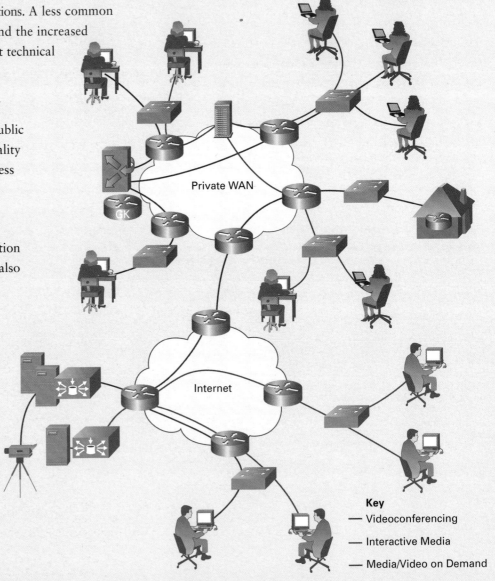

Private WAN

Internet

Key
— Videoconferencing
— Interactive Media
— Media/Video on Demand

Internet Application: E-Learning

E-learning allows remote users to experience the class as if they were present, and other students to view the class at a later time.

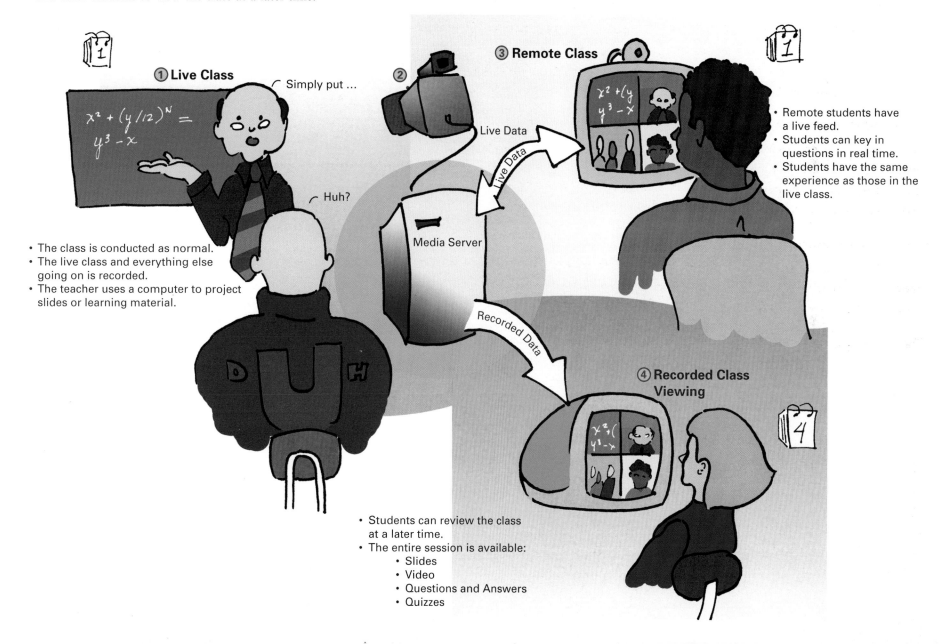

① Live Class

Simply put ...

Huh?

- The class is conducted as normal.
- The live class and everything else going on is recorded.
- The teacher uses a computer to project slides or learning material.

②

Live Data

Live Data

Media Server

Recorded Data

③ Remote Class

- Remote students have a live feed.
- Students can key in questions in real time.
- Students have the same experience as those in the live class.

④ Recorded Class Viewing

- Students can review the class at a later time.
- The entire session is available:
  - Slides
  - Video
  - Questions and Answers
  - Quizzes

Internet Application: E-Mail

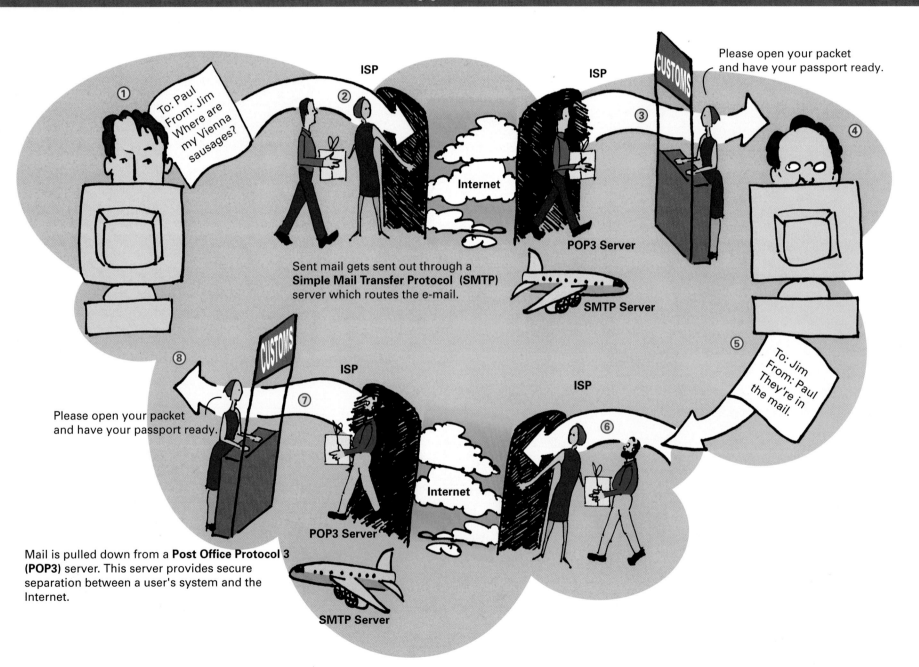

① To: Paul From: Jim Where are my Vienna sausages?

② ISP

Sent mail gets sent out through a **Simple Mail Transfer Protocol (SMTP)** server which routes the e-mail.

SMTP Server

Internet

POP3 Server

③ ISP

CUSTOMS

Please open your packet and have your passport ready.

④

⑤ To: Jim From: Paul They're in the mail.

⑥ ISP

Internet

POP3 Server

⑦ ISP

SMTP Server

CUSTOMS

⑧ Please open your packet and have your passport ready.

Mail is pulled down from a **Post Office Protocol 3 (POP3)** server. This server provides secure separation between a user's system and the Internet.

Internet Application: Peer-to-Peer Sharing

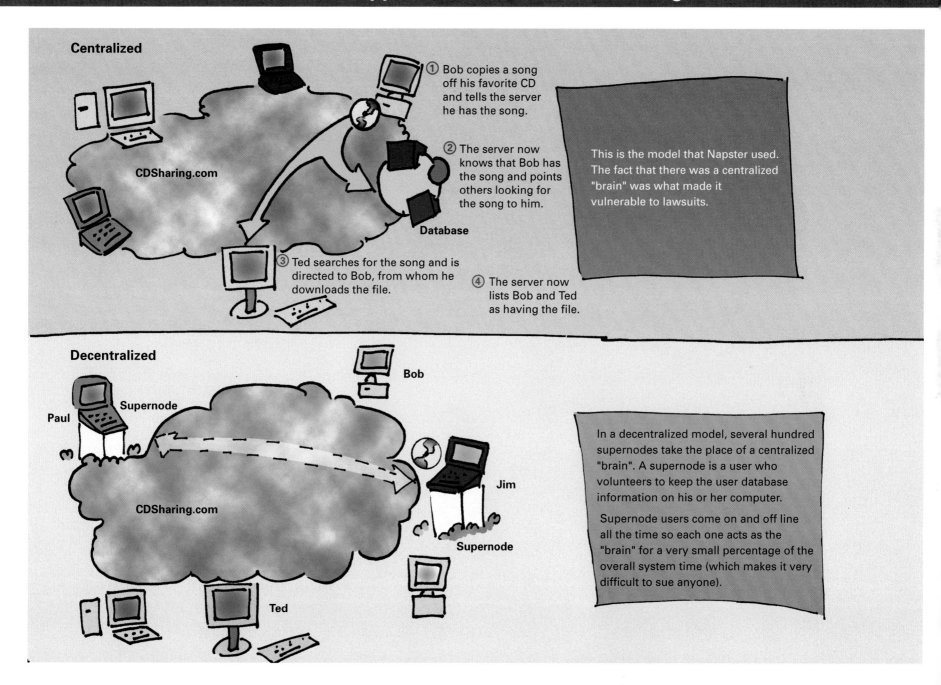

Centralized

CDSharing.com

① Bob copies a song off his favorite CD and tells the server he has the song.

② The server now knows that Bob has the song and points others looking for the song to him.

Database

③ Ted searches for the song and is directed to Bob, from whom he downloads the file.

④ The server now lists Bob and Ted as having the file.

This is the model that Napster used. The fact that there was a centralized "brain" was what made it vulnerable to lawsuits.

Decentralized

Bob

Supernode

Paul

CDSharing.com

Jim

Supernode

Ted

In a decentralized model, several hundred supernodes take the place of a centralized "brain". A supernode is a user who volunteers to keep the user database information on his or her computer.

Supernode users come on and off line all the time so each one acts as the "brain" for a very small percentage of the overall system time (which makes it very difficult to sue anyone).

Part II

Telephones and Movies on the Internet

Traditional phone networks have been separate from traditional data networks. Phone calls have different needs from that of data transfer. With a phone, you expect an immediate dial tone when you take it off the hook. Hearing no dial tone indicates the network is down. When you talk, you expect the person on the other end to hear what you say in real time. Otherwise, the conversation is frustratingly incomprehensible (as when talking to someone on a cell phone in an area with horrible reception).

With data networks, you are more tolerant to delays in the network. When browsing a website, you tolerate a 10–20 second delay on occasion. This delay is unacceptable in the voice world.

With the Internet, Transmission Control Protocol/Internet Protocol (TCP/IP), and mechanisms such as quality of service (QoS) becoming the de facto networking protocol and transport, "convergence" can occur. Traditional protocols (such as voice) can converge (or tunnel) through an IP network.

Today's networks can ensure that voice traffic receives the high priority it requires to provide a real-time conversation. Now that bandwidth abounds on the Internet and corporate networks, they can also transmit video (which has similar traffic characteristics as voice, except a greater volume).

Traditional functions such as videoconferencing, telephony, call centers, and video transmission can now converge onto IP networks, creating new possibilities. In Part II, you learn why we can talk on the phone, participate in conference calls, and watch movies over the Internet.

IP Telephony

Making Calls Over the Net

Traditionally, voice traffic traveled across circuit-switched networks using private branch exchange (PBX) networks or networks of private lines and time-division multiplexers (TDMs). These traditional networks tended to be proprietary, closed systems that were expensive to maintain, upgrade, or scale.

Internet Protocol (IP) telephony integrates traditional voice services with today's IP networks. With this convergence, both data and voice traffic traverse the same physical network, which eliminates the need for two separate networks and two separate sets of networking skills.

Migrating to an IP-based telephony network reduces the total cost of ownership for voice services in the following ways:

- **Toll charges**—IP telephony carries traffic through a corporation's private IP network, thereby bypassing the dedicated, leased voice lines used to connect remote offices. Eliminating the use of dedicated leased voice lines lets a company avoid toll charges and monthly fees for these dedicated circuits and converge their voice traffic onto existing leased data lines.

- **Administration costs**—Because IP telephony shares the same network as data applications, you have only one network to manage. Traditionally, separate teams managed voice networks and duplicated the data network.

The convergence of voice and data networks also offers productivity not available from traditional voice networks:

- **Employee mobility**—Working from home or remote locations is a trend that has demonstrated increased employee productivity. Imagine conducting business over your work phone from home. With technologies such as virtual private networks (VPNs) and broadband services, employees can work from home or an airport using the tools (computers and phone) they use at work as if they were sitting at their office desks.

- **Application integration**—IP phones are incorporating extensible markup language (XML) browsers into their video interfaces. Therefore, a company can extend enterprise applications to employees who do not need a computer. Additionally, mobile employees can make calls across corporate phone services using their notebook computers and software-based phones. They can also retrieve their voice mail by simply downloading their e-mail.

Ultimately, it is the convergence of enterprise applications with IP telephony that will advance productivity and efficiency in ways not possible with traditional PBX networks.

Components of an IP Telephony Implementation

An IP telephony network consists of four distinct layers:

- **Client layer**—Actual devices a person interacts with: IP phones, IP video-conferencing equipment, software-based phones.

- **Infrastructure layer**—Traditional devices associated with data networks: routers, switches, and gateways.

- **Call-processing layer**—Redundant call control and directories.

- **Application layer**—Voice mail, unified messaging (imagine receiving voice mail in your e-mail box or listening to your e-mail over the phone), personal and business productivity applications.

Client Layer

The client layer consists of the phones, video equipment, and software-based phones. These are the devices people interact with.

One issue implementers face when trying to convert their traditional PBX systems to IP networks is how to provide power to the phones. Traditional phones simply plug a single cable into the wall for both power and voice services. Because IP phones plug into IP networks (usually via Ethernet), traditional data networks are not able to provide power. At first glance, an IP phone must have two cables: a network cable and a power cable.

However, several alternatives allow the phone to receive power through the network cable, thereby allowing IP phones to plug and play as their traditional counterparts do:

1. Receive inline power from the Ethernet switch they connect to. The Cisco switches can do this.

2. Receive power supplied from the patch panel.

Devices at the client layer are responsible for translating the audio stream into digital data. IP phones use digital signal processing (DSP) to "sample" the audio received from the headset and convert it into digital data. This process is similar to making an MP3 copy of an audio CD.

Infrastructure Layer

From the perspective of delivering the reliable voice services people expect in traditional PBX networks, the infrastructure layer is most critical. It is the job of the infrastructure to ensure that a call (in the form of IP traffic) is carried from source to destination in a reliable and timely manner. Proper provisioning and network design, as well as the implementation of quality of service (QoS) mechanisms, provide the ability of a traditionally data-based infrastructure to deliver voice traffic reliably with the sound quality associated with PBX networks.

Proper implementation of QoS mechanisms in an IP network is critical to the successful implementation of IP telephony. Data networks are traditionally tolerant of delay or some degree of packet loss. However, because calls happen in real time, calls with delayed or lost packets deliver frustrating audio to the receiver in which a call either becomes choppy or becomes dropped. Implementing QoS and properly provisioning a network ensures that the data network handles calls in the manner traditionally associated with traditional telephony.

Call-Processing Layer

The IP PBX is the center of the call-processing layer. The IP PBX fills the role of the traditional PBX in that it provides connectivity, signaling, and device control for IP phones and gateways. Gateways allow traditional voice traffic to tunnel through an IP network. In addition, IP PBXs perform operations, administration, maintenance, and provisioning (OAM&P).

Cisco IP PBX is responsible for establishing a call between two phones, but after the call is established, IP PBX removes itself and the phones talk to each other directly. The call control (ringing the phone, directing the call, providing dial tone, etc.) is handled separately from the actual content of the call. When someone picks up the receiver, the IP PBX provides a dial tone. When someone dials a number, the IP PBX looks up the number, rings the phone on the other end, and provides the ringing sound back to the person who dialed the number. Once the person at the other end picks up the phone, the IP PBX leaves the picture because the two phones communicate directly.

Telephony gateways bridge the worlds of traditional TDM telephony networks to IP telephony networks. Gateways have several purposes:

- Bridging the public switched telephone network (PSTN) to an IP network
- Connecting legacy PBXs to an IP network
- Tunneling legacy PBXs and phones to other legacy PBXs

IP PBX dial plans define the accessibility of all entities in a voice network. Dials plans also provide alternate path routing and policy restrictions.

An IP PBX also provides connection admission control (CAC) functionality. When a user places a call over an IP WAN, the IP PBX must determine whether enough bandwidth is available across the slower speed WAN. If the capacity exists, the IP PBX passes the call through. If not, the IP PBX then attempts to pass the call through the PSTN. The CAC and the dial plan must be tightly coupled to ensure calls are passed efficiently and appropriately through the network.

Other features also facilitate the linking of CAC and dial plans. For example, a worker in one state might dial the internal five-digit extension of a coworker in another state. If the IP WAN is filled to call capacity, the call is redirected across the PSTN. This process requires that the IP PBX append the other five digits of the phone number so the PSTN recognizes the phone number.

Application Layer

With the convergence of telephony and data networks, it is easy to create new applications that merge the worlds of phones, video, and computers. Examples of these applications include the following:

- **The ability to use speech recognition in combination with call-handling rules**—Users can set up personalized rules that provide call forwarding and screening on the fly. They can forward calls to other user-defined locations such as their homes or cellular phones. Additionally, users can use voice commands to receive, reply, record, skip, and delete messages.

- **The merging of voice, e-mail, and fax messaging into a single "inbox"**—Users can then access their voice, e-mail, and fax messages from their IP phones, cellular phones, or their PCs (via e-mail).

- **The mobility of a phone number**—A user can log into any phone and have it assume his phone number. Thus, an employee based in Greenville, SC, can travel to the company's Wheaton, IL, office and use the phone (with her Greenville, SC, phone number) as if she were home. This mobility presents issues that haven't existed before, such as how to handle a 911 call. If you make a call to 911 from a phone in Illinois using a phone number that is based in Greenville, SC, how is the 911 call properly directed to the local emergency services?

- **Call-center processing**

- **Integration of existing customer applications, such as (ERP), (CRM), and inventory management**

Deployment Models

IP telephony has four deployment models:

- **Single site**—IP telephony is implemented in a single location.

- **Multisite independent call processing**—IP telephony is implemented in multiple remote sites, but calls between the sites travel across the PSTN.

- **Multisite with distributed call processing**—IP telephony is implemented across multiple remote sites with call-processing and voice-messaging equipment present at each location. Calls travel across the IP WAN as the primary path, with the PSTN as a secondary path.

- **Multisite with centralized call processing**—IP telephony is implemented across multiple sites, with call processing and voice messaging centralized in a single location. This solution is often the most efficient for multisite enterprises.

The single-site and multisite with independent call-processing models are similar in that they rely primarily on the PSTN for any calls outside of a single site. These two models are often the first step when a company migrates from old-world telephony to IP-based telephony.

For multisite corporations, true independence from traditional PBX occurs when they implement either a distributed or centralized call-processing model. In both cases, the IP network is the primary path for all corporate calls, with the PSTN serving as backup when either the IP WAN is down or it has insufficient resources to handle calls.

The distributed model places call-processing and voice-messaging equipment at multiple corporate locations. The IP PBX, voice-messaging equipment, and other resources at each location act as a tightly coupled system with the other locations.

The centralized model places call-processing and voice-messaging equipment in a central location. Remote locations contain only the basic infrastructure, such as switches, routers, gateways, and endpoints such as IP phones. The centralized model is easier to administer and troubleshoot, requires less overall equipment, and provides a single-point dial plan. Implementing a robust redundant infrastructure requires the centralized model.

At-A-Glance—IP Telephony

Why Should I Care About IP Telephony?

Traditionally, voice traffic (telephony) traveled the circuit-switched, public switched telephone network (PSTN). Many large businesses and organizations also employed their own internal telephone systems using private branch exchanges (PBXs). Unfortunately, this setup meant that businesses not only deployed a separate network for data traffic (such as e-mail and Internet use), but also paid long-distance charges for calls to remote branches or partners.

Internet Protocol (IP) telephony is a method of operating a telephony service over a data (IP) network. Its advantages include the following:

• Reduced cost and complexity with only a single network to manage

• Reduced long-distance charges (toll bypass)

• Ease of adding or moving people because phone numbers are provisioned in software rather than hard-switch connections

• Additional services such directory lookup, video conferencing, and call-center applications

What Are the Problems to Solve?

Customers who move away from circuit-switched voice technology can consolidate their separate networks into one network, reducing the number of circuits in a facility. Integrating IP technologies with existing technologies allows lets you carry some services over the data network, decreasing the need for separate PSTN circuits.

Explaining Toll Bypass

Toll bypass describes the ability of IP telephony users to avoid (or bypass) long-distance (toll) charges.

This figure illustrates where the fees are levied.

Traditional telephony—Access to local phone carriers is one cost. In addition, a long-distance provider collects a fee for transport over its system. If the company maintains a data network, it must also pay a different local provider for access to the data (IP) network.

IP telephony—A local service provider charges for access, but in this case, there is no charge for the long-distance transport of the packets or for time spent using the network.

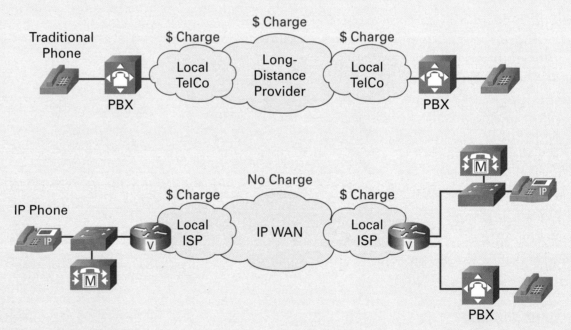

Call Admission Control

When an analog telephony system is overburdened, it degrades incrementally until the noise on the line (or static) becomes so great that the system is unusable. With digital or IP telephony, the system works near perfectly until it becomes overburdened and then all calls drop simultaneously. To prevent this dropping, IP telephony systems use *call admission control (CAC)*. With CAC, the call-processing agent checks the system to ensure that it has the capacity for another call. If it does not, the call is denied or routed through the PSTN.

At-A-Glance—Quality of Service and Making Calls

Quality of Service

The QoS chapter details quality of service (QoS), but its criticality to IP telephony warrants mention here.

QoS is a collection of methods designed to ensure reliable, timely delivery of voice and other real-time packets across an IP network. Unlike data files—which can be broken up, sent in random order, and reassembled at the receiving end—it is critical for voice packets to arrive in order with minimal delay. QoS ensures just that. Think of it as VIP treatment for packets.

Data Packets

QoS Policy

The Network

STOP

Voice Packets Go
to the Head of the Line

Blah...
Blah...

Making a Call on an IP Phone

This figure shows the steps involved in making a call from one IP phone to another. In this case, the call manager is in a centralized location. The steps alter slightly in cases where the phones are colocated or where each location has a call manager. In addition, if a call is made from an IP phone to a non-IP phone, the call is routed through a gateway to the PSTN. All of this routing is transparent to the users.

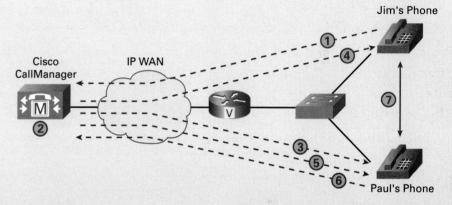

Jim's Phone

Cisco
CallManager

IP WAN

Paul's Phone

① Jim dials Paul's number.

② The CallManager looks up the dialed number and matches it to the IP address of Paul's phone.

③ A connection is set up between the two phones.

④ Jim hears a ring tone.

⑤ Paul's phone rings.

⑥ Paul picks up the phone. The two phones are connected via the IP switched network.

⑦ Jim asks Paul what he's going to wear to work tomorrow.

Anatomy of an IP Telephony Network

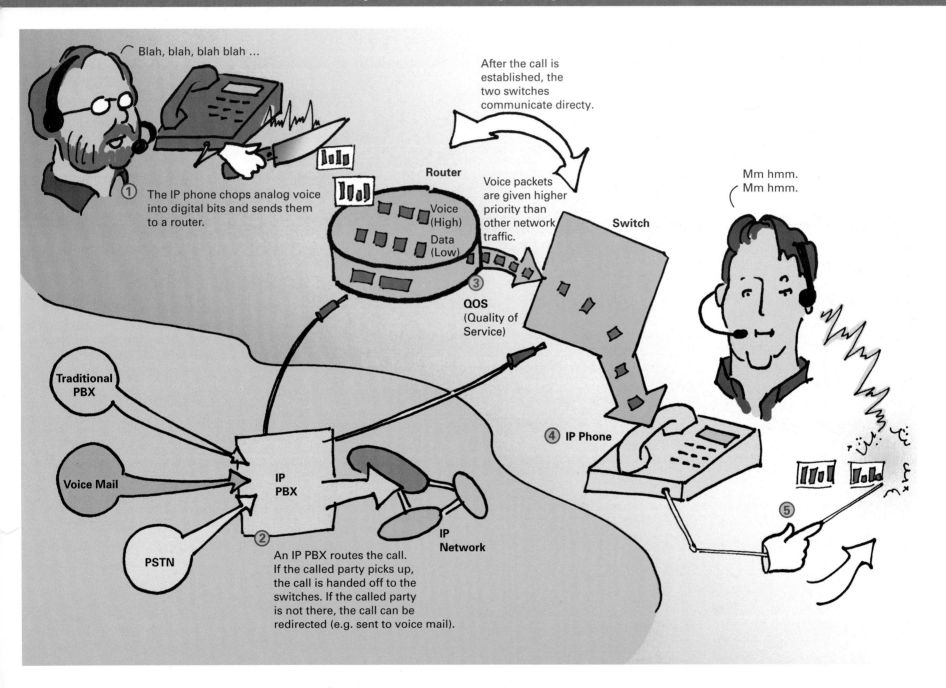

Blah, blah, blah blah ...

① The IP phone chops analog voice into digital bits and sends them to a router.

After the call is established, the two switches communicate directy.

Router

Voice (High)

Data (Low)

③

QOS (Quality of Service)

Voice packets are given higher priority than other network traffic.

Switch

Mm hmm.
Mm hmm.

Traditional PBX

Voice Mail

PSTN

IP PBX

② An IP PBX routes the call. If the called party picks up, the call is handed off to the switches. If the called party is not there, the call can be redirected (e.g. sent to voice mail).

IP Network

④ **IP Phone**

⑤

Toll Bypass—Saving Money on Long-Distance Calls

Regular Phone

Each party involved in processing a call will collect a toll. Typically, a long-distance carrier will take the most (depending upon many factors).

Dad? Dad?

$ Charged on a Per Use Basis

PSTN

PBX

Long-Distance Carrier

PSTN

PBX

Phone Bill $ $ $

Slam!

Regular Phone

Mon Cheri!

Access Charge Only

Private WAN or (Internet)

IP PBX

Router

ISP $

ISP

$ Router

IP PBX

IP Phone

Boston 0$ Paris 0$

IP Phone

With IP telephony, the public infrastructure is used for long-distance transport, which is free. The toll is bypassed.

Corporations or individuals only pay for access to a private WAN (which is primarily a data network). The WAN provider does not charge an additional toll for voice traffic over this data network, so the long-distance voice charge gets bypassed.

At-A-Glance—Voice over IP

Why Should I Care About Voice over IP?

Prior to Voice over Internet Protocol (VoIP), separate networks carried voice and data traffic: circuit-switched voice traffic and packet-switched data traffic. The two networks actually operated on the same types of wires, but the physical network infrastructure was optimized for the circuit-switched voice traffic because voice traffic existed first and accounted for the vast majority of the traffic.

Over the past 20 years, however, the volume of data traffic has increased exponentially. Studies suggest that data traffic began to exceed voice traffic some time between 2002 and 2003.

Because bandwidth is a limited and therefore expensive resource, there is continuous pressure to use it more efficiently. One of the best ways to efficiently use bandwidth is to converge voice and data networks. Convergence also reduces training and operational costs because you have only one network to maintain.

Because the primary network is now packet (data) based, it makes more sense to modify voice signals to traverse data networks than vice versa.

What Are the Problems to Solve?

Converting analog voice signals to digital packets—All sounds (including speech) are analog waves of one or more frequencies.

A Pure Tone

Someone Making an "Ahhh" Sound

VoIP networks must convert these analog signals into digital packets before carrying them over the IP network. Once transported, the signals are recreated into sound waves for your listening pleasure.

Transporting Packets in Real Time

Because of the near worldwide existence of circuit-switched telephony, VoIP will always be compared to its circuit-switched predecessor.

The sound quality of VoIP is based on the network's ability to deliver packets with a high success rate (more than 99 percent) and minimal delay (less than 150 msec end to end). There are well-established standards for quality. Although some people using VoIP might be willing to tolerate lower-quality sound in exchange for free long distance, VoIP quality must match that of circuit-switch telephony in business applications.

Analog Voice to Digital Conversion

Traditional telephony systems convert the sound waves produced by the human voice to electrical signals, which are easily transmitted down a wire. On the receiving end of the connection, the electric signals excite a diaphragm, which produces a very good representation (or an analogy) of the original signal.

Analog signals consist of continuously variable waveforms having an infinite number of states; therefore, you can theoretically replicate them exactly. Digital telephony (including VoIP) must convert the original signal to a digital stream (or series of packets) on the transmitter and then recreate it on the receiving end.

Analog to digital conversion (A/D) happens through sampling.

Sampling is the process of taking instantaneous measurements of an analog signal. If you take enough samples, you can replicate the original analog signal by "connecting the dots" of the instantaneous measurements.

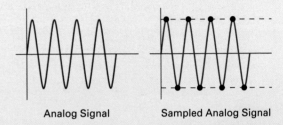

Analog Signal   Sampled Analog Signal

To correctly replicate the original signal, you must take the proper ratio of samples. If you take too few samples, more than one signal (frequency) can connect the dots. This process is called *aliasing*. Taking too many samples, however, is not always better. *Over-sampling* can improve the accuracy of the replicated signal, but at some point, it consumes too many resources (CPU and bandwidth) without yielding additional benefits.

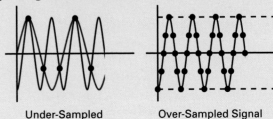

Under-Sampled Signal with Aliasing   Over-Sampled Signal

At-A-Glance—Voice over IP, Continued

It turns out that the ideal sampling rate for any signal is twice that of the signal's highest frequency. In other words, you can accurately recreate a 2 cycles per second signal by sampling it 4 times per second. This rate is called the Nyquist rate, named after the AT&T engineer who discovered it. The Nyquist theorem states that you can digitally recreate any analog signal by sampling it at twice the rate of the highest frequency contained in the signal. Typically, devices sample signals at just over the Nyquist rate.

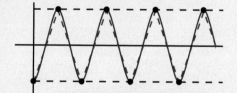

Correctly Sampled Signal with Approximated Recreation

One of key issues with VoIP is the conservation of bandwidth. Because the routing information contained in VoIP packets can more than double the size of the packet, it is important to compress the voice data as much as possible. Compression has three levels, or orders. The first order is to simply not transmit what can't be heard. A typical conversation is mostly silent (hard to believe but true). These silent parts of speech are not transmitted.

The second order of compression is to get the most out of the digital conversion of the analog signal. Remember that the analog signal has infinite number of states, but the digital representation must be a series of 1s and 0s and is limited by the number of bits used. More bits means more levels (a good thing) and more bandwidth required (a bad thing). For example, an 8-bit digital signal could represent 256 levels. Any instantaneous measurement in the A/D process is represented by one of these levels. This process is referred to as *quantization*. It turns out that by stacking more levels at low amplitudes (rather than evenly spacing them out), you can use fewer bits to get the same quality you would get by using more levels (without consuming additional bandwidth).

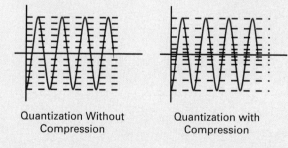

Quantization Without Compression   **Quantization with Compression**

Finally, the third order is to not send the actual voice data. You can model speech signals using pitch and tone. There are wide variances of tone and pitch data, but you can store them in lookup tables. Modern computing techniques and impressive statistical modeling let you send the table location (or vectors) of the pitch and tone information across the network. The receiving end applies the vectors to the tables and recreates the sound.

Comfort Noise

The digital signals in VoIP are usually much "cleaner" than the analog signals used in circuit-switch telephony. In analog systems, any amplification of the signal also amplifies noise, resulting in static heard in the background during calls. Digital signals can clean out noise and achieve a purer sound. This improvement might seem like a good thing, but it actually causes problems.

It turns out that on analog calls, the slight background noise is an indication of a good connection. Because most of the world's phone users were trained to hear this noise, the absence of the static bothers people and makes some wonder if the connection is still live ("Hello?"). To mitigate this "problem," digital systems inject static on the receiving end to let users know they still have a good connection. This injected static is called *comfort noise*.

IP Call Center

Why Can't I Talk to a Real Person?

"Press 1 to use our automated attendant; press 2 to speak with a representative." Customer service, support, and sales are sophisticated in how they handle and direct calls to the appropriate representative. From an automated attendant answering the phone, to the automated redirection of a call, to the interaction of phone and computer application, call-center applications allow a company to efficiently and effectively manage customer calls. Although this setup is possible in traditional voice networks, the convergence of voice with Internet Protocol (IP) networks opens new possibilities and an ease of administration not previously available.

Anatomy of a Call Center

Whether you call a computer company for support, an insurance company to make a claim, or an airline to check the status of a flight, you interact with a call center in some fashion. Likewise, when you receive a phone call during dinner asking whether you want to buy a subscription to a newspaper, a call center is interacting with you. The goal of a call center is to efficiently route a call to the appropriate person or call service while managing call queues when there are more calls than call-center employees available.

The primary components of a call center follow:

- **Private branch exchange (PBX)**—Provides traditional call-handling functionality.
- **Interactive voice responder (IVR)**—Affectionately known as "Silicon Sally," IVR is computer software that provides a series of audible menus for the caller to interact with. The IVR interprets key presses and, recently, voice responses to walk the caller through a series of menus. Based on the caller's selections, the IVR can return information to the user, ending the call, or provide a return code that directs the call appropriately.

- **Automatic call distribution (ACD)**—Depending on the vendor, ACD provides any of the following functionality:
  - Call distribution based on customizable rules
  - The ability to hold callers in a queue
  - Music-on-Hold, customizable messages and advertisements that play while the caller waits in a queue
- **Computer telephony integration (CTI)**—Allows computer applications to interface with the telephone equipment. For call centers, the caller's phone number, account number, or any piece of information the caller provides can serve as the key for an application. For example, when a customer calls her insurance company with questions, the call agent application can intercept the calling phone number and automatically display the customer's personal account information when the agent receives the call.

You can put all these components together in endless combinations; no two call centers operate the same. Vendors provide the functionality described here in different packaging and levels of functionality.

From the Caller to the Agent, and Back Again

Call centers can exist in many forms, but in general, a caller interacts with one of two models: inbound or outbound. The goal is to redirect the call to the appropriate live person or audible application that serves the caller.

With an *inbound* call center, the customer initiates the call to the company. Examples of inbound calls include contacting the following:

- An insurance company to make a claim
- An airline to check a flight schedule
- A bank for account information
- A computer company for technical support
- A mail-order company to make a purchase
- The power company to report a power outage

A traditional ACD determines where to route the call. With an IP-based call center, the IVR, intelligent contact management (ICM), and PBX are like a virtual ACD. Generally, the caller interacts with an IVR first. The IVR replaces the traditional switchboard operator or receptionist by giving the caller a list of options. Based on the caller's responses, the IVR either returns a code to the ACD or runs an application that addresses the caller's need.

With the application, the caller either receives the information he needs and hangs up or interacts further. When the IVR returns a code, the ACD then determines where to route the call, which might eventually be a group of call agents.

When managing calls destined to a group of agents, the ACD typically provides a series of functions that assist in managing a queue of callers. The caller remains on hold, and might hear music, status messages, and advertisements while waiting in the queue. When an agent becomes available, the ACD transfers the call to the PBX, finally linking the customer to a live person. With an IP call center, the IVR might serve as the queue point rather than the traditional ACD.

The other model, *outbound*, lets a system dial many numbers and then transfer the call to a live agent after it finds a number to ring or a person to answer. It appears that the agent called the caller directly. Examples of this method include the following:

- Subscriptions solicitations from a the local newspaper
- Special offers from insurance companies
- A public-opinion poll conducted by a political agency
- A loan company pursuing delinquent customers

With this model, an outbound dialer device parses through lists of phone numbers and dials each one. Based on defined rules, the dialer device hands the call to the ACD after it finds a live person, an answering machine, or simply a ring. The ACD transfers the call either to an automated recording or to a live agent. The call then proceeds.

Generally, for both methods, time is of the essence. Callers become frustrated and angry when forced to talk to recordings or sit in queues for any period of time. So the various systems that make up the call center must be tightly integrated and fast.

Managing Caller and Call Agent Efficiency

As companies conduct business across multiple time zones and countries, they need to provide call center services that do the following:

- Balance loads across multiple call centers.
- Provide support wherever the sun is shining (around the globe).
- Allow call agents to seamlessly work in remote locations. (You never know where your call is actually directed, except perhaps through the accent of the agent you interact with.)

New Methods for Customer Interaction

The Internet created new methods for customers and companies to interact. Aside from the telephone, customers need to be able to contact a company through the web and e-mail. Interactive web-based "chat" type support is popular. As various industries adopt these additional contact methods, customers begin to expect all other industry competitors to do so as well.

To the customer, it should not matter whether she uses e-mail, interactive chat, web submission, or the telephone: a company should respond with the same quality and priority regardless of the method. For the company with a traditional phone-based call center, migrating to this multiple-method model can be difficult.

Today's IP-based call-center software manages e-mail, phone calls, and other contact methods all from the same set of tools.

At-A-Glance—IP Call Centers

Why Should I Care About IP Call Centers?

If you have ever called an 800 number for customer service, chances are you have been routed through a call center. Call centers have been around for many years, but with the advent of Internet Protocol call centers (IPCCs), they have become incredibly powerful and flexible tools for customer service, ordering, and technical support.

What Are the Problems to Solve?

All call centers handle the tasks of receiving calls, collecting caller information, queuing callers, and routing callers to the agents on duty. In addition, IPCCs often provide an additional layer of sophistication in the form of integrated computer applications, which display caller information to the agents at the moment they are connected to the users.

IPCCs must also be capable of receiving and processing calls from traditional telephony systems.

IPCC Equipment

This section details the primary components of an IPCC. In many cases, several of these functions reside in a single box, but the following list outlines them separately for clarity:

- **Intelligent contact management (ICM)**— Distributes voice and data information to the Call Manager and interactive voice responder (IVR) systems and agent desktops.

- **Call Manager**—Provides traditional private branch exchange (PBX) telephony features, such as basic call processing, signaling, and connection services.

- **Peripheral gateway (PG)**—Provides a connection between IPCC components, such as the Call Manager and IVR, to the ICM. The PG serves as a traffic director between the devices.

- **Computer telephony integration (CTI) server**—Provides the connection to the agent's desktop. The CTI server provides incoming call information, receives agent activity reports (log in, available, wrap-up, etc.), and performs call-control functions (answer, hold, transfer, release).

- **IVR**—Prompts users for information, collects caller-entered digits, and generates announcements such as queuing information. ("Your call will be answered in approximately five minutes.")

- **Voice over Internet Protocol (VoIP) gateway**—Provides a traditional telephony connection into the IPCC.

At-A-Glance—Call Flow and Other Cool Stuff

Simple Call-Flow Example

① A customer dials a toll-free telephone number over a traditional public switched telephone network (PSTN) line. The call is routed through a voice gateway. The ICM receives such information as the dialed number (DN), the calling line ID (CLID), and any caller-entered digits (CED).

② The ICM kicks off a user-defined routing script to choose the most appropriate IVR (there could be several across a region or country) and queues the call.

③ The caller chooses a transaction that can be completed with only the IVR, so she is not routed to a live agent.

① A second customer dials the call center from an IP phone. The ICM again routes the call to the most appropriate IVR and queues the call. The IVR can collect additional information (account number, order info, Social Security number, etc.) or simply inform the customer of the approximate wait time. The CM reserves the agent for the incoming call.

② When the ICM detects that an agent is available, it sends a message (which includes the call context information) to the CM. The CM instructs the CTI server to notify the agent desktop of the incoming call.

③ The agent receives a notification that the call is coming in, along with the collected user information, which appears on the agent's computer screen.

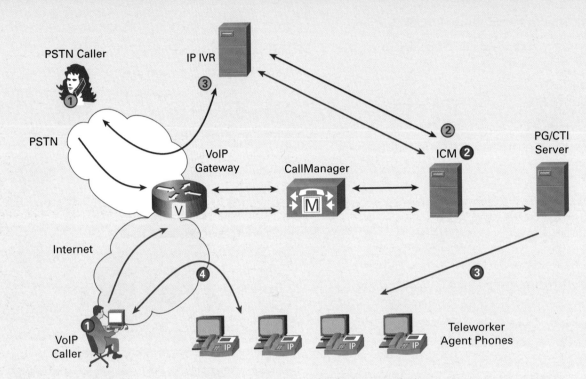

④ The CM connects the call to the agent. Because the caller is online, the agent can also share computer applications with the caller.

Other Cool Stuff

Routing to specialized agents—In some cases, a call center should route VIP customers directly to specialized agents (a $1M investor calling a brokerage house, for example). The IPCC routes them quickly and easily, and with the CTI server, the agent has the user's information on his computer screen before the call is even connected.

Following the sun—Using an IPCC, a company can avoid expensive third-shift costs by migrating its call-center operations from east to west as the day goes on. Remote agents handle calls until a local shift staffs up, at which time the local call center begins handling all the operations and call distribution.

Remote workers—IPCC offers a powerful solution to companies with seasonal spikes in call-center activity (such as a catalog company during the holidays). With the widespread availability of high-speed Internet access, temporary workers can work from home with the same effectiveness as those working at a physical call center.

Call Center—Telemarketer

Call Center—Tech Support

IP Convergence with Tunneling

Pushing All Traffic Types Through an IP Network

The Internet uses Internet Protocol (IP) as its exclusive Layer 3 network protocol. Corporate networks, however, have run many other protocols over the past 20 years and find themselves wanting to migrate to an IP-only network. IP has become the de-facto network protocol for nearly every data-based application.

However, other network protocols still in existence are Layer 3 routed protocols such as the NetWare Internetwork Packet Exchange (IPX) and AppleTalk and layer-bridged protocols such as Systems Network Architecture (SNA) and NetBIOS. Today's routers and switches allow these other protocols and IP to coexist on the same physical network.

Managing multiple networks adds complexity and extra cost. Companies are working to converge as much network traffic as they can into single-protocol IP networks. The advantages to a converged network include the following:

- Reduced equipment costs and design complexity
- Reduced training
- More predictable traffic patterns and response times
- Singular quality of service (QoS) and availability strategy

The primary mechanism for converging traffic onto a common IP network involves *tunneling*. Simply put, IP tunneling is the process of putting one type of packet into an IP packet. The packet traverses the IP network to the IP destination, in which the receiving device extracts the original packet from the IP packet and then passes it onto the destination device on its native network.

Cisco is a prominent player in multiple non-IP network markets primarily because of its ability to tunnel. Examples of technologies that can tunnel through IP networks include the following:

- **SNA (Systems Network Architecture)**—Developed by IBM for IBM mainframes
- **Telephony**—Traditional voice traffic between phones
- **Storage**—Protocols that allow servers to communicate with disk drives over a network

Because these technologies tunnel through IP networks, they benefit from IP services such as QoS and availability functions such as Hot Standby Router Protocol (HSRP). As a result, you can apply a single comprehensive strategy for prioritizing important traffic and handling network outages across application types.

The singular approach also presents problems that network designers must address. Certain SNA protocols require quick and consistent response time. As a result, network congestion that prevents tunneled SNA traffic from achieving expected response times can result in loss of connectivity to a mainframe.

The same applies to tunneling telephony. Network congestion can detrimentally affect the quality of one or more calls. The caller whose call meets congestion will experience strange choppy conversations or notice his call drop altogether. For companies consolidating their telephony and IP networks, a lack of quality can prohibit a successful rollout.

As a result, you must give special consideration when migrating one network technology, such as SNA or telephony, onto another such as IP. You must design the network in such a way that the network devices have enough bandwidth and processing power to deliver time-sensitive traffic while throttling back less sensitive traffic.

You can also use tunneling for security purposes. For example, corporations might want their employees to access the corporate network from the Internet. Although firewalls and other systems can protect the internal networks, corporate traffic traversing a public network can still be a problem. With readily available tools, hackers can intercept and perhaps alter the traffic as it travels between the Internet-based employee and the corporate network.

Through the use of protocols such as Internet Protocol Security (IPSec), the corporation can encrypt (scramble) the traffic such that it cannot be recognized unless the user knows certain keys. IPSec essentially tunnels the corporate traffic in the following way: Before traffic hits the Internet, a device (such as a router or PC) encrypts the contents of the traffic.

Generic routing encapsulation (GRE) is a type of tunneling that lets you tunnel any type of traffic. GRE is often used to tunnel unroutable protocols through an IP network.

Aside from tunneling, application and file server vendors are migrating their traditionally proprietary protocols to IP. For example, Novell NetWare and AppleTalk operate natively over IP.

At-A-Glance—IP Convergence

Why Should I Care About Internet Protocol Convergence?

Over the past several years, many protocols have competed for a dominant position among users, and the Internet Protocol (IP) is the winner. With the positive results of network effects (where more users create the need for more applications and services, which draws still more users, and so on), most companies have converted their networks to IP. Virtually all new networks and devices, from computers, to phones, to wristwatches, are compatible with IP.

IP has many benefits over other protocols, especially with the ability to transport non-IP protocols. This benefit helps companies still using legacy systems because it gives them the ability to fully convert to IP at a pace that makes sense for them.

What Are the Problems to Solve?

Converting to IP can be a slow and expensive process, and many companies want to use IP to transport their information across a WAN but keep their legacy systems in place. Using IP as a third-party transport requires that the original data be modified in some way. IP uses a process called *encapsulation* to transport the data through point-to-point tunnels (tunneling).

Although all this movement toward convergence is good for IP, the huge increase of traffic on IP networks sometimes results in congestion, which can seriously affect the quality of time-sensitive information such as live voice data. IP's ability to use quality of service (QoS) allows network administrators to prioritize certain types of traffic, which can be expedited through the network.

IP convergence can also address the issue of security. IP uses a public network for long-haul transport of information, which means that companies risk their private information being eavesdropped or stolen. Security schemes such as Internet Protocol Security (IPSec) allow strong encryption so that if information is stolen, it is unreadable.

Who's the So and So Guy?

One of the biggest issues with maintaining separate networks is the staffing requirements for maintenance, upkeep, and after hours (on-call) personnel. Whenever assistance is needed, the first question tends to be "Who is the so and so guy?" where "so and so" refers to the network in question. By running separate networks, companies spread their support resources thin among competing interests such as IP, time-division multiplexing (TDM) voice, and other legacy systems such as Systems Network Architecture (SNA), AppleTalk, or other proprietary protocols. The choice then becomes hiring additional staff or overworking existing staff, risking burnout.

With IP convergence, you can train all IT staff on a single protocol and support a single converged network.

At-A-Glance—IP Convergence, Continued

IP convergence is the concept of tunneling one type of network through another. Examples include the tunneling of SNA through an IP network, and encrypting IP traffic and tunneling the encrypted data through an unsecure IP network.

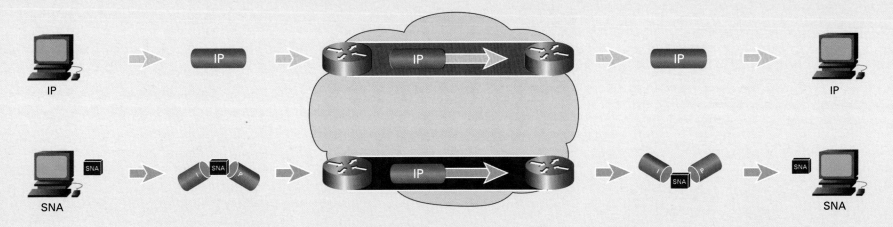

The sender drops a packet in its native language into a standard IP packet, which is then sent across the IP network to its destination. At the IP destination, the native packet is extracted from the IP packet, and then sent on its native way.

The key to tunneling is to make the IP network in the center invisible to the endpoints.

Multicast

Watching Movies Without Flooding the World

IP multicast is a bandwidth-conserving technology based on the IP protocol in which a data intended for multiple receivers is efficiently transmitted with a single stream. IP multicast best serves streaming audio, video, and data applications such as software distribution or stock-quote broadcasts.

Take this example: A corporate officer needs to deliver a live video broadcast to the company's employees. Doing so across an IP network using traditional IP protocols would require that the video feed be replicated once for every user. For a branch office across a wide-area network (WAN) link, 20 employees watching the video on their computers would result in the video stream being replicated 20 times across the WAN. The original data stream then must be replicated 20 times across the single WAN connection. Not only is this highly inefficient, but the WAN link would not be able to handle the sheer amount of traffic being transmitted.

IP multicast protocols allow users to request a particular multicast service (which can be audio, video, or data). The network then determines the source of the multicast transmission and routes the multicast stream to its destination. Multicast protocols ensure that only one copy of the stream is transmitted across any given link. Therefore, in the previous branch-office example, only one copy of the video broadcast would be transmitted over the WAN and then replicated to each user at the local-area network (LAN) level.

Multicasts relate to the concept of a group. The receivers who express an interest in receiving a particular data stream define the group. A receiver must join the group by using the Internet Group Management Protocol (IGMP), which requires that routers and switches must support IGMP to communicate with the receiver. Not until the receiver joins the group can she receive the data stream.

A multicast IP address identifies a group. The Internet Assigned Numbers Authority (IANA) assigns multicast IP addresses using the IP Class D address space 224.0.0.0–239.255.255.255.

The routers in a network are responsible for identifying the most efficient, shortest path from the multicast transmitter to its group of receivers. The Layer 2 LAN switches are responsible for receiving the singular transmission and replicating it to each of the registered receivers.

Of the multicast-related routing protocols, the primary protocol is Protocol Independent Multicast (PIM). The routers use the PIM protocol to make forwarding decisions. PIM determines the shortest path for each multicast group based on the IP routing protocol running on the router (such as Enhanced Interior Gateway Routing Protocol, EIGRP, or Open Shortest Path First, OSPF). Using Reverse Path Forwarding (RPF), routers use the existing unicast routing table to determine upstream and downstream neighbors and eliminate any loops.

PIM operates in three different modes: sparse, dense, and sparse-dense. The mode determines when the routers start forwarding packets to the group. Sparse mode employs a "pull" model, and dense uses a "push" model.

In sparse mode, packets are not transmitted through the network until a receiver specifically requests to join the group. In dense mode, packets are transmitted throughout the network without regard to registered users, and the network prunes transmission to parts of the networks where no receivers are registered. Sparse mode is more efficient in that traffic goes only where requested, whereas dense mode blasts everywhere initially. Sparse-dense mode is the third mode (developed by Cisco) in which the network intelligently determines which mode to use as opposed to configuring just one or the other.

Sparse mode is generally implemented for standard video and audio transmission in corporate networks. A core component of a sparse implementation is the *rendezvous point (RP)*. The RP is the central clearinghouse for multicast transmitters and group receivers. Multicast transmitters register themselves with the RP, and the network forwards requests from group receivers to the RP. The RP then facilitates the transmission of the data stream to the receivers.

If the RP fails or disappears from the network, receivers cannot register with senders. Therefore, a network needs multiple RPs. Anycast-RP is a protocol based on the Multicast Source Discovery Protocol (MSDP) that facilitates the fault-tolerant implementation of multiple RPs.

Dense mode floods traffic to every corner of the network. This brute-force method only makes sense when there are receivers on every subnet in a network. After traffic begins flowing, routers then stop the flow of (or prune) traffic to subnets that have no receivers. Companies generally do not implement dense mode except for special circumstances because of its fire-hose approach to data-stream replication.

Although PIM makes sense in a corporate network, it requires that a network be planned and configured to handle the particular implementation of PIM properly. This setup is not practical across the Internet and shared IP networks for which there is no guarantee that multicast is configured consistently or properly. Multiprotocol Border Gateway Protocol (MBGP) allows the scalable advertising and transmission of MBGP routes through the Internet.

At-A-Glance—IP Multicast

Why Should I Care About Internet Protocol Multicast?

Many applications in modern networks require that you send information (voice, video, or data) to multiple end stations. When you target only a few end stations, sending multiple copies of the same information through the network (unicast) causes no ill effects. However, as the number of targeted end stations increases, the harmful effects of duplicate packets becomes dramatic. Deploying applications such as streaming video, financial market data, and Internet Protocol (IP) telephony–based Music-on-Hold without enabling network devices for multicast support can cause severe degradation to a network's performance.

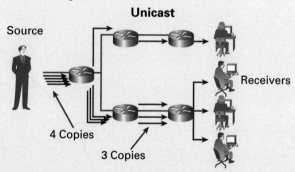

Unicast

Source

4 Copies

3 Copies

Receivers

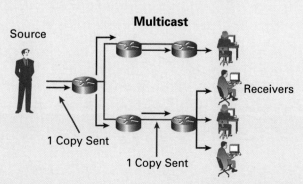

Multicast

Source

1 Copy Sent

1 Copy Sent

Receivers

What Are the Problems to Solve?

Multicasting requires methods to efficiently deploy and scale distributed group applications across the network. Multicasting uses protocols that reduce the network load associated with sending the same data to multiple receivers and alleviate the high host/router processing requirements for serving individual connections.

Internet Group Membership Protocol

Internet Group Membership Protocol (IGMP) allows end stations to join what is known as a multicast group. Joining a multicast group is like subscribing to a session or service that uses multicast. IGMP relies on Class D IP addresses for the creation of multicast groups.

When a multicast session begins, the host sends an IGMP message throughout the network to discover which end stations have joined the group. The host then sends traffic to all members of that multicast group. Routers "listen" to IGMP traffic and periodically send queries to discover which groups are active or inactive on particular LANs. Routers communicate with each other using one or more protocols to build multicast routes for each group.

Multicast Distribution Trees

Multicast-capable routers create *distribution trees* that control the path that IP multicast traffic takes through the network to deliver traffic to all receivers. The two basic types of multicast distribution trees are source trees and shared trees.

With *source trees* (also known as shortest-path trees), each source sends its data to each receiver using the most efficient path. Source trees are optimized for latency but have higher memory requirements because routers must keep track of all sources.

Shared trees send the multicast data to a common point in the network (known as the rendezvous point [RP]) prior to sending it to each receiver. Shared trees require

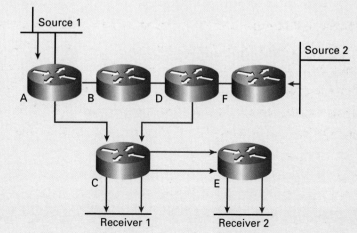

Source 1

Source 2

A B D F

C E

Receiver 1 Receiver 2

At-A-Glance—Multicast Protocols

less memory in routers than source trees but might not always use the optimal path, which can result in packet delivery latency.

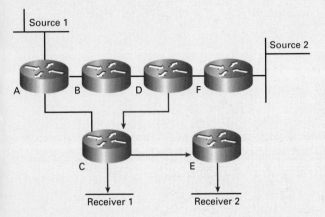

Layer 2 Multicast

A Layer 2 switch forwards all multicast traffic, which reduces network efficiency. Two methods, Cisco Group Management Protocol (CGMP) and IGMP Snooping, mitigate this inefficient switch behavior.

Cisco Group Management Protocol

CGMP allows catalyst switches to make Layer 2 forwarding decisions based on IGMP information. When configured on switches and routers, CGMP ensures that IP multicast traffic is delivered only to ports that are attached to interested receivers or multicast routers. With CGMP running, any router receiving a multicast join message via a switch replies to the switch with a CGMP join message. This message allows Layer 2 forwarding decisions.

IGMP Snooping

IGMP Snooping improves efficiency by enabling a Layer 2 switch to look at Layer 3 information (IGMP join/leave messages) sent between hosts and routers. When an IGMP host report travels through a switch, the switch adds the port number of the host to the associated multicast table entry. When the switch hears the IGMP leave group message from a host, the switch removes the table entry of the host. IGMP requires a switch to examine all multicast packets and therefore should only operate on high-end switches.

Multicast Forwarding

In unicast routing, traffic moves from the source to the destination host. The router scans through its routing table for the destination address and then forwards a single copy of the unicast packet out the correct interface.

In multicast forwarding, the source sends traffic to several hosts, represented by a multicast group address. The multicast router must determine which direction is the upstream direction (toward the source) and which one is the *downstream* direction (toward the hosts). When there is more than one downstream path, the router chooses the best downstream path (toward the group address). This path might not be the same path chosen for a unicast packet. This process is called *Reverse Path Forwarding (RPF)*. RPF creates distribution trees that are loop free.

Protocol Independent Multicast

Protocol Independent Multicast (PIM) is IP-independent and can leverage whichever unicast routing protocols populate the unicast routing table. PIM uses this unicast routing information to perform the multicast forwarding function. Although PIM is called a multicast routing protocol, it actually uses the unicast routing table to perform the RPF check function instead of building up a completely independent multicast routing table. It includes two different modes of behavior for dense and sparse traffic environments, dense mode and sparse mode.

PIM dense mode—In dense mode, the multicast router floods traffic messages out all ports (referred to as a "push" model). If a router has no hosts or downstream neighbors that are members of the group, a prune message tells the router not to flood messages on a particular interface. Dense mode only uses source trees. Because of the flooding and pruning behavior, dense mode is not recommended.

PIM sparse mode—PIM sparse mode uses an "explicit join" model. This model sends traffic only to hosts that explicitly ask to receive it. The router sends a join message to the RP.

Anycast RP provides load balancing, redundancy, and fault tolerance by assigning the same IP address to multiple RPs within a PIM sparse mode network multicast domain.

Bandwidth Conservation

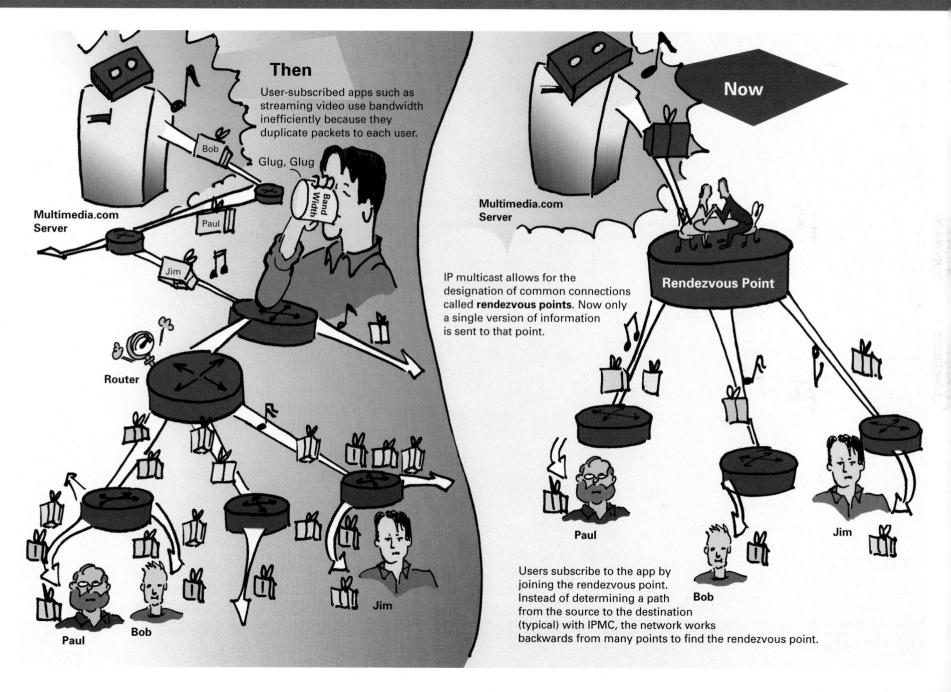

Then

User-subscribed apps such as streaming video use bandwidth inefficiently because they duplicate packets to each user.

Glug, Glug

Multimedia.com Server

Band Width

Router

Paul

Bob

Jim

Now

Multimedia.com Server

IP multicast allows for the designation of common connections called **rendezvous points**. Now only a single version of information is sent to that point.

Rendezvous Point

Paul

Bob

Jim

Users subscribe to the app by joining the rendezvous point. Instead of determining a path from the source to the destination (typical) with IPMC, the network works backwards from many points to find the rendezvous point.

Videoconference

Conducting Videoconferences Across the Net

Videoconferencing is similar to a voice conference call in that multiple people connect to a central site to communicate with each other. Videoconference networks are converging onto IP networks, thus allowing greater flexibility and lower cost.

Traditional videoconferencing systems use a protocol called H.320, which allows the transmission of video across public telephone lines using ISDN. Typically, companies build expensive videoconference rooms that are shared, requiring reservations in advance. During the videoconference, people want to share presentations and images and view notes or whiteboard scribbles. The cost of videoconferences was high both in the investment in equipment and the monthly cost for ISDN.

Although the cost of creating these videoconference nodes is high, the expense is still less than that of flying a group of people to a common location, putting them up in hotels, and so on, especially for international meetings.

Typical uses of videoconferences include the following:

• Executive broadcasts and communications

• High-impact meetings

• Training

With the convergence of video and voice over IP networks, videoconferencing was a natural technology to transfer to traditional data networks.

The introduction of videoconferencing over IP networks had to resolve two issues:

• Providing videoconferencing equipment that could operate on traditional data networks (using TCP/IP over Ethernet networks, for instance)

• Connecting existing H.320 videoconference locations to the IP-based systems

The International Telecommunications Union (ITU) H.323 protocol is the standard for real-time multimedia communications and conferencing over IP networks.

For videoconferencing, H.323 breaks the dependence on expensive conferencing equipment, costly monthly network fees, and dedicated facilities. H.323 lets you connect videoconferencing equipment anywhere there is a traditional data-network connection. Individuals and teams can plug inexpensive video cameras into the corporate network, or across the Internet, and conduct videoconferencing essentially anywhere without dedicated facilities.

Although H.323 addresses the real-time transmission of video and audio, users still want to write and view whiteboard notes, exchange files, or share an application. The ITU T.120 protocol addresses these tasks. The standard identifies how to reliably and efficiently distribute files and graphical information in real time during a videoconference.

As with any real-time or multimedia application, the data network design must accommodate the requirements of these protocols. For videoconferencing, the network must ensure that the video and data transmissions reach their destinations in a timely manner, with minimal loss and delay. To accomplish this task, the networks use quality of service (QoS) prioritization and queuing mechanisms. Traditional application traffic is tolerant of network delays or drops because networks can always retransmit the data.

Videoconferencing traffic has a different traffic profile from that of data but is similar to voice traffic. There is no need to retransmit video frames if some are lost because the video and audio continue to move forward. However, network delay or loss cause the videoconference to look choppy or, worse, appear to lock up. Participants in a videoconference can find the delay frustrating and even unproductive.

Aside from QoS, the network must also handle the sheer capacity of videoconferencing traffic. Video and multimedia generate a high amount of network traffic. Therefore, videoconferencing might not be possible on slow WAN links or congested network connections.

IP-Based Videoconferencing Components

Videoconferencing multipoint control unit (MCU)	The "central meeting place" for a videoconference. Videoconference participants connect to this server via IP. The server facilitates full multipoint, multimedia conferences between three or more parties. The MCU also provides rate matching, enabling the conferencing of slow and higher-speed transmission rates.
Videoconferencing gateway	Lets users interconnect IP-based H.323 videoconference endpoints with legacy ISDN-based H.320 systems.
Video terminal adapter	Allows traditional H.320 locations to attach directly to IP networks using H.323.
T.120 data conferencing application	Lets users share applications, whiteboard notes, and files.
H.323 gatekeeper and proxy	Enables network managers to control bandwidth and priority settings for H.323 videoconferencing services based on individual network configurations and capacities. Cisco provides gatekeeper functionality in Cisco IOS.
H.323 endpoints	Cameras, microphones, and application-sharing tools that people use to participate in a videoconference. It can be as simple as a cheap camera and microphone connected to a PC.

Videoconferencing: All the Talking Heads Come Together

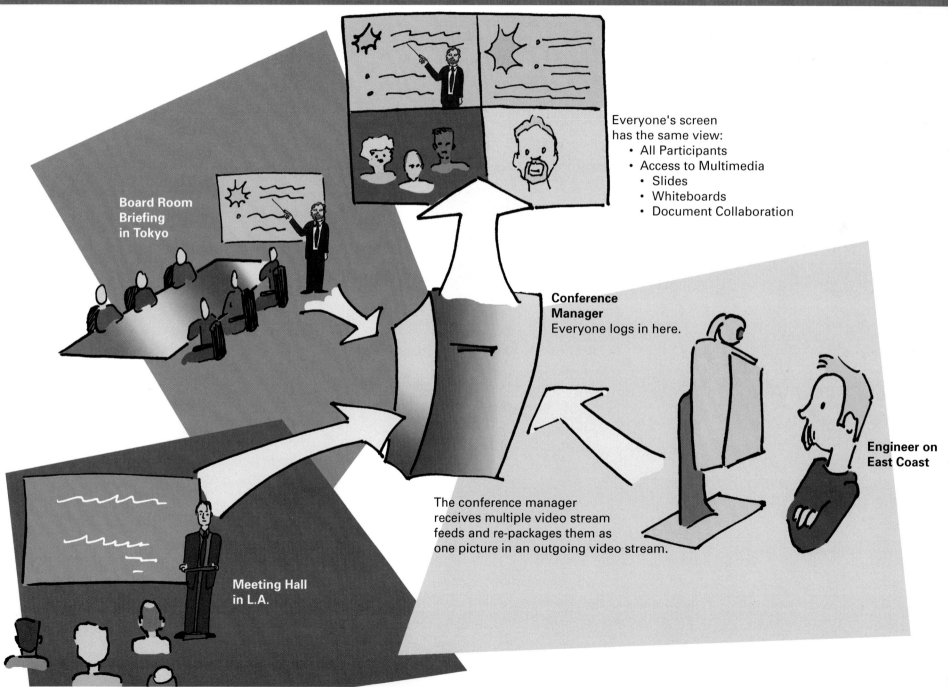

Everyone's screen
has the same view:
- All Participants
- Access to Multimedia
  - Slides
  - Whiteboards
  - Document Collaboration

**Board Room
Briefing
in Tokyo**

**Conference
Manager**
Everyone logs in here.

**Engineer on
East Coast**

The conference manager
receives multiple video stream
feeds and re-packages them as
one picture in an outgoing video stream.

**Meeting Hall
in L.A.**

At-A-Glance—Videoconferencing

Why Should I Care About Videoconferencing?

Traditional videoconferencing consisted of room-based systems that connected to other room-based systems via satellite or Integrated Services Digital Network (ISDN) connections. These fixed systems were expensive and proprietary and provided little flexibility or data-sharing capability. Even with these limitations, videoconferencing provides a good alternative to traveling to remote sites for meetings and were good vehicles for executive communication.

Alternatively, you can conduct Internet Protocol (IP) videoconferencing from any PC or connected location, providing application sharing and whiteboard capabilities cheaply and effectively over corporate and public IP networks.

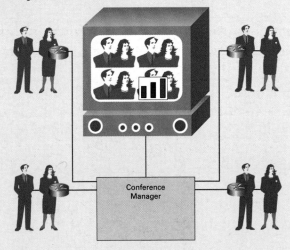

With videoconferencing, all parties can see each other at the same time. With conference management, all parties can also view and manipulate applications.

What Are the Problems to Solve?

Bandwidth—Videoconferencing requires a great deal of bandwidth. A LAN typically has sufficient bandwidth to accommodate videoconferencing, making the WAN (and the physical connection to the WAN) the critical constraint.

Quality of Service (QoS)—Regardless of the amount of bandwidth available, it is always preferable to employ QoS design practices. Most networks are intentionally over-provisioned, but even those are prone to instantaneous congestion. A good QoS design is one of the best ways to use the available bandwidth most efficiently.

Legacy systems—Many legacy systems are still in use today. The migration strategy for converting to an IP videoconferencing system must take legacy systems into account. Tools exist for this purpose.

Videoconferencing Equipment

Endpoints are the cameras, microphones, and application-sharing tools that people use to participate in a videoconference. They can be as simple as a cheap camera and microphone connected to a PC.

 A multipoint control unit (MCU) allows multiparty conferences with three or more participants.

 The H.320 video gateway allows communication between H.323 and H.320 (legacy) video terminals.

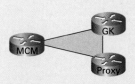

The gatekeeper (GK) provides address resolution and bandwidth management, whereas the proxy provides traffic classification and security.

H.323

The H.323 protocol was developed specifically for multimedia communications over a packet-switched network. Multimedia in this case refers to audio, video, and general data communication.

The benefits of H.323 include the following:

- Standardized compression of audio and video allowing multivendor equipment and support
- Hardware and operating-system independence
- Efficient use of bandwidth with multipoint conferencing (multicast)
- Bandwidth-management features

T.120

The T.120 protocols define the methods for document conferencing and application sharing (also known as data conferencing) within a multimedia conference. The standards specify how to efficiently and reliably distribute files and graphical information in real time during a multipoint multimedia meeting. T.120 ensures interoperability between end terminals in the absence of prior knowledge about the other terminals. The standard also allows data-sharing applications such as whiteboards, graphic displays, and image exchanges.

At-A-Glance—Videoconferencing: Zones

Zones

If the network has no gatekeepers, endpoints can directly call each other if they know the network addresses. This approach requires a full-mesh design, however, so it is only suitable for very small networks.

Single Zones

When gatekeepers are present in the network, all video endpoints and equipment must register with the closest gatekeeper, which controls traffic on the network. Each cluster of terminals and equipment controlled by a single gatekeeper comprises a zone. Once defined, the gatekeeper acts as the central point for all calls within its zone, providing address resolution, admission control, and call-control services to registered endpoints.

A single zone is suitable for small- to medium-size campuses or for several small WAN-separated campuses.

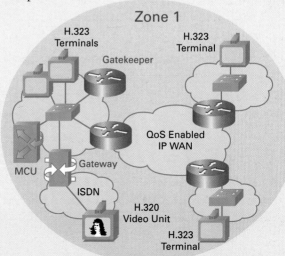

Multiple Zones

Large campuses or WAN-separated campuses with multiple endpoints require a multizone solution. Intrazone communication follows the same procedure as a single-zone solution. However, for communication across different zones, the gatekeepers of each zone must establish a communication link.

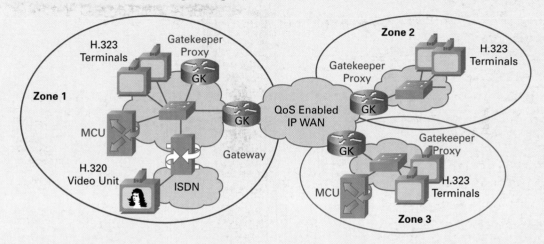

More complex networks require a hierarchical gatekeeper scheme to provide end-to-end connectivity for all gateways and terminals. The higher-level gatekeeper is a directory gatekeeper. This figure illustrates the importance of the directory gatekeeper in network efficiency and simplicity.

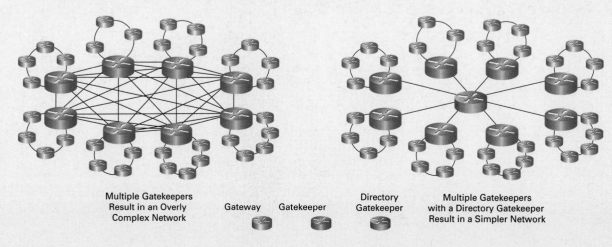

Multiple Gatekeepers Result in an Overly Complex Network

Gateway   Gatekeeper

Directory Gatekeeper

Multiple Gatekeepers with a Directory Gatekeeper Result in a Simpler Network

> **Part III**

Making the Network Safe

The Internet has opened boundless avenues for new forms of conducting business and trade. Such business and trade does not come without its drawbacks, however. We buy books and cars and other things on the Internet, but concerns remain about the credit-card numbers, personal information, or passwords being stolen from the Internet. In addition, employees want the ability to connect back to the corporate network from anywhere at any time; but there are many instances of commerce sites that have been hacked or bombarded with bogus traffic.

Why does all that happen? Quite simply: Because the Internet is inherently unsecure.

Fortunately, some mechanisms reduce the threat of these problems. Although these methods can be effective, people who want to break security measures are always developing new techniques that break existing protections. You need to be armed with both tools and common sense to help keep your stuff secure.

Home broadband customers and corporations protect their computers and users by installing firewalls between them and the Internet. When conducting commerce and confidential transactions across a public network such as the Internet, the sender and receiver need a way to ensure that each is who she says she is and that no one can eavesdrop on the transactions. Client authentication, encryption, and hashing achieve these goals, and you learn about them and much more in Part III.

Security

Network Security

The following sections describe the different categories of network security.

Identity

Identity is the identification of network users, hosts, applications, services, and resources. Examples of technologies that enable identification include Remote Authentication Dial-In User Service (RADIUS), Kerberos, one-time passwords, digital certificates, smart cards, and directory services.

Perimeter Security

Perimeter security ontrols access to critical network applications, data, and services so that only legitimate users and information can access these assets. Examples include access lists on routers and switches, firewalls, virus scanners, and content filters.

Data Privacy

The ability to provide secure communication is crucial when you must protect information from eavesdropping. Digital encryption technologies and protocols such as Internet Protocol Security (IPSec) are the primary means for protecting data, especially when implementing virtual private networks (VPNs).

Security Monitoring

Regardless of how security is implemented, it is still necessary to monitor a network and its components to ensure that the network remains secure. Network-security monitoring tools and intrusion detection systems (IDSs) provide visibility to the security status of the network.

Policy Management

Tools and technologies are worthless without well-defined security policies. Effective policies balance the imposition of security measures against the productivity gains realized with little security. Centralized policy-management tools that can analyze, interpret, configure, and monitor the state of security policies help consolidate the successful deployment of rational security policies.

A company's network is like any other corporate asset: It is valuable to the success and revenue of that company. More than ever, the corporate computer network is the most valuable asset of many companies. Therefore, it must be protected. Generally, middle- to large-size companies appoint a chief security officer, whose job is to develop and enforce corporate security policies.

Security threats present themselves in many forms:

- A hacker breaking into the network to steal confidential information or destroy corporate data
- A natural disaster such as a fire, tornado, or earthquake destroying computer and network equipment
- A disgruntled employee intentionally trying to modify, steal, or destroy corporate information and devices
- A computer virus
- An act of war or terrorism

Common security threats introduced by people include the following:

- Network packet sniffers
- IP spoofing
- Password attacks
- Distribution of sensitive internal information to external sources
- Man-in-the-middle attacks

Internet security is also a big concern given the exposure of corporate data resources to the publicly accessible Internet. Traditionally, you could achieve security by physically separating corporate networks from public networks. However, with corporate web servers and databases—and the desire to provide access to corporate resources to employees over the Internet—companies must be especially diligent in protecting their networks.

Another recent area for security concern is wireless networking. Traditional networking occurred over physical wires or fibers. However, the current trend is to provide networking services over radio frequencies. Companies are installing wireless networking in their buildings so employees can link to the corporate network from conference rooms and other shared locations from their laptop computers. Additionally, service providers are now offering public wireless Internet services.

Identity and Network Access Control

You can define identity terms of *authentication* and *authorization*:

- A computer or computer user identifies itself to the network or network resources.
- Authorization occurs after authentication. After the computer or user successfully identifies itself, the network or server authorizes the individual or computer to perform certain things with a certain level of access.

802.1x is a link layer protocol used for transporting higher-level authentication protocols defined by the Institute of Electrical and Electronic Engineers (IEEE).

One form of authentication occurs through the exchange of passwords. This form is generally a one-way transaction in which a user or computer identifies itself to a network or server.

A popular method for securely identifying a machine or individual uses *digital signatures*. For example, if you send an e-mail to someone, he might want to verify that you were indeed the originator of the e-mail. Algorithms such as Secure Hash Algorithm (SHA), Message Digest 5 (MD5) (similar to checksum), and triple Digital Encryption Standard (3DES) encrypt and securely "sign" the message. Then, the sender and receiver match public and private keys. The combination of these methods allows both parties to trust (or not trust) each other when exchanging information.

At-A-Glance—Security

Why Should I Care About Network Security?

A company's network is like any other corporate asset: it has value, it is directly related to the success and revenue of that company, and, as such, it must be protected. One of the primary concerns of network administrators is the security of their network. Security attacks can range from malicious attacks to theft of information to simple misuse of company resources. Estimated losses attributed directly to network intrusions totaled more than $15 billion for 2001.

According to the FBI, the number of network attacks doubled from 2000 to 2001. They are expected to increase another 100 to 150 percent in 2002. It is believed that less than 50 percent of intrusions are actually reported. The majority of unauthorized access and resource misuse continues to come from internal sources. In addition, attacks from external sources continue to grow in number as less sophisticated hackers gain access to information and power tools designed for hacking. The figure below demonstrates this change.

What Are the Problems to Solve?

Security must be an inherent part of every network design based on the principles of protecting from the outside (perimeter security) and controlling the inside (internal security). In other words, keep the outsiders out, and keep the insiders honest. You should think of the network performing the dual roles of "gatekeeper" (perimeter) and a "hall monitor" (internal).

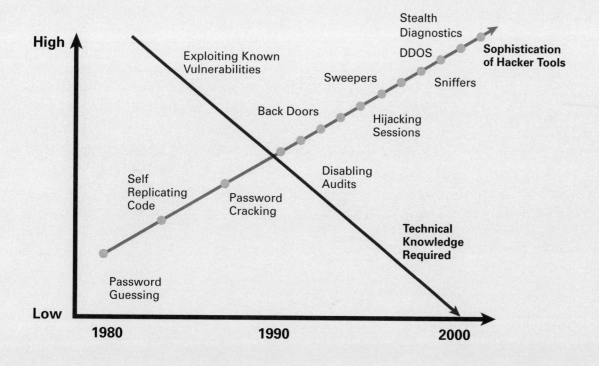

At-A-Glance—Security, Continued

Balancing Trust and Security

Security and trust are opposing concepts. Trust is necessary for applications to run, but open access can expose a network to attacks or misuse. On the other hand, a very restrictive security policy might limit exposure but also reduce productivity. When security is a primary design consideration, you can determine a trust boundary on a per-user basis and strike the proper balance.

Establishing Identity

The first part of any security design is determining who is on the network. Without some knowledge of who the users are, you would have to make the network policies generic so they would likely be too open or too restrictive. Identity can include

- User identity based on password, smart card, fingerprint, etc.
- Device identity (e.g. IP phone) based on Internet Protocol (IP) or Media Access Control (MAC) address.
- Application identity based on IP address or Transmission Control Protocol/User Datagram Protocol (TCP/UDP) port number.

Identity is tightly linked with authentication. After you establish identity, you can apply, monitor, and enforce the proper policy for that user, device, or application.

Perimeter Security

Perimeter security refers to controlling access to critical network applications, data, and services so that only legitimate users and network information can pass through the network. You typically control access with access control lists (ACLs) enabled on edge routers and switches, as well as with dedicated firewall appliances. A *firewall* is a device that permits only authorized traffic to pass (according to a predefined security policy). Other tools, such as virus scanners, content filters, and intrusion detection systems (IDSs), also help control traffic.

Policy Management

As networks grow in size and complexity, the requirement for centralized policy management grows as well. Regardless of the existence of sophisticated tools, companies must employ a sound policy with clear guidelines for enforcement. Generally, middle- to large-size companies appoint a chief security officer whose job is to develop and enforce corporate security policies.

At-A-Glance—Security, Continued

Data Privacy

Much of the information passing through a network is confidential. Whether it is business-specific (engineering or financial) or personnel (human resources correspondence) information, it must be protected from eavesdropping. You can implement encryption and data privacy schemes in Layer 2 (Layer 2 Tunnel Protocol (L2TP)) or Layer 3 (IP Security (IPSec) for encryption), Multiprotocol Label Switching (MPLS) for data privacy). This type of protection is especially important when implementing virtual private networks (VPNs).

Security Monitoring

Enabling security measures in a network is not enough. Network administrators must regularly test and monitor the state of security solutions. Using a combination of network vulnerability scanners and IDSs, the network administrator can monitor and respond to security threats in real time.

Top 13 Security Vulnerabilities

1. Inadequate router access control.

2. Unsecured and unmonitored remote access points, providing easy access to corporate networks.

3. Information leakage revealing operating-system and application information.

4. Hosts running unnecessary services.

5. Weak, easily guessed, and reused passwords.

6. User or test accounts with excessive privileges.

7. Misconfigured Internet servers, especially for anonymous FTP.

8. Misconfigured firewalls.

9. Software that is outdated, vulnerable, or left in default configurations.

10. Lack of accepted and well-promulgated security policies, procedures, guidelines, and minimum baseline standards.

11. Excessive trust domains in UNIX and NT environments, giving hackers unauthorized access to sensitive systems.

12. Unauthenticated services such as the X Window System.

13. Inadequate logging, monitoring, and detection capabilities.

Comparing Physical and Logical Security

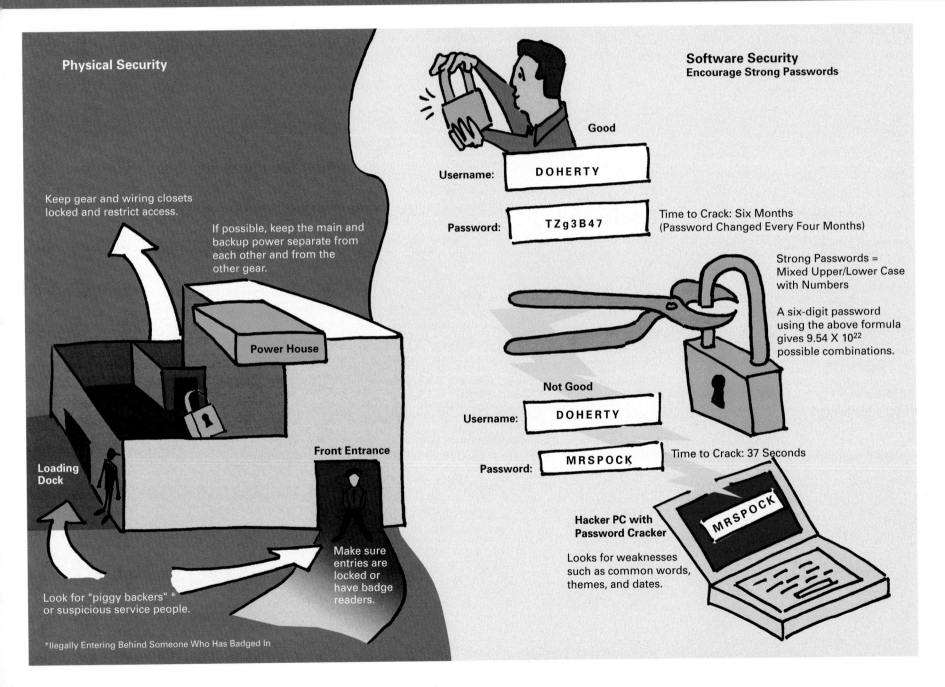

Physical Security

Keep gear and wiring closets locked and restrict access.

If possible, keep the main and backup power separate from each other and from the other gear.

Power House

Loading Dock

Front Entrance

Make sure entries are locked or have badge readers.

Look for "piggy backers" * or suspicious service people.

*Ilegally Entering Behind Someone Who Has Badged In

Software Security
Encourage Strong Passwords

Good

Username: DOHERTY

Password: TZg3B47

Time to Crack: Six Months
(Password Changed Every Four Months)

Strong Passwords = Mixed Upper/Lower Case with Numbers

A six-digit password using the above formula gives 9.54×10^{22} possible combinations.

Not Good

Username: DOHERTY

Password: MRSPOCK

Time to Crack: 37 Seconds

Hacker PC with Password Cracker

Looks for weaknesses such as common words, themes, and dates.

MRSPOCK

Protecting Networks from Theft and Evil

At-A-Glance—Identity

Why Should I Care About Identity?

The majority of resource misuse and unauthorized access to traditional networks comes from internal sources. Identifying users and devices attempting to access the corporate network is the first step of any security solution.

Validating the *identity* of users and devices can also let network administrators provision services and allocate resources to users based on their job functions.

To be truly effective, the security policy must use identity in a way that does not disrupt business or make authorized access prohibitively difficult.

What Are the Problems to Solve?

A comprehensive network-security policy must keep the outsiders out and the insiders honest. Specific goals should be

- Preventing external hackers from having free rein in the network
- Allowing only authorized users into the network
- Preventing network attacks from within
- Providing different layers of access for different kinds of users

Network Security Policy Spans the Network

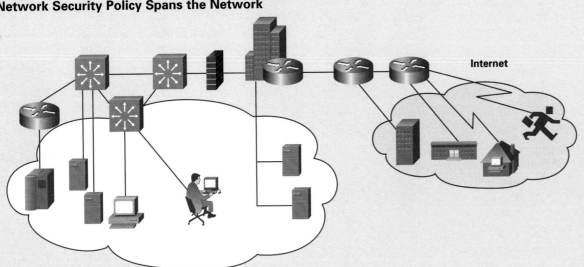

Internet

What Is 802.1x?

802.1x is a set of standards that describe a Layer 2 protocol used for transporting higher-level authentication protocols. It is language used to carry the information payload (e.g. name and password) between an endpoint (client) and the authenticator (server).

802.1x Header	EAP Payload

Extensible Authentication Protocol

The *Extensible Authentication Protocol (EAP)* is a flexible protocol that carries authentication information. The authentication information can include user passwords or predefined security keys.

The EAP typically rides on top of another protocol, such as 802.1x or Remote Authentication Dial-In User Service (RADIUS), which carries the authentication information between the client and the authenticating authority.

At-A-Glance—Benefits of Identity

What Does Identity Do for Me?

Identity not only prevents unauthorized access, but it also lets you know who and where your insiders are. After you know who is on the network, you can apply policies on a per-user basis. This solid, comprehensive security solution actually enhances the usability of the network rather than reduce it. Some examples of the advantages of an identity-based security solution appear in the following figure.

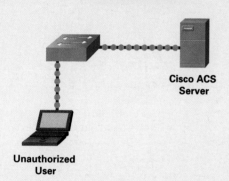

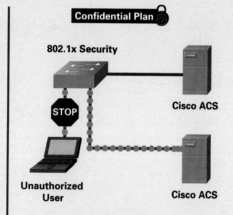

Without Identity
An unauthorized user can connect to the network and download confidential documents.

With Identity
802.1x, used with an access control server (ACS), prevents unauthorized users and outsiders from going where they do not belong.

Preventing Unwanted Access
Limiting Access to Networked Resources

With Identity
By using 802.1x with extensions, you can specify which networked resources the user can access. For example, only managers have access to HR information.

Without Identity
Access to Human Resources databases and other sensitive material is available to all employees.

User-Based Service Provisioning

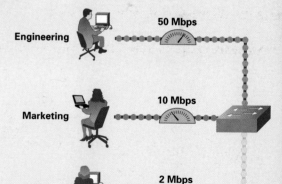

Without Identity
Hackers or malicious insiders might try to crash a network by overloading it with requests and traffic.

With Identity
By using 802.1x, the switch can allocate bandwidth and other services on a case-by-case basis. You can deal with an abuse quickly and easily.

Authentication

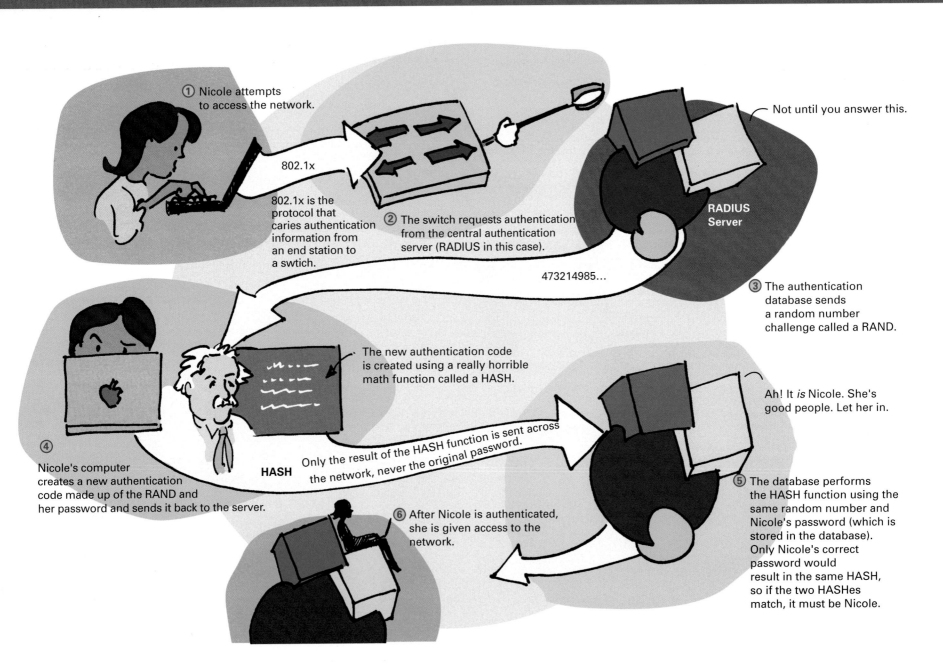

① Nicole attempts to access the network.

802.1x

802.1x is the protocol that caries authentication information from an end station to a swtich.

② The switch requests authentication from the central authentication server (RADIUS in this case).

Not until you answer this.

RADIUS Server

473214985...

③ The authentication database sends a random number challenge called a RAND.

The new authentication code is created using a really horrible math function called a HASH.

Ah! It *is* Nicole. She's good people. Let her in.

④ Nicole's computer creates a new authentication code made up of the RAND and her password and sends it back to the server.

HASH

Only the result of the HASH function is sent across the network, never the original password.

⑤ The database performs the HASH function using the same random number and Nicole's password (which is stored in the database). Only Nicole's correct password would result in the same HASH, so if the two HASHes match, it must be Nicole.

⑥ After Nicole is authenticated, she is given access to the network.

At-A-Glance—Authentication Servers

Working with Authentication Servers

802.1x is only half of the identity story. A service must authenticate the information carried by 802.1x. This authentication can come from name and password validation using a RADIUS or Terminal Access Controller Access Control System (TACACS) server or from digital signatures confirmed by a third-party validation service such as public-key infrastructure (PKI).

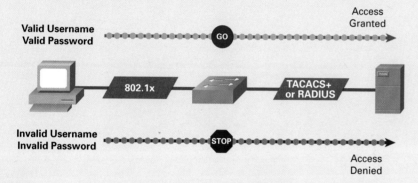

RADIUS

RADIUS is a protocol that communicates between a network device and an authentication server or database. RADIUS allows a network device to securely pass login and authentication information (username/password), as well as arbitrary value pairs using vendor-specific attributes (VSAs). RADIUS can also act as a transport for EAP messages. RADIUS refers to the server and the protocol.

PKI

PKI provides identity authentication between two parties via a trusted third party. A PKI certificate is "proof" of identity signed by the third party. It is the network equivalent of a valid passport trusted by the customs agents of other countries. Just as a passport signed by the passport office states your verified identity and citizenship, a PKI certificate signed by a certificate authority states your verified identity and network associations. Unlike passports, PKI certificates can't be forged.

Hacking

Why Should I Care About Hacking?

Anyone who accesses a public network should know about hackers and their methods. Failure to understand what they do can leave you and your network exposed.

Although thieves and opportunists always go after an easy target versus a difficult (or well-prepared) one, some hackers specifically choose difficult targets, such as government offices or networking companies, solely for bragging rights.

What Are the Problems to Solve?

Hacking really boils down to a few activities:

- **Breaking in**—Breaking into a private network is usually the first part of any hacking scheme. (A denial-of-service [DoS] attack is one notable exception.) Most break-ins require a password (which are guessed or stolen), but hackers find other ways to get in as well.

- **Breaking stuff**—Once in a network, many hackers (anarchists in particular) try to break or disable the entire network, or specific parts of it, such as web servers. If they destroy data or disrupt business, recovery can be expensive for the attacked company.

- **Stealing stuff**—Like most thieves, many hackers are motivated by greed. They might sell plans, schematics, or intellectual property to unscrupulous individuals, companies, or government agencies.

Hacks and Attacks

An *attack* in network speak refers to any attempt to break into a computer, network, or packet, as well as any attempt to launch a malicious or self-replicating program. Attacks fit into multiple categories, many of which are described here.

All network attacks are either active or passive.

Active attacks include injecting malicious files, altering data, or clogging the network. In theory, you can detect active attacks but not passive attacks.

Passive attacks such as eavesdropping do not actually cause harm to the network, but hackers can use them to obtain information that enables active attacks. People looking for passwords can tirelessly try every combination until they find a working password (a brute-force attack). Man-in-the-middle attacks occur when a hacker interposes between two valid users and eavesdrops for passwords. Passive attacks are difficult to detect.

Remote attacks are conducted by people outside the network (those without a network ID), whereas *local attacks* use an existing account to exploit the system.

Hit-and-run attacks quickly crash systems, whereas *persistent* attacks affect the victims only as long as the attack lasts.

At-A-Glance—Hacking Types

① Inside Jobs

Most security breeches originate inside the network that is under attack. *Inside jobs* include stealing passwords (which hackers then use or sell), performing industrial espionage, causing harm (as disgruntled employees), or committing simple misuse.

Sound policy enforcement and observant employees who guard their passwords and PCs can thwart many of these security breeches.

② Rogue Access Points

Rogue access points (APs) are unsecured wireless access points that outsiders can easily breech. (Local hackers often advertise rogue APs to each other.) Rogue APs are most often connected by well-meaning but ignorant employees.

③ Back Doors

Hackers can gain access to a network by exploiting *back doors*—administrative shortcuts, configuration errors, easily deciphered passwords, and unsecured dial-ups. With the aid of computerized searchers (bots), hackers can probably find any weakness in your network.

④ Viruses and Worms

Viruses and *worms* are self-replicating programs or code fragments that attach themselves to other programs (viruses) or machines (worms).

Both viruses and worms attempt to shut down networks by flooding them with massive amounts of bogus traffic, usually through e-mail.

⑤ Trojan Horses

Trojan horses, which are attached to other programs, are the leading cause of all break-ins. When a user downloads and activates a Trojan horse, the hacked software (SW) kicks off a virus, password gobbler, or remote-control SW that gives the hacker control of the PC.

⑥ Denial of Service

DoS attacks give hackers a way to bring down a network without gaining internal access.

DoS attacks work by flooding the access routers with bogus traffic (which can be e-mail or Transmission Control Protocol, TCP, packets).

Distributed DoSs (DDoSs) are coordinated DoS attacks from multiple sources. A DDoS is more difficult to block because it uses multiple, changing, source IP addresses.

⑦ Anarchists, Crackers, and Kiddies

Who are these people, and why are they attacking your network?

Anarchists are people who just like to break stuff. They usually exploit any target of opportunity.

Crackers are hobbyists or professionals who break passwords and develop Trojan horses or other SW (called warez). They either use the SW themselves (for bragging rights) or sell it for profit.

Script kiddies are hacker wannabes. They have no real hacker skills, so they buy or download warez, which they launch.

Other attackers include disgruntled employees, terrorists, political operatives, or anyone else who feels slighted, exploited, ripped off, or unloved.

⑧ Sniffing and Spoofing

Sniffing refers to the act of intercepting TCP packets. This interception can happen through simple eavesdropping or something more sinister.

Spoofing is the act of sending an illegitimate packet with an expected acknowledgment (ACK), which a hacker can guess, predict, or obtain by snooping.

At-A-Glance—Hacking Types, Continued

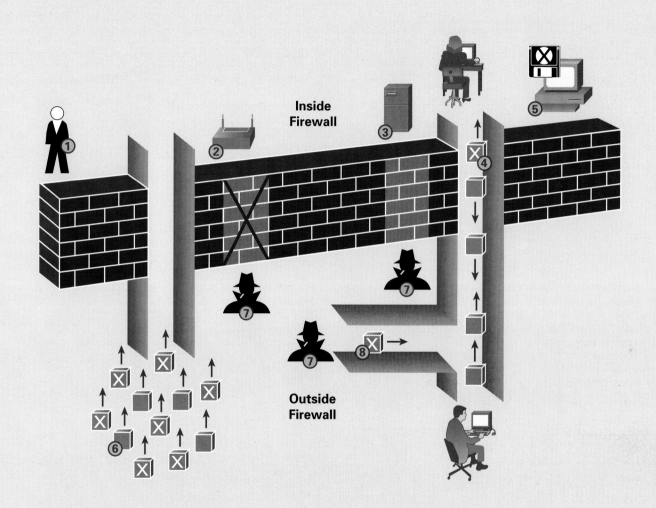

Denial of Service (DoS) Attacks

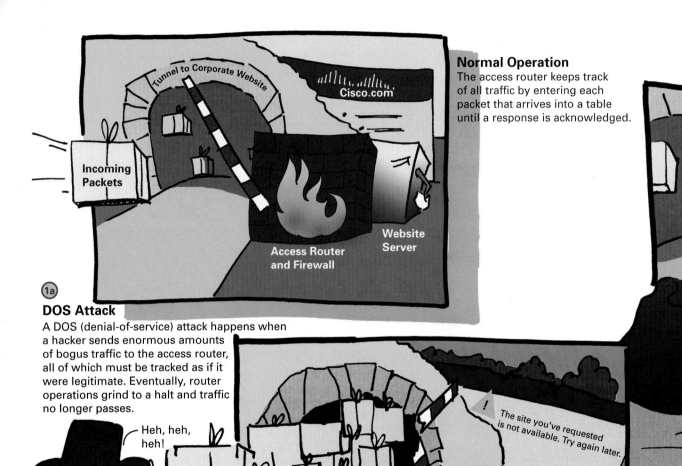

Normal Operation
The access router keeps track of all traffic by entering each packet that arrives into a table until a response is acknowledged.

DOS Attack
A DOS (denial-of-service) attack happens when a hacker sends enormous amounts of bogus traffic to the access router, all of which must be tracked as if it were legitimate. Eventually, router operations grind to a halt and traffic no longer passes.

Blocking a Suspect Source
In a DOS attack, the web server identifies the suspect source and blocks any more incoming packets from it.

Denial of Service (DoS) Attacks

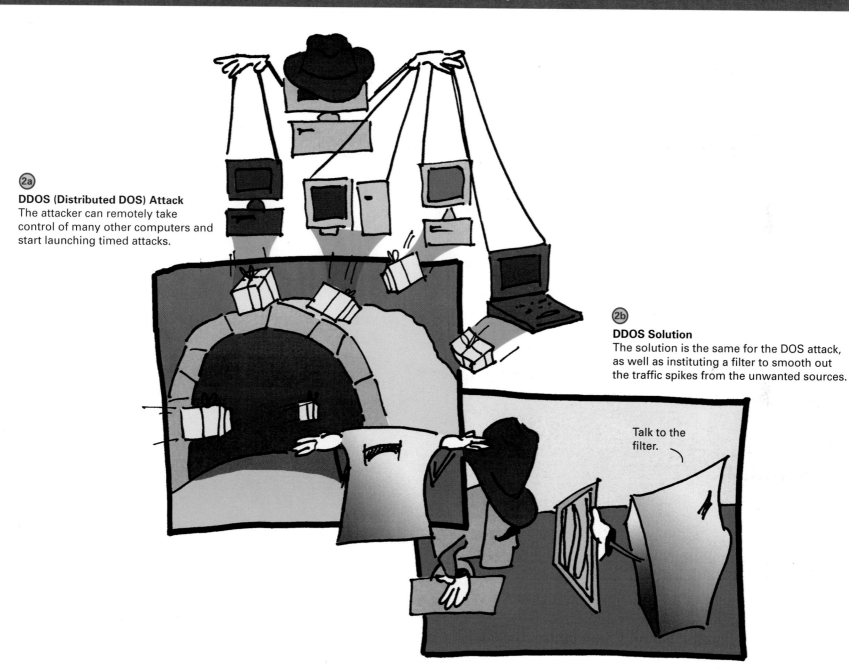

2a

DDOS (Distributed DOS) Attack
The attacker can remotely take control of many other computers and start launching timed attacks.

2b

DDOS Solution
The solution is the same for the DOS attack, as well as instituting a filter to smooth out the traffic spikes from the unwanted sources.

Talk to the filter.

Snooping and Spoofing

Ooh! Jim will love this one!

Doesn't he have any real work to do?

The hacker now sends his own packet that looks like part of a valid session.

After the hacker penetrates a system, he can easily gain access to information or attack other sites from a "clean" site.

Sniffer Software

Hacker

① The hacker can gain access to packets by physically accessing a network device such as a router, or by using software tools such as a trojan horse. A data capture tool (packet sniffer) finds the packets the hacker is interested in.

Prevention
Spoofing and snooping by an external source can be prevented by never allowing an address that is not in your address database to come from outside. Preventing spoofing and snooping by an internal source is typically handled with point-to-point encryption.

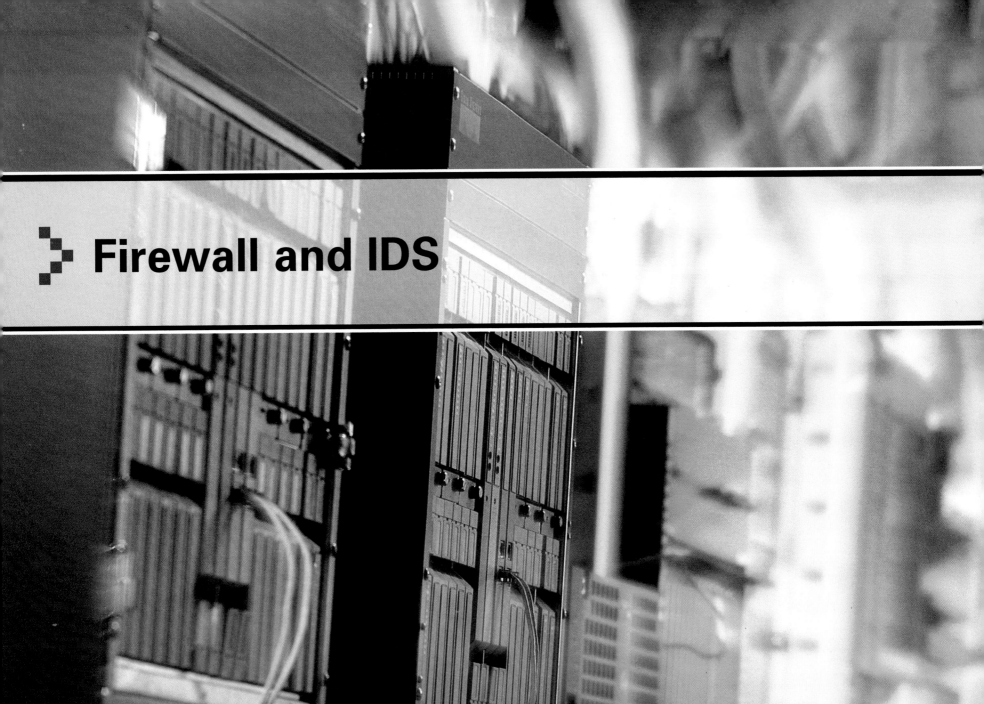

Firewall and IDS

Protecting the Perimeter

Businesses and home users are moving more of their network activities to the Internet. At a minimum, most users have a dialup connection to the Internet, but broadband technologies such as DSL and cable modems enable users to watch online movies, purchase items online, exchange digital photos, download software, and listen to online music over the Internet.

With more home computers and business networks connecting to the Internet, there is considerably more opportunity for malicious attacks from hackers and saboteurs. The same danger applies to internal corporate networks in that companies must protect their data centers and computing resources from internal and external attack.

News stories are common of website invasions, erased hard drives, stolen corporate data, and lethal viruses. And with home users migrating to broadband "always-on" networks, hackers have a whole playground of unsuspecting exposed home networks. Users accessing their corporate networks from home also creates the potential for compromising the corporate network.

Network attacks occur for a variety of reasons: extortion, fraud, espionage, sabotage, or simple curiosity. The acts themselves involve a range of activities, including misuse of authorized systems, system break-ins, equipment theft, interception of network traffic, and reconfiguration of computer systems to allow for future access. Because of the nature of global networks, these attacks can (and often do) cross network and national boundaries.

How can home users and corporations protect themselves?

Get Off the Net!

The most secure way to avoid attack is to not connect to a network. Although physical security (such as keeping computers behind locked doors) remains an issue, going off the net is the most secure way to reduce exposure to security risks.

Clearly, removing yourself from the net is not a practical option.

Instead, consider the concept of perimeter security. Traditionally, a firewall provides perimeter security. Firewalls sit between an unsafe, "dirty" side and a safe, "clean" side.

Suppose a home user puts a firewall between his computer and the Internet connection. The side of the firewall that connects to the Internet is the dirty side (meaning the traffic cannot be trusted), and the side of the firewall that connects to the home network is the clean side (where the traffic can be trusted). The firewall inspects packets going in either direction and determines whether it should permit or drop the traffic.

The firewall is the central location to perform any perimeter-related activities.

Firewalls for Your Protection

Firewalls are designed to combat network-related security threats. Examples of such threats include the following:

- **Passive eavesdropping**—Attackers use packet-capture programs to glean sensitive information or steal username/password combinations.
- **IP address spoofing**—An attacker pretends to be a trusted computer by using an IP address within the accepted range of internal IP addresses. This tactic is similar to assuming another identity.
- **Port scans**—Servers "listen" for traffic on different ports. For example, port 80 is where servers listen for web HTTP traffic. Attackers find ways to infiltrate servers through individual server ports.

- **Denial-of-service attack**—The attacker attempts to block valid users from accessing servers by creating TCP SYN packets that exhaust the server so it cannot handle any valid requests.
- **Application-layer attack**—These attacks exploit the weaknesses of certain applications to obtain illicit access to the hosting server.

Firewalls provide the ability to block these and other attacks by inspecting traffic, tracking valid sessions, and filtering traffic that looks suspect so it cannot pass.

Intrusion Detection Systems

Firewalls provide a barrier for traffic. However, some traffic might look legitimate, and some traffic might in fact be legitimate but unbeknownst to the user carry devious viruses or attack programs.

Although a firewall is sufficient for home use, corporations tend to have more at risk and choose to invest in extra measures to detect traffic patterns that a firewall can't catch. Intrusion detection provides this ability.

Intrusion detection systems (IDSs) analyze data in real time to detect, log, and hinder misuse and attacks. Host-based IDSs monitor server operations for any mischievous events, and network-based IDSs monitor network traffic on a specific segment.

Network-based IDSs monitor traffic in real time, looking at each packet for mischievous data profiles. When a particular data flow is suspect, the IDS logs the finding and notifies the receiving router to deny the traffic and any future traffic from that source.

Keeping Up with the Times

New viruses and new forms of attacks are introduced to networks regularly. For each security measure put in place, motivated attackers always find a way to work around it. There is no such thing as a foolproof security measure.

For that reason, network administrators and home users must be diligent in regularly updating their security software and profiles. Firewall updates can block newly found vulnerabilities. IDS updates can detect new forms of viruses or attacks.

The Internet is anarchy in a good and bad way. Companies and individuals have the burden of protecting themselves from probing individuals.

At-A-Glance—Firewalls and Intrusion Detection Systems

Why Should I Care About Firewalls and IDSs?

Firewalls and *intrusions detection systems (IDSs)* provide the perimeter defense of corporate and personal networks. As hackers become more sophisticated (and aggressive) in their attacks, so has the technology behind keeping networks safe. Firewalls and IDSs are a direct response to hackers.

With the advances in technology comes a great deal of innovation around the deployment of these systems, which is important to companies with public websites.

What Are the Problems to Solve?

The main goal with perimeter security is to keep the bad guys out of the network. The way to be absolutely sure of perimeter security is to not connect to anything. However, most companies rely on the Internet, and for some, it is a critical aspect of their business. The problem then is how to maintain an external presence and still stay relatively safe against attacks.

The answer is the three-part firewall system, which places external-facing servers into an intermediate zone in the network between two separate firewalls.

What Does a Firewall Do?

Firewalls keep both corporate and personal networks safe from attack by inspecting packets for known attack profiles and by acting as a proxy between you and the rest of the world.

Service companies sell packages of profiles they discover.

The proxy function works by using a "third party" address whenever you communicate with the world so that no one knows your actual IP address, the discovery of which is the basis of many attacks.

Are You a Good Packet or a Bad Packet?

In terms of a firewall system, good packets fall into two categories:

 Good outbound packets are those sent by inside users to approved external locations.

Good in-bound packets originate outside the external firewall and either correspond to a Transmission Control Protocol (TCP) session originated by an inside user (that is, it can only be a response packet) or access publicly available services such as web traffic.

 Bad packets are pretty much everything else, and firewalls discard them for the safety of the network.

At-A-Glance—Three-Part Firewall System

Clean Net

The clean net is the interior corporate network. The only "outside" packets allowed in have been inspected and have the acknowledgment to a TCP packet generated from an inside computer.

Inside Filter (Firewall System Part One)

The *inside filter* performs the functions of both firewall and IDS. In addition to blocking attacks such as denial of service (DoS), it inspects every packet, making sure that no externally initiated TCP sessions reach the clean net. (Hackers can gain access by spoofing a session.) The inside filter trashes any packets of questionable origin. It also inspects outbound packets to ensure compliance with corporate policy.

Isolation LAN (Firewall System Part Two)

The *isolation LAN* or demilitarized zone (DMZ) acts as a buffer between outside-facing (web) applications and the clean LAN. Servers in the isolation LAN are called bastion hosts, and outsiders use them for access to public web pages or FTP servers. These servers are secure, but are still prone to hackers.

Outside Filter (Firewall System Part Three)

The *outside filter* is a firewall that screens for TCP replies and UPD packets assigned to port numbers associated with whatever bastions hosts are present. This firewall should only have static routes assigned, and simple rules because complicated processes are prone to errors and hackers love errors!

The Dirty Net

The Internet is often referred to as "the dirty net" by network and security admins who, in the interest of network security, assume every packet was sent by a hacker until proven otherwise. The majority of users are honest, but this attitude can and does prevent disasters.

Hackers and Their Evil Ways

Hackers use a number of tools and tricks to exploit networks, including (but not limited to) DoS attacks, IP address spoofing, viruses, worms, Trojan horses, and e-mail bombs. The chapter, "Hacking" discusses this subject in detail.

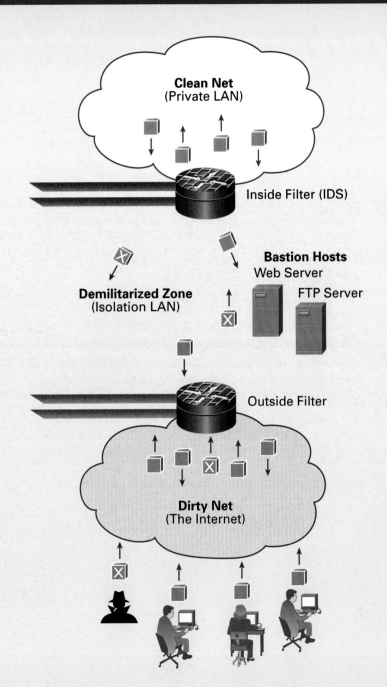

Firewalls and IDS

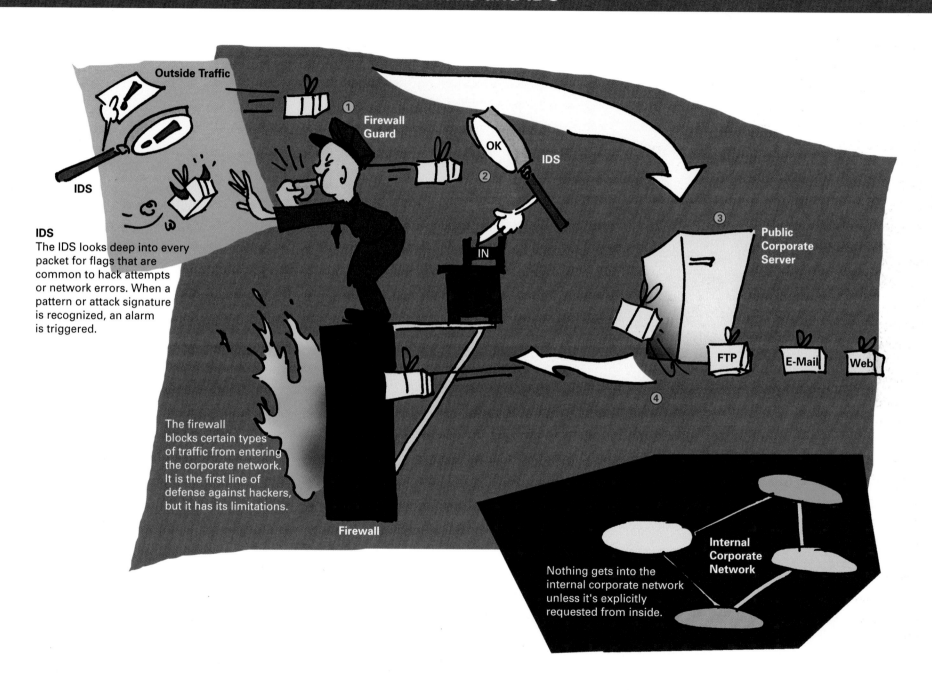

Outside Traffic

IDS

IDS
The IDS looks deep into every packet for flags that are common to hack attempts or network errors. When a pattern or attack signature is recognized, an alarm is triggered.

① **Firewall Guard**

OK

② **IDS**

IN

③ **Public Corporate Server**

FTP **E-Mail** **Web**

④

The firewall blocks certain types of traffic from entering the corporate network. It is the first line of defense against hackers, but it has its limitations.

Firewall

Internal Corporate Network

Nothing gets into the internal corporate network unless it's explicitly requested from inside.

Firewall Protection Schemes

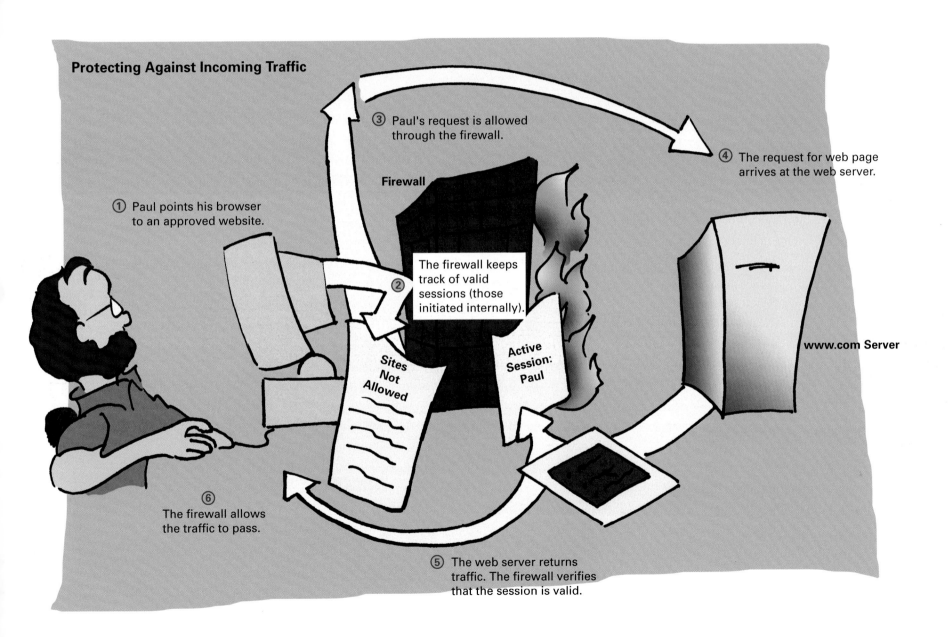

Protecting Against Incoming Traffic

③ Paul's request is allowed through the firewall.

④ The request for web page arrives at the web server.

Firewall

① Paul points his browser to an approved website.

The firewall keeps track of valid sessions (those initiated internally).

②

Sites Not Allowed

Active Session: Paul

www.com Server

⑥ The firewall allows the traffic to pass.

⑤ The web server returns traffic. The firewall verifies that the session is valid.

Firewall Protection Schemes

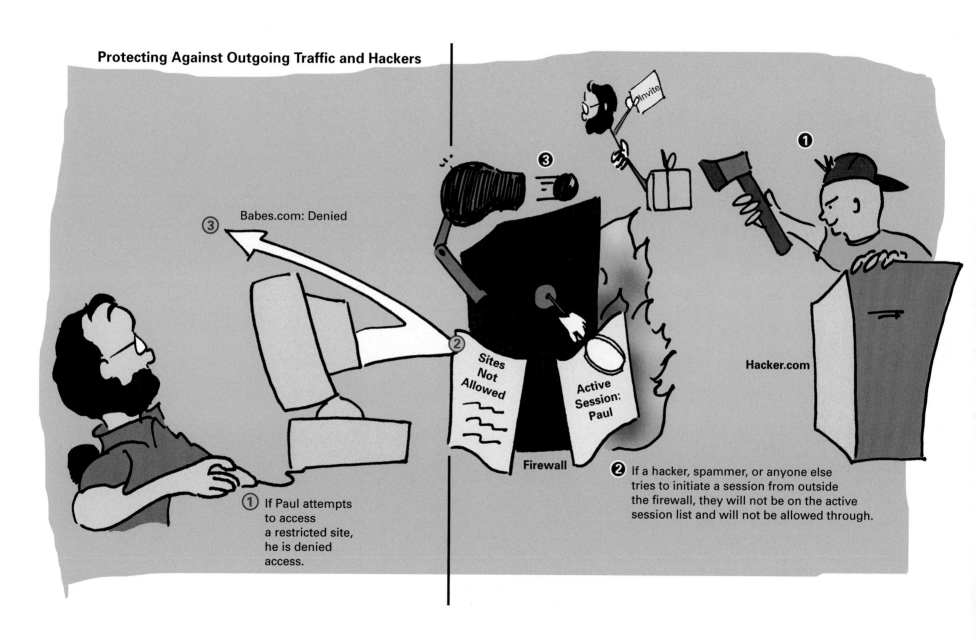

Protecting Against Outgoing Traffic and Hackers

Babes.com: Denied

Sites Not Allowed

Active Session: Paul

Firewall

Hacker.com

① If Paul attempts to access a restricted site, he is denied access.

② If a hacker, spammer, or anyone else tries to initiate a session from outside the firewall, they will not be on the active session list and will not be allowed through.

VPNs

Secure Networking Over the Internet

Traditional WAN networking involved dedicated circuits running Frame Relay or leased lines. Although prices have recently decreased, the cost of these private circuits continues to be high.

In addition to dedicated WAN connections, corporations had to maintain large banks of dialup modems (or outsource the dial-in to a vendor) so that workers could remotely access the corporate network with modems. In both cases, the goal was to extend the corporate network to remote locations and individuals.

With the widespread implementation of the Internet, IP connectivity is accessible both from people's houses as well as public locations, such as airports and coffee shops. Service providers find it more cost-effective to offer IP-based WAN services as opposed to dedicated circuits. Corporations must provide extensive Internet services to their employees, partners, and customers to remain competitive.

Given the confluence of IP public and corporate networks, extending the corporate network to places other than the main campus is more economical and practical.

Virtual private networks (VPNs) allow corporations to replace their dedicated private networks (such as Frame Relay, ATM, and leased line) with "virtually" private networks. This means their data traverses public IP networks but is secure due to authentication and encryption. Because of the Internet and service-provider IP networks, networks of equivalent bandwidth end up being cheaper than dedicated services.

With the availability of Internet connectivity, VPNs allow users to access their corporate networks securely from homes, hotels, businesses, and other public locations. VPNs also provide the ability to "work from home," creating "telecommuters." For example, call-center employees can answer phones from home (using IP-based call center and IP phones).

With the convergence of voice, video, and data, VPNs add value not previously available from dialup and WAN services. IP connectivity to the corporation eliminates the need for separate fax, data, phone, and video lines. However, because using a VPN involves heavy data crunching to encrypt traffic, and data typically traverses the public Internet, unpredictable delay and jitter can affect voice and video quality.

The term VPN actually defines two different concepts for virtual networks. To corporations, a VPN typically means encrypted traffic (using IPSec, IP Security) is tunneled through public IP networks. To service providers, VPN typically describes a tag-switching–based IP service, which does not involve encryption. This discussion focuses on IPSec-based VPNs.

The three types of VPN connectivity follow:

- **Site-to-site**—Connects remote corporate locations to the corporate network. The remote site typically has multiple users sharing access to the corporate network.

- **Remote user**—Individual users gain access to the corporate network either over dialup or broadband network. Also called teleworker.

- **Extranet**—Similar to site-to-site, except the VPN connects separate companies. Security concerns increase because both companies must protect their networks from each other.

Making Secure IPSec Connections Secure

Because they traverse public IP networks, VPNs introduce security considerations that were not necessary with private dial-in or WAN topologies. In general, providing security means encrypting corporate-bound traffic using secure authentication. For site-to-site VPNs, providing security means adding firewalls, intrusion detection, and NAT/PAT.

IPSec provides a way to manage encryption between multiple hosts using secure communications. Encrypting devices (such as routers or end-station PCs) inspect traffic ready to be transmitted. A set of rules on the device determines whether a particular packet must be encrypted. For example, a packet destined for the Internet can be left unencrypted, but a packet destined for the corporate network must be encrypted.

If a packet is to be encrypted, the device scrambles the contents, rendering them unreadable. Different encryption algorithms determine how difficult an encrypted packet is to crack: an encryption scheme that is more difficult to decode by an intruder requires more computing cycles than one that is less difficult.

VPNs are point-to-point, meaning every connection has only two endpoints. A single device (such as an WAN aggregation router) can have multiple remote sites, and users terminate their connections on the one box, but there is still one connection (or tunnel) per pair.

For each encrypted tunnel, the two endpoints must first authenticate each other and ensure that the other end is whom it claims. In encryption terms, this means that each endpoint must establish a security association (SA) with the other. Essentially, this involves the trusted exchange of information between the two hosts that allow each to verify the identity of the other. This process is called *Internet Key Exchange (IKE)*.

After both sides determine that the other side is whom it claims and that they can trust each other, they can then send encrypted data across the VPN.

At-A-Glance—Virtual Private Networks

Why Should I Care About VPNs?

A *virtual private network (VPN)* refers to a set of solutions and technologies designed to make secure (encrypted) site-to-site and remote-access connections over public networks. These connections provide low-cost alternatives to dedicated private WANs and allow telecommuters to connect to the corporate network via cable, digital subscriber line (DSL), or dialup.

You can set up VPN connections quickly over existing infrastructures and provide an excellent alternative to dedicated private networks such as Frame Relay and Asynchronous Transfer Mode (ATM).

The benefits of using a VPN include the following:

- **Cost savings**—VPNs use cost-effective public IP networks to connect remote-office users to the main corporate site, eliminating expensive dedicated WAN links.

- **Security**—VPNs provide a high level of security using advanced encryption and authentication protocols.

- **Scalability**—You can set up VPNs easily over the existing Internet infrastructure, allowing corporations to add capacity without adding significant infrastructure.

- **Compatibility with broadband technology**—VPNs allow mobile workers, telecommuters, and day extenders to take advantage of high-speed broadband connectivity such as DSL and cable for corporate connectivity.

- **Ease of access**—You can provide network access from anywhere in the world with local Internet access points of presence (POPs).

VPNs offer almost the same level of information security as traditional private networks and can be simpler to set up, less expensive to operate, and easier to administer.

What Are the Problems to Solve?

The two primary technical issues in setting up VPNs are

- **Tunneling**—Tunneling is encapsulating the protocol header and trailer of one network protocol into the protocol header and trailer of another. Prior to the packet traversing the network, it is encapsulated with new header information that allows an intermediary network to recognize and deliver it. When the transmission ends, the tunneling header is stripped off, and the original packet is delivered to the destination.

- **Encryption**—Although tunneling lets a third-party network carry data, it does not protect data against unauthorized inspection or viewing. To ensure tunneled transmissions are not intercepted, you encrypt traffic over a VPN. It is important to realize, however, that hackers can still intercept encrypted data and attempt to decrypt what they capture.

Deployment Modes

Site-to-site VPNs link company headquarters, remote locations, branch offices, and e-business partners to an internal network over one shared infrastructure. Site-to-site VPNs can be intranets or extranets. It is not uncommon for extranets to traverse multiple service providers.

Remote-access VPNs allow corporate users and mobile workers to access a corporate intranet securely by using their cable, DSL, or Internet service provider (ISP) to dial in and connect to the network. Leveraging local ISP dial-up infrastructures enables companies to reduce communications expenses and increase productivity due to the robust technology that supports the Internet and other public networks.

At-A-Glance—VPN Architecture

VPN Architecture

Several methods (both Layer 2 and Layer 3) and technologies serve those who want to establish a VPN. You can establish and manage VPNs on the customer site or over the network with a service provider. As if that were not enough, you can combine several methods at once to meet a specific need.

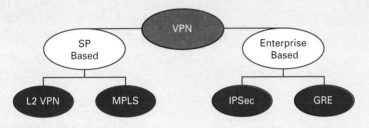

Putting It All Together

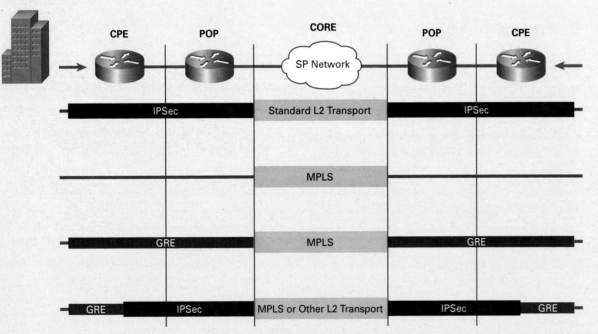

General Routing Encapsulation

General routing encapsulation (GRE) is a workaround method for routing packets over an IP network that are otherwise not routable. You can also use GRE for routing multicast packets over incompatible networks. GRE can route non-IP protocols (e.g. AppleTalk, Internetwork Packet Exchange, or IPX) over IP networks. The next figure illustrates the concept of encapsulating a packet. When the GRE packet reaches the destination network, the GRE header and trailer are stripped off and the original protocol works as usual.

IPSec tunnels over a service-provider network— This setup is a trusted, virtual, point-to-point connection.

MPLS VPN—When they enter the service-provider network, packets are assigned labels, and they are routed according to forwarding instructions.

Simple GRE over an L2 transport—You can use this setup to transport AppleTalk over an IP network. A company that needs to send AppleTalk over a secure link can implement this setup using a service provider and MPLS or another method.

This scenario could be implemented by a company needing to transport AppleTalk over a secure link.

At-A-Glance—IP Security and MPLS

IP Security

IP Security (IPSec) is an Internet standard for establishing and managing data privacy between network entities over unprotected networks such as the Internet.

IPSec security services are provided at the network layer, allowing simple and effective encryption of IP traffic. Prior to IPSec, you encrypted data on an application basis or added hardware (HW) encryptors to the network. None of these security steps was standardized at the time, so companies tended to use proprietary solutions, limiting how they could share secure information with trusted partners, customers, and resellers.

With IPSec networks, tunnels essentially serve as point-to-point "virtual circuits" through a service provider's network.

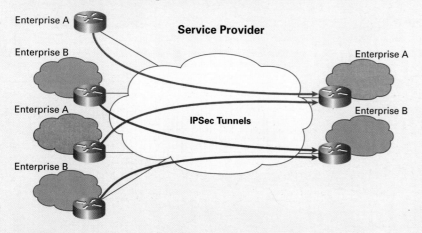

Multiprotocol Label Switching

Multiprotocol Label Switching (MPLS) uses a method of forwarding packets that is based on labels. The labels can correspond to IP destination networks, as in traditional IP forwarding, but they can also represent other parameters, sources addresses, quality of service (QoS), or other protocols. MPLS implements label swapping between different modules within the network. The two main components in an MPLS network are the control plane and the data plane. The control plane takes care of routing exchanges and exchanging labels between adjacent devices. The data plane, which forwards packets based on labels, is independent of routing or label-exchange protocols.

You can use MPLS on virtually any media and Layer 2 encapsulation. For frame-based encapsulations, MPLS inserts a 32-bit label between the Layer 2 and Layer 3 headers ("frame-mode" MPLS).

MPLS allows service providers to offer enterprises similar services as those in Frame Relay or ATM networks, with the conveniences of an IP network.

With MPLS networks, VPNs operate as logical "ships in the night" across a common routed backbone. The VPN appears as a privately routed WAN to the enterprise.

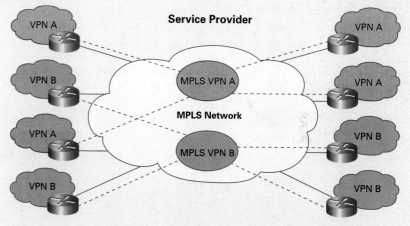

VPN: Establishing an IPSec Connection

Employees often need to connect to the corporate network from a remote location. IPSec provides a secure way to make these connections. This whiteboard illustration shows the process of establishing an IPSec connection.

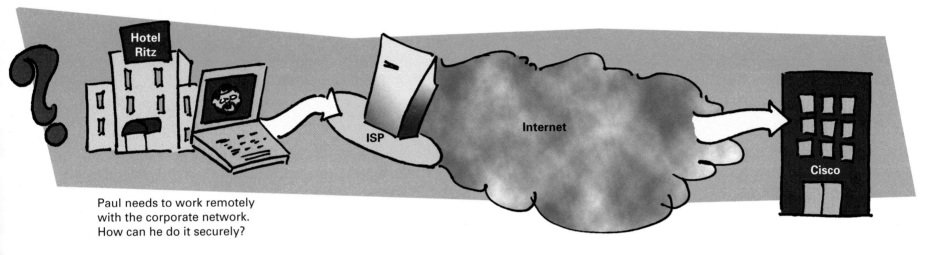

Paul needs to work remotely with the corporate network. How can he do it securely?

1 Establishing Identity

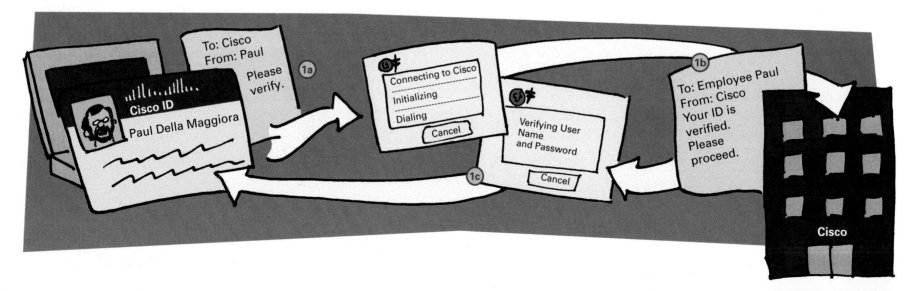

VPN: Establishing an IPSec Connection

② Initiating Communication and Security

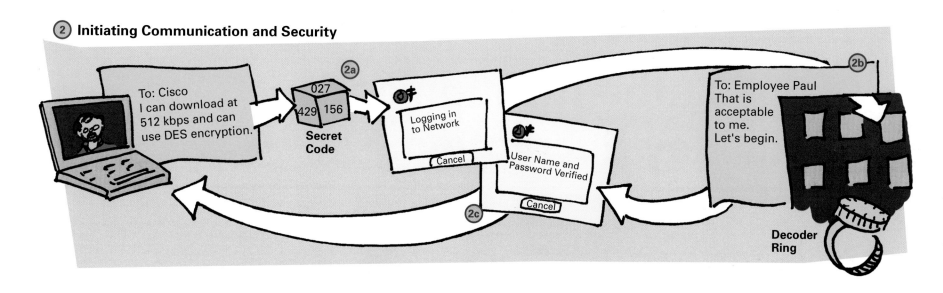

③ Communication

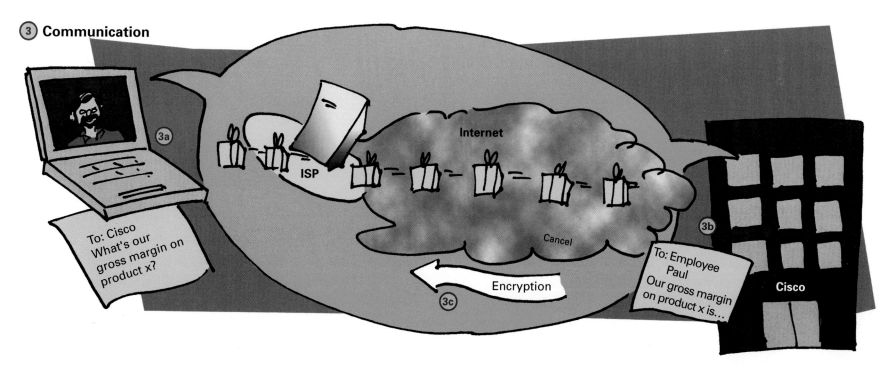

Client Authentication and Public Key Encryption

Why Should I Care About Encryption?

Data that travels across unsecured networks is vulnerable to anyone who wants to read, alter, or forge information. Using easily obtained tools such as protocol analyzers, just about anybody can read packets and gain access to classified information. Hostile parties can tamper with packets, hinder delivery, or prevent network communications.

Encryption provides a means to scramble and protect information as it travels across an otherwise unsecured network. Different levels of encryption can keep anyone from deciphering the message or figuring out the message's origin and destination.

What Are the Problems to Solve?

Almost all methods of encryption rely on two basic items, codes and keys.

First, you must develop a mathematical *code* so that only those processing the right keys to the equation can properly code and decode messages. Extremely complicated mathematic functions are used in the following way.

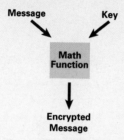

The mathematics are so complex that without knowing both the encryption code and the right key, it is virtually impossible to figure out the original message.

The second key piece of encryption is the distribution and protection of keys. There are a number of methods for key exchanges; the following At-A-Glance sheet focuses on the Diffie-Hellman method.

Bullets, Bombs, and Secret Codes

It might surprise you at first: Encryption codes and cryptography methods have the same export laws as guns, ammunitions, and explosives!

However, it does start to make sense when you think about the damage that could come from someone unraveling the myriad encrypted messages sent across the Internet every minute of every day. Access to this information could compromise military operations or expose the information that businesses and organizations keep secret.

What might happen if one company knew every other company's marketing plans, or if your insurance company could track all your credit-card purchases? In dollars and cents, the damage could be as bad or worse than what a bomb could do.

At-A-Glance—DES and Key Exchange

DES and Triple DES

The *Data Encryption Standard (DES)* is a fixed-block algorithm, which is a fancy way of saying it performs a complicated math function on a standard length of bits (referred to as a block). The DES algorithm splits the blocks in two, encrypting one half using a key value and a complicated algorithm. The two halves are rejoined and then re-split; the process is repeated a number of times before the output is secure. Think of it as an extremely complicated way of shuffling bits.

Triple DES (3DES) encrypts message using three seperate passes of the DES algorithm. 3DES provides a high degree of message security, but depending on processor speeds, it can take up to three times longer than standard DES to encrypt a data block. However, with the increased availability of cheap, fast processors, this method is becoming a popular option.

Clear Text

Our Quarterly Sales

Shared Secret Key

DES or 3DES Algorithm

Ουρθυ αρτλψ Σαλεσ Λιαφσβ Ηβαγσ Ιφαη

Encrypted Text

Clear Text

Our Quarterly Sales

Digital Signature Standard

The process of encrypting and decrypting data happens through the use of keys. Without the correct key, third parties are unable to unscramble a coded message. (Of course, you can eventually crack any code given enough computing power and time.) *Digital Signature Standard (DSS)* uses a public key/private key pair to identify users and code and decode messages. A public key is mathematically derived from the private key using a mathematical method called factoring. A detailed explanation of factoring is beyond the scope of this paper, but the nature of factoring makes it nearly impossible to figure out a private key by looking at the public key.

The results of an encryption is a *hash*. Using a private or session key, you can code messages. The public keys ensure that the message is authentic and unchanged, and the private key decodes the message.

Diffie-Hellman Key Exchange

Understanding how DSS uses keys is only half the battle. You must also have a secure way to obtain session keys without any third party obtaining them, even when you exchange the keys over unsecure links. The Diffie-Hellman key exchange protocol was designed for just this purpose. The exchange is secure because keys are never transmitted in clear text, and they are exceptionally difficult to figure out. Diffie-Hellman prevents key interception using two known prime numbers that have a special mathematical relationship to one another. Is it possible for two parties to agree on a shared secret key but impossible for eavesdroppers to determine what this secret key is (even if they know the shared primes). Here is a basic example of how it works:

N = Prime number   G = A Root of N

User 1 creates very large random number A.

User 2 creates very large random number B.

User 1 sends a to User 2.

User 2 sends b to User 1.

a = GA * (crazy math function using N)

b = GB * (crazy math function using N)

Both parties can now figure out the key (K) as

K = ([A]) b * (crazy math function using N)

K = ([B]) a *(crazy math function using N)

At-A-Glance—Encryption and OSI Layers

Where You Encrypt Matters

You can implement encryption at one of three OSI layers: the application, the data link, or the network. Each layer has advantages and disadvantages.

For application layer encryption, you must upgrade each application to support encryption, and all hosts that communicate with the applications must speak the same encryption language. This setup can often mean replacing all the hosts in a network, but it does not necessarily require any network upgrades because traffic is unaffected.

You can do network layer encryption anywhere in the network (at the ingress and egress, for example). You do not have to upgrade the hosts. It also leaves pertinent Layer 3 and Layer 4 information in the clear for use in routing. Network layer encryption has a good balance of security and cost.

Data link layer encryption is very secure because it encrypts everything (including IP addresses). The downside is that each router must decrypt the traffic at every link and then re-encrypt it once the correct path is determined. This process is very slow.

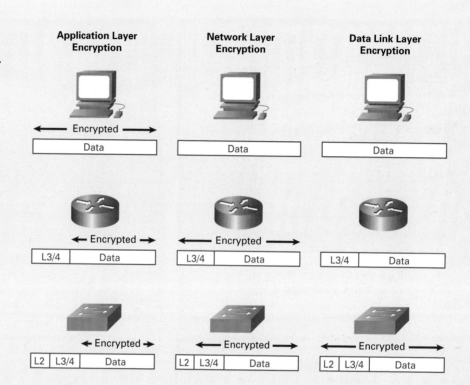

Client Authentication

① Jill wants to buy something on XYZ with her credit card.

② XYZ sends Jill a certificate (cert) signed by a trusted third party certificate authority (CA) to prove to Jill she is really talking to XYZ. This certificate contains a public key.

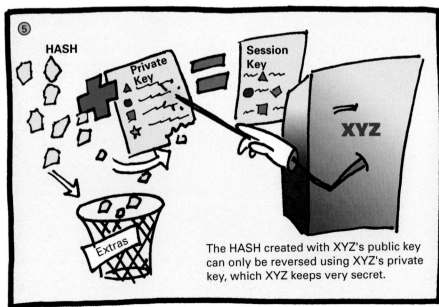

⑤ The HASH created with XYZ's public key can only be reversed using XYZ's private key, which XYZ keeps very secret.

⑥ Even if the original certificate was forged (which is possible), without access to the private key, Jill's information cannot be read.

Client Authentication

③ Now that Jill has verified that she is talking to XYZ, she will need to generate a session key that will be used to encrypt the information sent back and forth between her and XYZ.

Question: But how can Jill share the session key with XYZ without everyone else seeing it too?

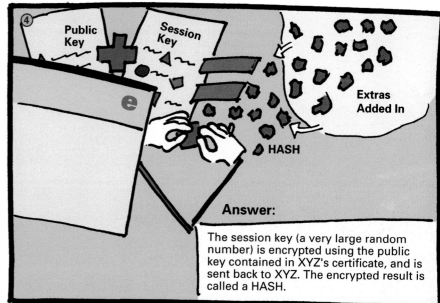

④ Public Key · Session Key · Extras Added In · HASH

Answer:

The session key (a very large random number) is encrypted using the public key contained in XYZ's certificate, and is sent back to XYZ. The encrypted result is called a HASH.

⑦ Now both Jill and XYZ know the session key that encrypts all their communication for the length of their communication.

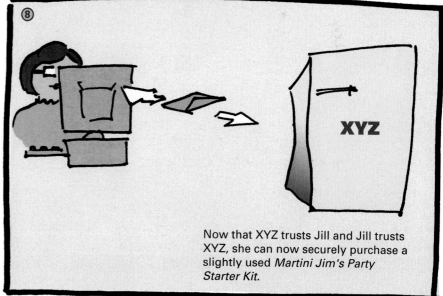

⑧ Now that XYZ trusts Jill and Jill trusts XYZ, she can now securely purchase a slightly used *Martini Jim's Party Starter Kit.*

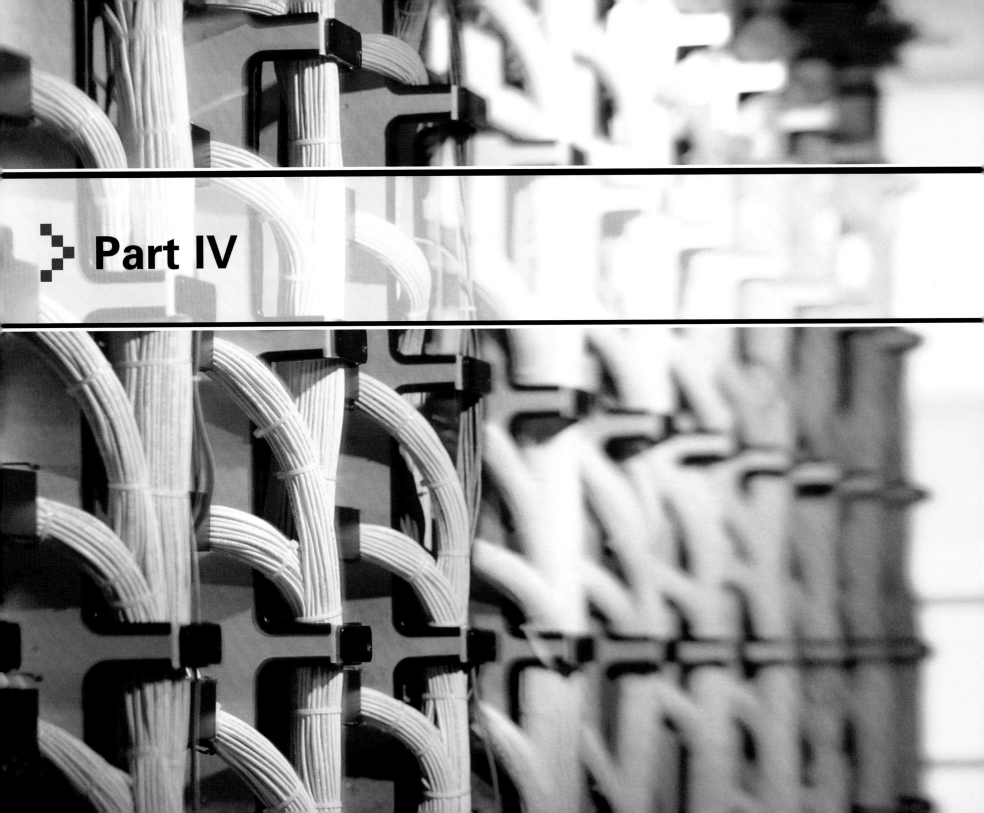

Part IV

How Traffic Gets from Here to There

Cisco Systems is in the business of computer networking. Computer networks are responsible for moving traffic from a source to a destination. When you type http://www.cisco.com/, the network must know how to move the request from your computer to the server at Cisco that contains the web page you want. The same process applies to dialing a phone number on a phone.

At their most basic level, networks move electric signals, light waves, and radio signals across copper cables, fiber, and the airwaves (respectively). Cables, fibers, and wireless interfaces connect devices to form a network. A device can be a computer, phone, or networking device such as a router or switch. Protocols running over these networks facilitate communication between applications and network devices.

Different types of network devices have different levels of intelligence, but ultimately they all act in concert to intelligently move traffic from there to here and back again.

Recently, a new method to transmit traffic is changing how people view networking: wireless. Mobile phones, wireless PCs, and organizers are examples of devices that no longer need a wall with a cable.

In Part IV, you learn about routers, switches, and the other means by which traffic gets from here to there.

Ethernet

History of Ethernet

Robert Metcalfe developed Ethernet at the famous Xerox Palo Alto Research Center (PARC) in 1972. The folks at Xerox PARC had developed a personal workstation with a graphical-user interface and needed a technology to network these workstations with their newly developed laser printers. (Remember, the first PC, the MITS altair, was not introduced to the public until 1975.)

Metcalfe originally called the network Alto Aloha Network but changed the name in 1973 to Ethernet to make it clear that any type of device could connect to his network. He chose the name "ether" because the network carried bits to every workstation in the same manner that scientists once thought waves were propagated through space by the "luminiferous ether." Robert's first external publication concerning Ethernet was available to the public in 1976.

Metcalfe left Xerox, and in 1979, he got Digital Equipment Corporation (DEC), Intel, and Xerox to agree on a common Ethernet standard called DIX. In 1982, the Institute of Electrical and Electronic Engineers (IEEE) adopted a standard based on Metcalfe's Ethernet.

Ethernet took off in academic networks and some corporate networks: it was cheap, and public domain protocols such as Internet Protocol (IP) ran natively. However, one major company wanted the world to adopt its protocol instead. That company was IBM, and its protocol was called Token Ring.

Before switching was introduced, Ethernet was more difficult to troubleshoot than Token Ring because Ethernet devices occupied the same cable or hub. Although Ethernet was less expensive to implement, larger corporations chose Token Ring because of their relationship with IBM and the ability to more easily troubleshoot problems.

The battle for the LAN continued for more than ten years, until eventually Ethernet became the predominant technology. Arguably, it was the widespread adoption of Ethernet switching that drove the final nail in Token Ring's coffin.

Other LAN technologies have been and continue to be introduced, but Ethernet prevails as the predominate technology for local high-speed connectivity.

What Is Ethernet?

Ethernet describes a system that links the computers in a building. It consists of hardware (a network interface card), software, and cabling used to connect the computers together. All computers on an Ethernet are attached to the same cable, as opposed to the traditional point-to-point networks in which a single device connects to another single device.

Because all computers share the same cable on an Ethernet network, the network needs a protocol to handle contention if multiple computers want to transmit data at the same time. (Only one can talk at a time.) Metcalfe's invention introduced the carrier sense multiple access collision detect (CSMA/CD) protocol. CSMA/CD defines how a computer should listen to the network before transmitting. If the network is quiet, the computer can transmit its data.

However, a problem arises if more than one computer listens, hears silence, and transmits at the same time: the data collides. The collision-detect part of CSMA/CD defines a method for transmitting computers to back off when collisions occur and randomly attempts to restart transmission.

Ethernet originally operated at 3 Mbps, but today operates at speeds ranging from 10 Mbps to 10 Gbps.

Evolution of Ethernet

When Metcalfe originally developed Ethernet, computers were connected to a single copper cable. The physical limitations of a piece of copper cable carrying electrical signals restricts the distance computers could be from each other on an Ethernet. Repeaters help alleviate the distance limitations. *Repeaters* are small devices that regnerate an electrical signal at the original signal strength. This process allows an Ethernet to extend across an office floor that might exceed the Ethernet distance limitations.

The addition or removal of a device to the Ethernet cable disrupts the network for all other connected devices. A device called an Ethernet *hub* solves this problem. First, each port on a hub is actually a repeater. Secondly, hubs let computers insert or remove themselves nondisruptively from the network. Finally, hubs simplify Ethernet troubleshooting and administration.

As networks grow larger, companies need to fit more and more computers onto an Ethernet. As the number of computers increased, the number of collisions on the network increases. As collisions increase, network traffic decreases. Networks come to a grinding halt when too many collisions occur.

Ethernet *bridges* resolve this problem by physically breaking an Ethernet into two or segments. This arrangement means that devices on one side of the bridge do not collide with devices on the other side of the bridge. Bridges evolved so that they learn which devices were on each side and only transfer traffic to the network containing the destination device. A two-port bridge also doubles the bandwidth previously available because each port is a separate Ethernet.

Ethernet bridges evolved to solve the problem of connecting Ethernet networks to Token Ring networks. This process of translating a packet from one LAN technology to another is called *translational bridging*. Translational bridging facilitates the migration of Token Ring networks to Ethernet.

As Ethernet networks continue to grow in a corporation, they become more complex, connecting hundreds and thousands of devices. Ethernet switches allow network administrators to dynamically break their networks into multiple Ethernet segments.

Initially, switches operated as multiport Ethernet bridges. But eventually, as the cost per port decreased significantly, Ethernet switches replaced hubs, in which each connected device receives its own dedicated Ethernet bandwidth.

Collisions are no longer an issue because connections between computer and switch can be point-to-point, and the Ethernet can both send and receive traffic at the same time. This ability to send and receive simultaneously is called *full duplex*, as opposed to traditional Ethernet, which operated at *half duplex*. Half duplex means a device can receive or transmit traffic on the network, but not at the same time. If both happen at the same time, a collision occurs.

At-A-Glance—Ethernet

Why Should I Care About Ethernet?

Ethernet was developed in 1972 as a way to connect newly invented computers to newly invented laser printers. Although recognized even at that time as a remarkable technology breakthrough, few people would have wagered that the ability to connect computers and devices would change communication on the same scale as the invention of the telephone and change business on the scale of the Industrial Revolution. Several competing protocols have emerged since 1972, but Ethernet remains the dominant standard for connecting computers into LANs.

What Are the Problems to Solve?

Ethernet is a shared resource where all end stations (computers, servers, etc.) all have access to the transmission medium at the same time. The result is that only one device can send information at a time. Given this limitation, there are two viable solutions:

- **Use a sharing mechanism**—If all end stations are forced to share a common wire, then rules must ensure that each end station waits its turn before transmitting, or, in the event of simultaneous transmissions, follows rules for retransmitting.

- **Divide the shared segments and insulate them**—Another solution is to use devices that reduce the number of end stations sharing a resource at any given time.

What They Gave Away

In the 1970s, Xerox Corporation assembled a group of talented researchers to investigate new technologies. The new group was located in the newly opened Palo Alto Research Center (PARC), well away from the corporate headquarters in Connecticut.

In addition to developing Ethernet, the brilliant folks at the PARC invented the technology for what eventually became the personal computer, the graphical user interface (GUI), laser printing, and very large scale integration (VLSI).

Inexplicably, Xerox failed to recognize the brilliance (and commercial viability) of many of these home-grown innovations and let other companies (such as Intel, Microsoft, and Apple) use and market these technologies.

Ethernet Collisions

In a traditional LAN, several users all share the same port on a network device and compete for resources (bandwidth). The main limitation of such a setup is that only one device can transmit at a time. Segments that share resources in this manner are called *collision domains* because if two or more devices transmit at the same time, the information collides and both endpoints must resend their information. Typically, the devices both begin a random countdown before attempting to retransmit.

This method works well for a small number of users on a segment, each having relatively low bandwidth requirements. As the number of users increases, the efficiency of collision domains decreases sharply, to the point where overhead traffic (management and control) clogs the network.

Smaller Segments

You can divide segments to reduce the number of users and increase the bandwidth available to each user in the segment. Each new segment created results in a new collision domain. Traffic from one segment or collision domain does not interfere with other segment, thereby increasing the available bandwidth of each segment. In the following example, each segment has greater bandwidth, but all segments are still on a common backbone and must share the available bandwidth.

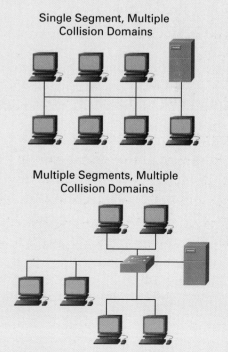

Single Segment, Multiple
Collision Domains

Multiple Segments, Multiple
Collision Domains

At-A-Glance—Ethernet, Continued

The basic tools for segmenting an Ethernet LAN into more collision domains follow:

- Bridges
- Routers
- Switches

This At-A-Glance sheet discusses segmenting using bridges and routers.

Increasing Bandwidth

In addition to creating segments to increase available bandwidth, you can use a faster medium such as optical fiber or gigabit Ethernet. Although these technologies are faster, they are still shared media; collision domains still exist and eventually experience the same problems as slower media.

Ethernet Segment

A *segment* is the simplest form of network, where all devices are directly connected. In this type of arrangement, disconnecting or adding a computer disables the segment.

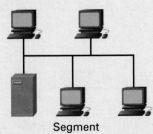

Segment

Hubs

Hubs enable you to add and remove computers without disabling the network but do not create additional collision domains.

Repeaters

Repeaters simply extend the transmission distance of an Ethernet segment.

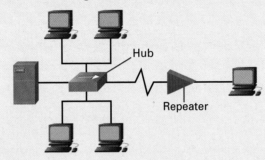

Hub

Repeater

Bridges

Bridges are simple Layer 2 devices that create new segments, resulting in fewer collisions. Bridges must learn the addresses of the computers on each segment to avoid forwarding traffic to the wrong port.

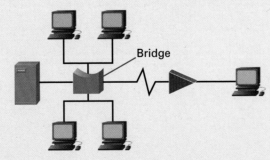

Bridge

Switched Ethernet

You can think of a LAN switch as a high-speed, multiport bridge with a brain. Switches not only give each end station a dedicated port (meaning there are no collisions), but they also allow end stations to transmit and receive at the same time, greatly increasing the efficiency of the LAN.

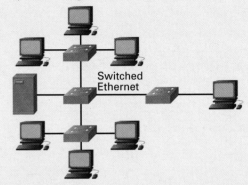

Switched Ethernet

LAN Routers

LAN-based routers greatly extend the speed, distance, and intelligence of Ethernet LANs. Routers also allow traffic to travel along multiple paths.

Routers, however, do require a common protocol between the router and end stations.

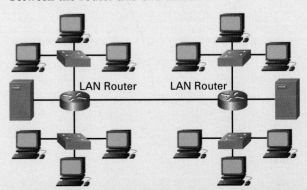

LAN Router   LAN Router

Ethernet—Shared Medium and the Problems with Phasing Out Collisions

When End Stations Share a Single Switch

① LAN Wait Wait Send

Before sending data, end stations "listen" for other traffic. If they hear none, it's OK to send.

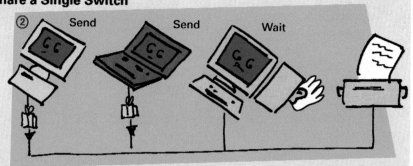

② Send Send Wait

Sometimes, two or more end stations will hear nothing and send data simultaneously.

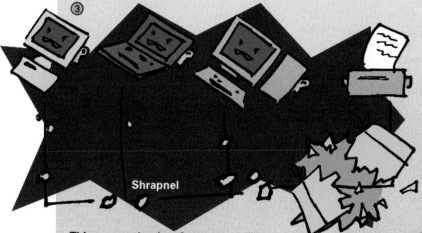

③ Shrapnel

This causes the data frames to collide, destroying all the frames (which must be resent).

④ After the collision, each end station starts a random timer that must expire before it can try to resend the data.

The Switch Port Option

Switch ports have become relatively inexpensive, so now each end station gets a dedicated port. The result: no more collisions.

LAN Switching

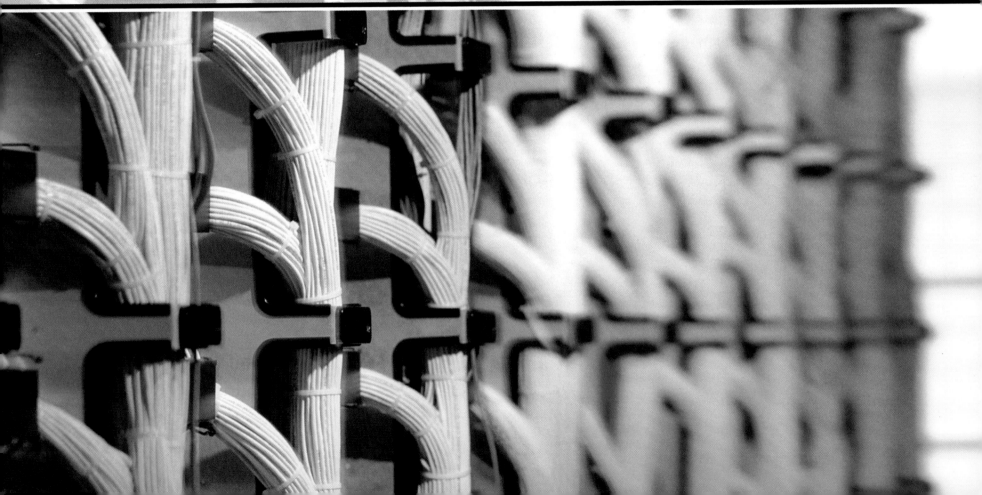

Fast Computers Need Faster Networks

The personal computer (PC) emerged as the most common desktop computer in the 1980s. Local-area networks (LANs) emerged as ways to network PCs in a common location. Networking technologies such as Token Ring and Ethernet allowed users to share disks and printers and exchange files with each other.

As originally defined, Ethernet and Token Ring provided network access to multiple devices on the same segment or ring. These LAN technologies had predefined limitations for how many devices could connect to a single segment, as well as for the physical distance between computers.

Desktop computers got faster, the number of computers grew, operating systems became *multitasking* (allowing multiple tasks to operate at the same time), and applications became more network-centric. All these advancements resulted in the congestion of LANs.

To address these issues, two device types emerged: repeaters and bridges. *Repeaters* are simple Open System Interconnection (OSI) Layer 1 devices that allow networks to extend beyond their defined physical distances. *Bridges* are OSI Layer 2 devices that physically split a segment into two and reduce the amount of traffic on either side of the bridge. This setup allows more devices to connect to the LAN and reduces congestion.

LAN switches emerged as a natural extension of bridging, revolutionizing the concept of local-area networking.

Switching Basics—It's a Bridge

The term *switching* originally described devices that made packet-forwarding decisions in wide area networks (WANs). Today, LAN switching describes technologies that are an extension of traditional bridges.

Bridges connect two or more LAN segments and make forwarding decisions on whether to transmit packets from one segment to another. When a packet arrives, the bridge inspects the destination and source Media Access Control (MAC) addresses in the packet. (This is an example of *store-and-forward switching*.) It places an entry in a table indicating that the source MAC address is located off the bridge interface in which the packet arrived. The bridge then consults the same table for an entry for the destination MAC address.

If it has an entry for the destination MAC address, and the entry indicates the MAC address is located on a different port from which the packet was received, the bridge forwards the packet onto the specified port.

If the bridge table indicates the destination MAC address is located off the interface for which it was received, then the bridge drops the packet. Why send it back onto the segment from which it came? This decision is where a bridge reduces congestion.

Finally, if the destination MAC address is not in the bridge's table, then that indicates the bridge has not seen a packet destined to this MAC address. The bridge then forwards the packets out all other ports (called *flooding*) except the one in which the packet was received.

At their core, switches are multiport bridges. However, switches have radically matured into intelligent devices, replacing both bridges and hubs. Switches not only reduce traffic through the use of bridge tables, but also offer new functionality that support high-speed connections, virtual LANs (to be explained shortly), and even traditional routing.

Switching Ethernets

Before the introduction of switches, the use of hubs and bridges improved Ethernet network performance. Multiple devices connected to a single Ethernet by connecting to Ethernet hubs. Hubs are Layer 1 devices that essentially provide two things: nondisruptive addition and removal of devices to an Ethernet and repeater functionality.

Ethernet, by specification, allows for multiple devices to connect to a single Ethernet. A device cannot transmit a packet if it is receiving traffic. This ability, called *half-duplex*, is similar to the idea that you can't hear what someone is saying if you are talking. Two devices transmitting at the same time causes a *collision*. When a collision is detected, both devices back off and retransmit at random intervals.

Each Ethernet port on a switch, like a bridge, is a separate Ethernet, with its separate collision domain and its own bandwidth. Collisions on one switch port are not seen on other switch ports.

As switch Ethernet ports became less expensive, switches replaced hubs in the wiring closet. Initially, when switches were first introduced, network administrators plugged hubs (containing multiple hosts) into switch ports. But eventually, it became cost-effective to plug the hosts directly into a switch port. This arrangement gives each host its own dedicated Ethernet and removes the possibility of collisions. Because a dedicated switch connection has only two hosts (the switch and the host), you can configure an Ethernet switch port as *full duplex*, which means a device can both receive incoming traffic and transmit traffic simultaneously.

End stations have considerable more bandwidth when they use switches. Ethernet has the capability to run at multiple speeds: 10 Mbps, 100 Mbps, 1 Gbps, and 10 Gbps, and therefore switches can provide connectivity at these speeds.

However, network applications and the web create considerably more network traffic, re-introducing new forms of congestion problems. Switches can use quality of service (QoS) and other mechanisms to help the congestion issue.

Virtual LANs

A virtual LAN (VLAN) is a group of hosts or network devices that form a single broadcast domain. Layer 2 trunking protocols such as 802.1q and Inter-Switch Link (ISL) allow a VLAN to extend across multiple network devices, including routers and LAN switches.

VLANs group related users regardless of where their physical hosts connect to the network. You might group users according to their functional team or location. The goal is to group users into VLANs so their traffic stays within the VLAN. This grouping provides the following benefits:

- Broadcast control
- Security
- Performance
- Network management

Switches communicate with each other using a *trunking* protocol such as Cisco's ISL or the public domain 802.1q. These trunking protocols preserve the VLAN identification associated with a packet so that VLANs can extend across multiple switches. Routers can also recognize trunking and route amongst the VLANs.

Switches Take Over the World

As switches established themselves in networks, vendors added increasing functionality. Switches can perform forwarding decisions based on traditional Layer 3 routing and can even make forwarding decisions based on Layer 4 and above. Switches can provide power to IP-based phones.

Even though switches can perform the functions of other higher-layer devices such as routers and content switches, you must still separate these functionalities to avoid single points of failure.

All in all, switches are the workhorse of networks, providing functionality across almost all layers of the OSI model reliably and quickly.

At-A-Glance—LAN Switching

Why Should I Care About Switching?

The advances in switching technology combined with the decrease in switch prices have made computer networks a common and increasingly important aspect of business today.

What Are the Problems to Solve?

Switches must learn about the network to make intelligent decisions. Due to the size and changing nature of networks, switches learned how to discover network address and keep track of network changes.

Switches must make decisions about what to do with traffic. The decisions are based on the switch's knowledge of the network.

Switches must also have mechanisms for segmenting users into logical groupings to allow efficient provisioning of services.

Broadcast and Collision Domains

From time to time, a device on the network wants to communicate with all other "local" devices at the same time. Typically, this communication occurs when a device wants to query the network for an address, when a device is newly added to a network, or when there is a change in the network.

A group of devices that receive all broadcast messages from members within that group is called a *broadcast domain*. Network broadcast domains are typically segmented with Layer 3 devices (routers).

A group of devices that share a common access medium, and can therefore interfere with each other when transmitting simultaneously, define a *collision domain*. Traditionally, each broadcast domain had multiple collision domains. Modern switches, however, have a low price/port ratio, making it feasible to dedicate a port to a single end device, effectively removing all collision domains.

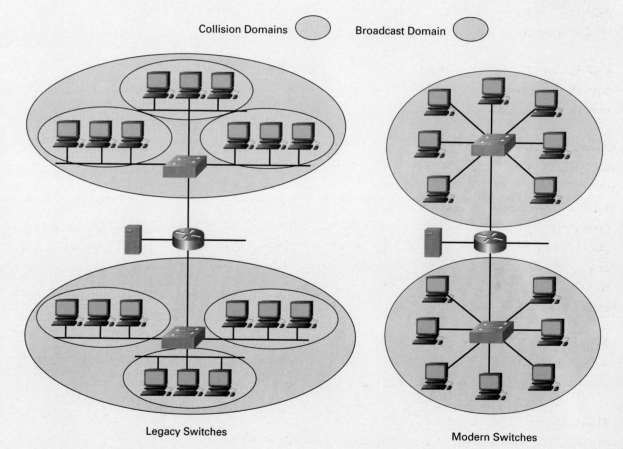

Collision Domains

Broadcast Domain

Legacy Switches

Modern Switches

At-A-Glance—LAN Switching, Continued

Forwarding and Filtering

A switch always does something when it receives traffic. The preference is to send the traffic out a specific port (called *filtering*), but that only works when the location of the intended destination is known. When the destination address is not known, the switch forwards the traffic out every port, except the one on which the traffic was received. This process is called *flooding*.

From a network efficiency standpoint, it is much better for the network when the switch knows all the addresses on every port, but it is not always practical to enter this information manually. As the network grows and changes, all the port addresses are almost impossible to track.

Address Learning

A switch must therefore learn the addresses of the devices attached to it. It does so by inspecting the source address of all the traffic sent though it and then associates the port the traffic was received on with the Media Access Control (MAC) address listed. The following example illustrates this concept. (The MAC addresses, shown for clarity only, are not the correct format.)

- **Time 0**—The switch shown has an empty MAC address table.

- **Time 1**—The device attached to port 2 sends a message intended for the device on port 0. This message kicks off two actions within the switch: The switch now knows the address associated with the device on port 2, so it enters the information in its table; and because it does not have an association for the device the traffic is intended for (namely the computer on port 0), it floods the message out all ports except the one on which it was received.

- **Time 2**—The device on port 0 replies to the message. The switch now associates the source address of the message with port 0.

This process happens all the time in every switch.

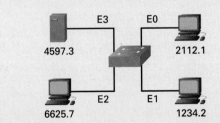

Time 0	
Port	Address

Time 1	
Port	Address
E2	6625.7

Time 2	
Port	Address
E2	6625.7
E0	2112.1

Frame Transmission Modes

Switches are typically Layer 2 devices. (Some switches now perform Layer 3 functions.) According to the OSI model, the data unit processed by a switch is called a *frame*. Switches must balance speed and accuracy (no errors) when processing frames because they are typically measured on both attributes.

The three primary frame switching modes follow:

- **Cut-through**—The switch only checks the destination address and then immediately begins forwarding the frame. This process can decrease latency but can also transmit frames containing errors.

- **Store and forward**—The switch reads the entire frame and performs a cyclic redundancy check (CRC) before forwarding. If the CRC is bad, the switch discards the frame. Although this method does increase latency (processing time), it tends to minimize errors.

- **Fragment-free (modified cut-through)**—The switch reads the first 64 bytes before forwarding the frame. The switch needs a minimum of 64 bytes to detect and filter out collision frames.

At-A-Glance—Virtual LANs

Virtual LANs

Virtual LANS (VLANs) provide the means to logically group several end stations with common sets of requirements. VLANs are independent of physical locations, meaning that two end stations connected to different switches on different floors can belong to the same VLAN. Typically, the logical grouping follows workgroup functions such as engineering or finance, but you can customize them as well.

With VLANS, it's easier to assign access rules and provision services to groups of users regardless of their physical location. For example, using VLANs, you can give all members of a project team access to project files by virtue of their VLAN membership. This ability also makes it easier to add or delete users without re-running cables or changing network addresses.

VLANs also create their own broadcast domains without the addition of Layer 3 devices.

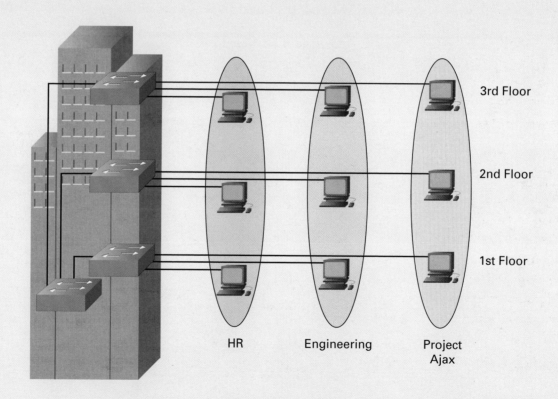

HR   Engineering   Project Ajax

3rd Floor

2nd Floor

1st Floor

Routing and Switching

Network devices have one primary purpose: to pass network traffic from one segment to another. (There are exceptions, of course, such as network analyzers, which inspect traffic as it goes by.) With devices that independently make forwarding decisions, traffic can travel from its source to the destination. The higher up the Open System Interconnection (OSI) model a device operates, the deeper it looks into a packet to make a forwarding decision.

Railroad-switching stations provide a similar example. The switches enable a train to enter the appropriate tracks (path) that take it to its final destination. If the switches are set wrong, a train can end up traveling to the wrong destination or traveling in a circle.

Bridges and Switches

Bridges and *switches* are networking devices that operate at OSI Layer 2. Bridges became popular in the 1980s and enabled packet forwarding between homogenous networks. More recently, bridges and switches forward frames among different types of networks.

Switching technology has emerged as the evolutionary replacement for bridging. Switches provide all the features of traditional bridging and more. Compared to bridges, switches provide superior throughput performance, higher port density, and lower per-port cost.

The different types of bridging include the following:

- Transparent bridging primarily occurs in Ethernet networks.
- Source-route bridging occurs in Token Ring networks.
- Translational bridging occurs between different media. For example, a translational bridge might connect a Token Ring network to an Ethernet network.

Bridging and switching occur at the data link layer, which means bridges control data flow, provide transmission error handling, and enable access to physical media. Basic bridging is not complicated: A bridge or switch analyzes an incoming frame, determines where to forward the frame based on the packet's content, and forwards the frame toward its destination. With transparent bridging, forwarding decisions happen one hop at a time. With source-route bridging, the frame contains a predetermined path to the destination.

Bridges and switches divide networks into smaller, self-contained units. Because only a portion of traffic is forwarded, bridging reduces the overall traffic devices see on each connected network. The bridge acts as a kind of firewall in that it prevents frame-level errors from propagating from one segment to another. Bridges also accommodate communication among more devices than are supported on a single segment or ring. Bridges and switches essentially extend the effective length of a LAN, permitting more workstations to communicate with each other within a single broadcast domain.

The primary difference between switches and bridges is that bridges segment a LAN into a few smaller segments. Switches, through their increased port density and speed, permit segmentation on a much larger scale. Modern-day switches have hundreds of ports per chassis. Additionally, modern-day switches interconnect LAN segments operating at different speeds.

Routers

Whereas switches and bridges operate at OSI Layer 2 (data link layer), *routers* primarily operate at OSI Layer 3 (network layer). Like bridging, the primary act of routing involves moving packets across a network from a source to a destination. The difference involves the information that is used to make the forwarding decisions. Routers make decisions based on network layer protocols such as Internet Protocol (IP) and Novell NetWare Internetwork Packet Exchange (IPX).

Routing gained popularity in the mid to late 1980s as a result of internetworks growing beyond the capability of bridges. Before this popularity, networks were relatively small and isolated, and bridges were able to handle the jobs of forwarding and segmentation. However, as networks grew, routers facilitated larger scaling and more intelligent growth across wider physical distances. Although routers are more expensive and complex than bridges, routing is the core of the Internet today. (As a side note, Cisco as a company made its name through routing.)

Routing involves two processes: determining optimal routing paths through a network and forwarding packets along those paths. Routing algorithms make the optimal path determination. As they determine routes, tables on the router store the information.

Routing algorithms fill routing tables with various types of information. The primary piece of information relevant to routing is the *next hop*. Next-hop associations tell a router that it can reach a particular destination by sending a packet to a particular router representing the next hop on the way to its final destination. When a router receives a packet, it attempts to associate the destination network address in the packet to an appropriate next hop in its routing table. In addition to next-hop associations, routers store other pertinent information in routing tables. For multiple paths to a destination, a routing table might contain information that allows the router to determine the desirability of one path over another.

Routers communicate with each other and maintain their routing tables through the exchange of messages over the network. Routing updates are one particular type of message. A *routing update* contains all or part of another router's routing table and allows each router to build a detailed picture of the overall network topology.

Once a router determines an optimal path for a packet, it must forward the packet toward the destination. The process of a router moving a packet from its received port to the outgoing destination port is called *switching*. Although the process of switching a packet on a router is similar to that of a Layer 2 switch, the decision criteria and the actual handling of the packet are different.

When a computer determines that it must send a packet to another host, it places the network address of the final destination host in the packet. However, it places the Layer 2 physical (Media Access Control [MAC]) address of the nearest router in the packet. When the router receives the packet, it first determines whether it knows how to reach the packet's stated destination network. If the destination is not known, the router typically drops the packet. If the destination is known, the router changes the destination physical address in the packet to contain that of the next hop. The router then transmits the packet out the destination interface.

The next hop can be either the final destination or another router. Each router in the process performs the same operation. As the packet moves through the network, each router modifies the physical address stored in the packet but leaves the network address untouched (because it determines the final destination).

Routers Bridge and Switches Route

In an ideal world, each thing does what it is defined to do. This is not the case for network devices. Routers can provide bridging functionality, and switches are quickly becoming the high-density port, high-speed router of the campus. Network devices, including switches and routers, make forwarding decisions on OSI layers higher than the network layer. For example, routers can provide firewall functionality in which the router inspects Layer 4 packet information, and switches such as content switches can perform forwarding decisions based on Layer 5–7 packet information (such as the URL in an HTTP packet).

Routers and Switches

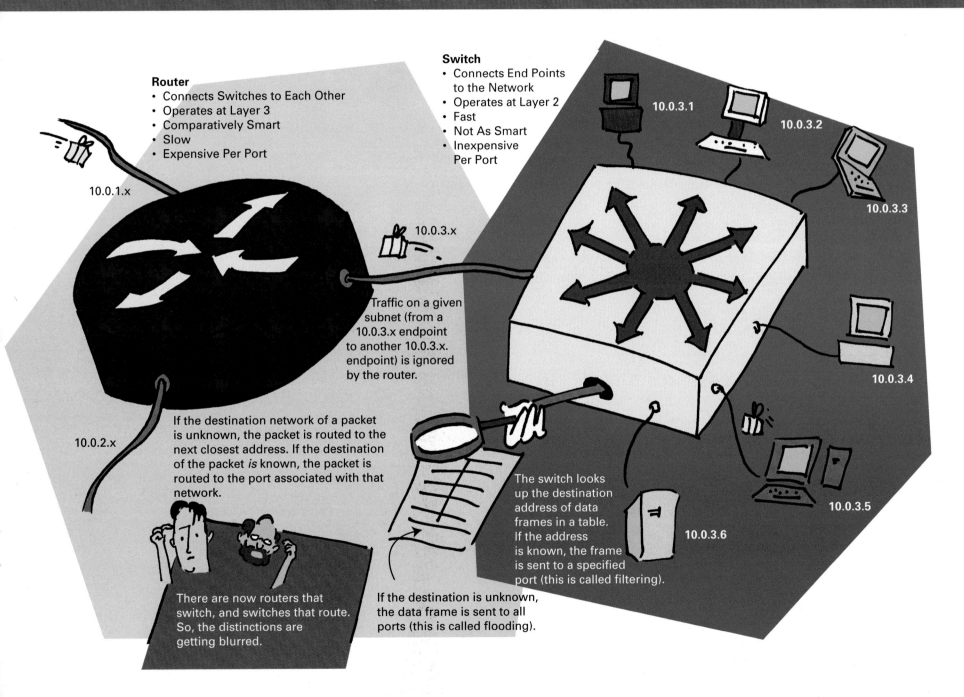

Router
• Connects Switches to Each Other
• Operates at Layer 3
• Comparatively Smart
• Slow
• Expensive Per Port

Switch
• Connects End Points to the Network
• Operates at Layer 2
• Fast
• Not As Smart
• Inexpensive Per Port

10.0.1.x

10.0.2.x

10.0.3.x

10.0.3.1
10.0.3.2
10.0.3.3
10.0.3.4
10.0.3.5
10.0.3.6

Traffic on a given subnet (from a 10.0.3.x endpoint to another 10.0.3.x. endpoint) is ignored by the router.

If the destination network of a packet is unknown, the packet is routed to the next closest address. If the destination of the packet *is* known, the packet is routed to the port associated with that network.

The switch looks up the destination address of data frames in a table. If the address is known, the frame is sent to a specified port (this is called filtering).

There are now routers that switch, and switches that route. So, the distinctions are getting blurred.

If the destination is unknown, the data frame is sent to all ports (this is called flooding).

Routers and Switches

Connectivity

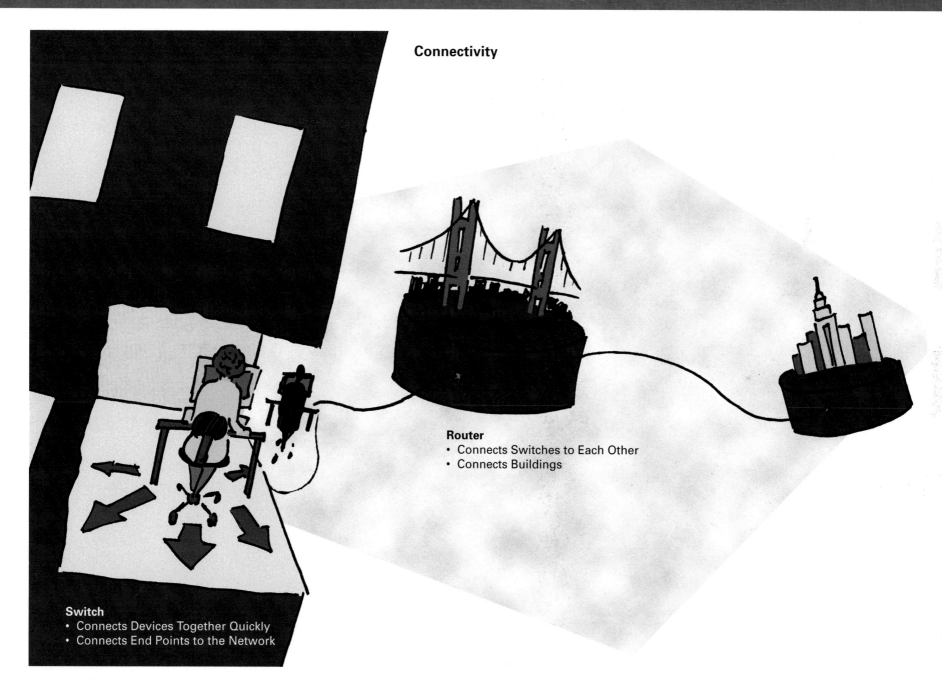

Router
- Connects Switches to Each Other
- Connects Buildings

Switch
- Connects Devices Together Quickly
- Connects End Points to the Network

At-A-Glance—Routing

Why Should I Care About Routing?

Routing is one of the fundamental aspects of networking. The ability of routers to learn possible routes (rather than make you manually configure and constantly update the routes) is one of the primary reasons that ARPANET, which originally connected seven sites, scaled into the modern Internet in only a few short years.

What Are the Problems to Solve?

Routed networks are often large and complex, and it would be prohibitively difficult to manage and update network information on all routers all the time. Several algorithms have been developed to help address these difficulties. These algorithms allow the routers to learn about the network and then make decisions based on that information.

To learn paths (or routes) through a network, and make decisions on where to send packets, a router must know the following information:

- **Destination address**—Typically the Internet Protocol (IP) address of the data's (packet) destination.
- **Source address**—Where the information came from (typically an IP address).
- **Possible routes**—Routes that can get information from its present location or source to some other location (the destination or closet known point).
- **Best route**—The best path to the intended destination. ("Best" can mean many things.)
- **Status of routes**—The current state of routes, which routers track to ensure timely delivery of information.

What Exactly Does "Best" Mean?

Routers often make decisions about the best possible path to get information from a source to a destination. "Best," however, is loosely defined, and it depends on what is valued by the network. These measurements of value are referred to as *metrics*. Which metrics are valued by the network is determined by the network administrator. Several metrics are listed here:

- **Hop count**—Number of times a packet goes through a router.
- **Delay time**—Time required to reach the destination.
- **Reliability**—Bit-error rate of each network link.
- **Maximum transmission unit (MTU)**—Maximum message length (or packet size) allowed on the path.
- **Cost**—Arbitrary value based on a network-administrator–determined value. Usually some combination of other metrics.

Static Versus Dynamic

Routers must learn about the network around them to make determinations on where to send packets. This information can either be manually entered (static routes) or learned from other routers in the network (dynamic routes):

- **Static routes**—When a network administrator manually enters information about a route, it is considered a *static route*. Only a network administrator can change this information. (That is, the router does not learn from, or update, its routing tables based on network events.) Static routes allow for tight control of packets but are difficult to maintain and prone to human error.
- **Dynamic routes**—Routers on a network can learn about possible routes and current route status from other routers in the network. Routes learned in this way are called *dynamic routes*. Routers in dynamic routes learn about changes in the network without administrative intervention and automatically propagate them throughout the network.

At-A-Glance—Routing: Flat Versus Hierarchical, Intradomain Versus Interdomain

Flat Versus Hierarchical

With *flat* networks, all routers must keep track of all other routers on the network. As networks grow, the amount of information contained in the routing tables increases.

Although this method is simple, it can result in poor network performance because the number of routing updates traffic grows with each new router.

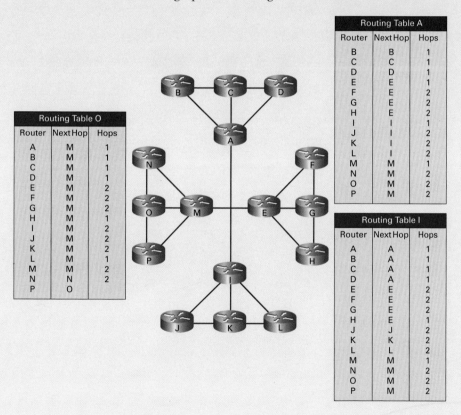

Routing Table O

Router	Next Hop	Hops
A	M	1
B	M	1
C	M	1
D	M	1
E	M	2
F	M	2
G	M	2
H	M	1
I	M	2
J	M	2
K	M	2
L	M	1
M	M	2
N	M	2
P	O	

Routing Table A

Router	Next Hop	Hops
B	B	1
C	C	1
D	D	1
E	E	1
F	E	2
G	E	2
H	E	2
I	I	1
J	I	2
K	I	2
L	I	2
M	M	1
N	M	2
O	M	2
P	M	2

Routing Table I

Router	Next Hop	Hops
A	A	1
B	A	1
C	A	1
D	A	1
E	E	2
F	E	2
G	E	2
H	E	1
J	J	2
K	J	2
L	K	2
M	L	2
N	M	1
O	M	2
P	M	2
	M	2

Hierarchical networks segment routers into logical groupings. This arrangement simplifies routing tables and greatly reduces overhead traffic.

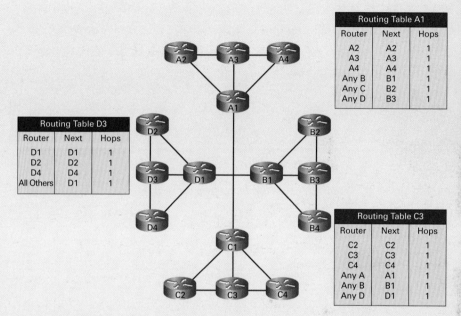

Routing Table A1

Router	Next	Hops
A2	A2	1
A3	A3	1
A4	A4	1
Any B	B1	1
Any C	B2	1
Any D	B3	1

Routing Table D3

Router	Next	Hops
D1	D1	1
D2	D2	1
D4	D4	1
All Others	D1	1

Routing Table C3

Router	Next	Hops
C2	C2	1
C3	C3	1
C4	C4	1
Any A	A1	1
Any B	B1	1
Any D	D1	1

Intradomain Versus Interdomain

You can easily understand intradomain and interdomain routing in the context of large-scale hierarchical networks. Think of each segment as its own autonomous network. Within each autonomous network, intradomain routing protocols, also called Interior Gateway Prototols (IGPs), exchange routing information and forward packets. Interdomain routing protocols, also called Exterior Gateway Protocols (EGPs), are used between autonomous networks.

At-A-Glance—Distance-Vector and Link-State Routing

Distance-Vector Versus Link-State Routing

The two main classes of routing are distant vector routing and link-state routing.

With *distance-vector routing*, routers share their routing table information with each other. Also referred to as "routing by rumor," each router provides and receives updates from its direct neighbor. In the following figure, Router B shares information with Routers A and C. Router C shares routing information with Routers B and D. A distance vector describes the direction (port) and the distance (number of hops or other metric) to some other router. When a router receives information from another router, it increments whatever metric it is using. This process is called *distance accumulation*. Routers using this method know the distance between any two points in the network, but they do not know the exact topology of an internetwork.

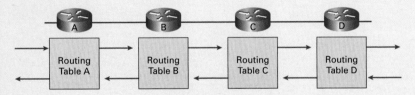

Discovering Information with Distance Vectors

Network discovery is the process of learning about indirectly connected routers. During network discovery, routers accumulate metrics and learn the best paths to various destinations in the network. In the example, each directly connected network has a distance of 0. Router A learns about other networks based on information it receives from Router B. Routers increment the distance metric for any route learned by an adjacent router. In other words, any distance information A learns about other routers from B, it increments by 1.

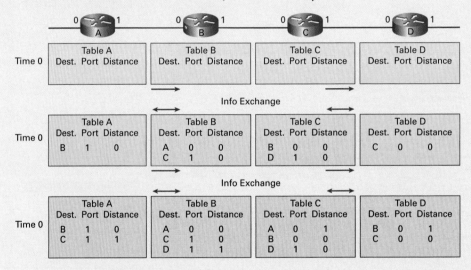

Link-State Routing

With *link-state routing*, also known as shortest path first (SPF), each router maintains a database of topology information for the entire network.

Link-state routing provides better scaling than distance-vector routing because it only sends updates when there is a change in the network, and then it only sends information specific to the change that occurred. Distance vector uses regular updates and sends the whole routing table every time. Link-state routing also uses a hierarchical model, limiting the scope of route changes that occur.

Mobility and Wireless Networks

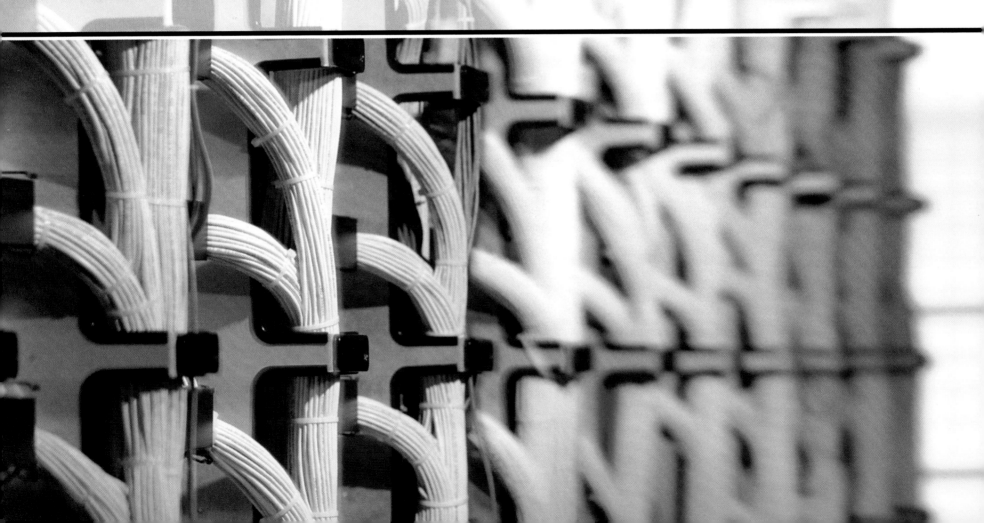

Throwing Away the Ties That Bind

The evolution of the telephone reveals one consistent evolving design principle: People do not want to be tied down to a particular location when using the phone. The first phones were attached to the wall, and people leaned down or stood on their toes to speak into the horn and listen to the response. Then the mouthpiece and listening device were combined into a single handset and connected to the phone by a chord; the phone still hung on the wall, but a person could rest the handset against his head and talk to the other person comfortably.

Finally, the phone was liberated from the wall. A cable attached to the phone itself allowed the caller to comfortably move the phone around the room. The caller was still restricted by the length of the phone cable, but at least she could lay on the couch while talking to a friend.

Then came wireless phones. Throw away the cable; the caller could be anywhere in the house, or even in the garden outside, and still comfortably speak with friends and family. This change was revolutionary in the independence it provided.

This principle of independence applies to wireless LANs. Notebook computers and personal digital assistants (PDAs) are commonplace in corporations; people take their computers with them to meetings, customer sites, airports, and hotels. Until recently, this mobility meant dragging a cable and being restricted to sitting somewhere near the wall where the cable plugged into the network.

With wireless networking, the computing user can easily access the network wherever he is as long as a wireless access point is nearby. Breaking the dependence on a cable and a wall jack is quite liberating.

Some benefits realized with the introduction of wireless networking include the following:

- Computer users can access the corporate network and Internet anywhere on campus. This offers unprecedented convenience and flexibility.
- Temporary networks are easier to set up when making moves, adds, and changes or when setting up war rooms or temporary workspaces.
- It is easier to collaborate on the spot. Users can exchange files or handle requests for information when in meetings, for example.
- Users can exchange data with servers directly rather than wait to download it from a wired connection. This flexibility is important in warehouse and manufacturing, for example.
- Recently, with the addition of LEAP and other security and encryption-related protocols, wireless LANs are as secure as wired LANs. Before the development of these protocols, hackers could easily join a wireless network and access corporate or personal data.

Wireless LANs are meant to complement existing wired networks. Wireless access points (similar to a traditional Ethernet hub) provide access to devices that have wireless network interface cards. The access points connect to an Ethernet switch and are typically configured on their own VLAN. Wireless bridges can provide wireless connectivity as well. This setup allows for longer distance connectivity between buildings, for example. The current wireless standards include 802.1a, 802.1b, and 802.1g.

In general, wireless LANs cannot achieve speeds as fast as wired networks. The size of the antenna and the transmission power setting of the interface card determine the distance, speed, and area between the transmitter and receiver. If you must achieve greater distance must be achieved, you can reduce the data rate. Tradeoffs occur between greater distance and faster transmission speeds.

As a user moves from one part of a building to another, the network must be able to switch which access point is associated with the user. This *roaming* happens automatically, invisibly to the user.

Security is a significant concern with wireless networking. Anyone with a wireless card can walk by a company building and possibly gain access to the corporate network. For example, a teleworker might be running a virtual private network (VPN) from her house to the corporate network and running wireless. Someone could easily access the corporate network with a wireless card from outside that person's house.

Wireless security consists of authentication and privacy. Authentication ensures that only authorized persons can access the wireless LAN. Privacy provides a means to securely encrypt the traffic on the wireless LAN so that it cannot be intercepted. These means are effective in preventing unauthorized access to the wireless network.

At-A-Glance—Wireless LANs

Why Should I Care About Wireless LANs?

A wireless local-area network (WLAN) is a network of computers or terminals connected by radio frequencies. Unlike traditional LANs, WLAN users are free to move about while staying connected to the network.

Because of this mobility, WLANs offers business great flexibility when implementing a new network or when looking for new office space. You can implement a wireless LAN in a building not set up for traditional networking, saving the time and expense of making a new space business-ready.

WLANs typically connect users to a corporate network, but they can also connect physically separated buildings. This implementation is referred to as a *building-to-building bridge system*.

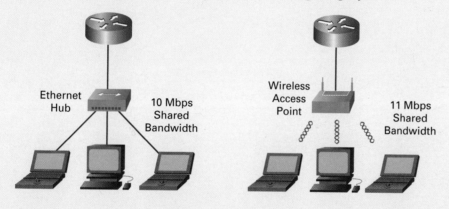

The following are the advantages of WLANs over traditional LANs:

- With LANs, PCs must plug into Ethernet jacks. On WLANs, PCs can access the network from anywhere on the campus.

- With LANs, temporary networks are difficult to set up. With WLANs, temporary networks are easy to set up.

- Users on LANs typically share data files after work sessions due to a lack of connections. On WLANs, users can easily share data and files during work sessions.

What Are the Problems to Solve?

Wireless LANs present network administrators with some new issues:

- Unlike fixed Ethernet, WLANs must trade off between throughput and the power consumption of mobile devices on battery power.

- One of the advantages of WLANs is mobility. Therefore, WLANs must employ schemes that allow users to remain connected as they move about a building or campus.

- WLANs present new security issues such as access control and data privacy.

In-Building Systems

In-building WLANs give employees the flexibility to move about freely while staying connected to the network.

The number of access points (APs) required depends on the size of the building and the desired throughput. You must make trade-offs between power, battery life, and transmission throughput. Remember that in addition to receiving a signal, the PC must transmit a signal to the nearest AP.

At-A-Glance—Wireless LANs and Roaming

Wireless transmissions cause a large power drain on a laptop battery.

This figure shows the trade-off between coverage and throughput.

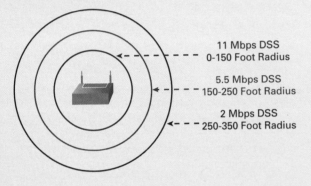

11 Mbps DSS
0-150 Foot Radius

5.5 Mbps DSS
150-250 Foot Radius

2 Mbps DSS
250-350 Foot Radius

Direct Sequence Spread Spectrum (DSS) is a wireless multiplexing scheme for combining multiple signals into the same block of frequencies.

WLAN Roaming

Because wireless APs are relatively inexpensive, and the desire for bandwidth is high, most companies opt for deploying multiple APs with a reduced transmission radius and increased throughput. This solution introduces the need for a WLAN roaming scheme. *Roaming* describes switching from the control of one AP to another. You should position APs so there are no "dead spots." As a user moves away from one AP, the power and signal quality decrease. A good roaming plan ensures that as this happens, another AP signal is sufficiently strong enough to take control of the wireless connection. The network controls this "handoff" transparently to the user.

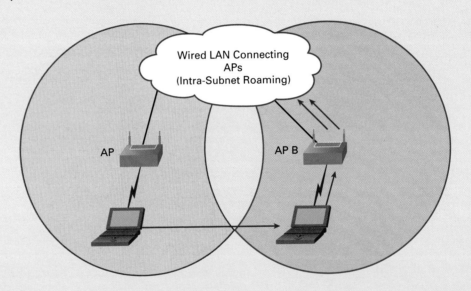

Wired LAN Connecting
APs
(Intra-Subnet Roaming)

AP

AP B

Wireless handoff can only occur on the same WLAN. If a user moves between two WLANs, connectivity is lost until the device authenticates on the new WLAN.

At-A-Glance—Wireless Bridges and Security

Building-to-Building Bridge Systems

Wireless bridges create a single LAN by linking remote networks together. For simple networks, the bridge connects to a hub or a switch on the LAN. If the network contains multiple subnetworks, the bridge is connected to a router. Wireless bridges are a convenient and cost-effective solution for rapidly growing companies or for users located in areas where a fixed connection is either expensive or impractical.

In some cases, building-to-building wireless bridges offer superior price and performance over the following competing technologies:

- Direct cable connections:
  - High installation costs
  - Difficulty overcoming physical barriers such as lakes, highways, and other buildings
  - Often require approval from local governments
  - Inflexible after deployment
- Telephone-line connections
  - High monthly service fees
  - High installation and equipment costs
- Microwave connections
  - Expensive
  - Require licensing
  - Difficult to install

Security Issues and Options

Security is a major concern for WLANs. The two main security issues for WLANs are

- **Access control**—Because WLANs use radio waves for access, any WLAN client in the area is capable of accessing the network. Some hackers access networks while sitting in a car outside of a building. Businesses should protect their networks with centralized user-authentication schemes to protect against unauthorized access.

- **Privacy**—Privacy is also an issue with WLANs. Unlike fixed connections, which send information point to point, WLANs broadcast information everywhere. Hackers can "scoop" this information out of the air. Therefore, it is essential to encrypt the data packets that transmit through the air.

Part V

Keeping the Network Running

Have you ever been in a traffic jam? Ever been in gridlock? Ever had to take a detour rather than the normal road to your destination?

Computer networks face similar traffic problems. A backhoe tractor might be digging ground for a new pipe and accidentally sever a network cable buried underground. A person might accidentally misconfigure a router, bringing the network crashing down. Or a building may lose power.

Network designers must anticipate these possibilities and design their networks accordingly. Redundant network paths (such as a road detour) and redundant devices ensure that if one device fails or one path becomes unavailable, you can select another with minimal delay. Protocols facilitate the quick recovery of a failure so that network devices can relearn the new paths to use.

Network redundancy is costly, so network designers must weigh the increased cost of implementing network redundancy and disaster recovery against the risk of not being able to recover from a failure. In this part, you'll learn about the methods, benefits, and costs of keeping the network running.

Disaster Recovery

What Happens When the Network Stops Working?

Disaster recovery (DR) is the planning process for how you restore network and computer services or continue operating in the event of a natural or human disaster. The process includes identifying the hardware and software required to run business-critical applications and the associated processes that provide a smooth transition from the event.

A DR plan assesses the loss of time and loss of data that are acceptable to the business. Within those limits, DR moves processing to an alternate location after a catastrophic event.

DR establishes an alternate processing location. The alternate location must have all the components of the production site already in place before the disaster. The move to an alternate location requires an understanding of five key components, as described in the following table.

Component	Description
Equipment	What equipment is affected? Which servers, disk, and networks?
Data	Which databases and data are affected? (Data includes application code.)
People	Who is responsible for recovery?
Location	Where does the recovery take place?
Network	How do we switch the network to the recovery location?

Statistically, fire is the leading cause of disaster. Examples of other possible disasters include storms, floods, earthquakes, chemical accidents, nuclear accidents, wars, terrorist attacks, cold winter weather, extreme heat, airplane crashes (loss of key staff), and avalanches. The planning process includes all the different locales and determines the political stability of the critical business locations.

For each possible disaster that could affect a site, the disaster team assesses the impact to the business in advance. The team addresses the following questions:

- How much of the organization's resources (including data, equipment, and staff) could be lost? What are the replacement costs?
- What efforts are required to rebuild?
- How long does it take to recover?
- What is the impact on the overall organization?
- What customers are affected? What is the impact on them?
- How much does it affect the share price and market confidence?

DR Planning

After outlining possible threats, the DR team ranks the services and systems according to three categories: mission critical, important, and not so important. The ranking determines the depth of planning, funding, and resiliency. A DR team takes the following steps:

1. Form a planning group.
2. Perform risk assessments and audits.
3. Establish priorities for the network and applications.
4. Develop recovery strategies.
5. Prepare an up-to-date inventory and documentation of the plan.
6. Develop verification criteria and procedures.
7. Implement the plan.

The team identifies recovery action for the applications staff, system administrators, database administrators, and network staff.

Resiliency and Backup Services

Business resiliency is the ability to recover from any network failure or issue, whether it is related to disaster, links, hardware, design, or network services. A highly available network (built for resiliency) is the bedrock of effective and timely disaster recovery.

Consider the following areas of the network for resiliency:

- Network links
  - Carrier diversity
  - Local loop diversity
  - Facilities resiliency
  - Building wiring resiliency
- Hardware resiliency
  - Power, security, and disaster
  - Redundant hardware and onsite spare equipment
  - Mean time to repair (MTTR)
  - Network path availability
- Network design
  - Layer 2 WAN designs
  - Layer 2 LAN design
  - Layer 3 IP design
- Network services resiliency
  - Domain Name System (DNS) resiliency
  - Dynamic Host Configuration Protocol (DHCP) resiliency
  - Other services resiliency

Preparedness Testing

The final step to any DR is testing processes and systems. Just as firefighters practice fighting different types of fires to hone their skills and reactions, the DR team should plan mock disasters to ensure that systems, network services, and data all transition as expected and that all the people involved understand their parts in the transition.

At-A-Glance—Disaster Recovery

Why Should I Care About Disaster Recovery?

System outages can be devastating to a business. Regardless of the cause, any outage can cost a company hundreds of thousands or even millions of dollars per hour of system downtime.

Disaster recovery is the planning and implementation of systems and practices to ensure that when disasters do occur, the core business functions continue to operate.

Many people prefer to use the term "business continuance" rather than disaster recovery, because the former term implies that you can actually avoid disaster (business stoppage) with the proper planning and implementation.

What Are Typical Causes of Disasters?

Disaster come in all shapes and sizes. For simplicity, we organized "typical" causes of business disruptions into a few categories:

- Natural disasters
  - Earthquakes
  - Flood
  - Hurricane or typhoon
  - Blizzard
- Unintentional man-made disasters
  - Backhoes
  - Fire
  - Illness (loss of staff)
  - Power outages

- Intentional man-made disasters
  - Acts of war
  - Hacking
  - Work stoppages

What Are the Problems to Solve?

A disaster-recovery plan has four phases: assessment, planning, testing, and implementation/recovery. You must put a plan in place for each risk assessed. Although disruptions can come in many forms, we concentrate on network services and critical applications and data.

Disruption	Solution
Phone service is interrupted.	Multichannel communications strategy.
Network service is disrupted.	Distributed, redundant network design.
Mission-critical application is down.	Business-continuity plan (standby data center, backup).
You can't commute to the office.	Secure remote access and flexible communications (mobility, telecommuting).
Productivity is constrained.	Innovative Internet Protocol (IP) applications.

Before Disaster Strikes

The first step in a business-continuance plan is to assess the business criticality and downtime impact of each business application. The risk assessment should consider how a temporary or extended loss of each application and function impacts the business, regarding the following:

- Financial losses (lost revenue)
- Operation disruption
- Customer satisfaction and retention
- Lost productivity
- Brand dilution
- Legal liability
- Stock price
- Credit rating

For each critical system, application, or function, you must implement a backup and recovery plan.

Planning for Disasters

After you identify and assess the critical systems, data, and applications, you must develop a plan. A business-continuance plan has two primary components: designing the network for high availability and backing up critical systems in geographically diverse buildings.

Networks designed for high availability are resilient to disruptions such as faulty hardware, disconnected or broken cables ("backhoe failures"), and power outages.

At-A-Glance—Disaster Recovery, Continued

More severe disasters (such as a building fire or earthquake), however, can wipe out entire data centers and application-server farms. The only way to recover gracefully from such an event is to have a completely backed-up secondary data center, as shown in this figure.

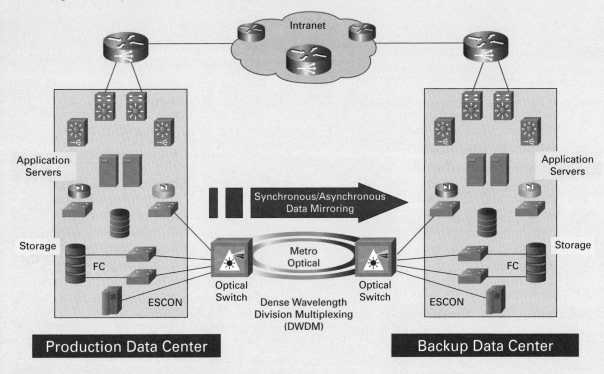

Backing Up Systems

You can back up data centers and application farms in many ways. Some companies back up systems each night after the close of business hours. When they do, the worst-case data loss is a single day. Another backup scheme is called *synchronous data mirroring*. Synchronous data mirroring allows companies to perform real-time backups with no lag, ensuring that they lose virtually no data in the event of a disaster. An added benefit of synchronous data mirroring is that both systems can be online at the same time, providing load and application sharing, which can increase overall productivity. The main challenge with synchronous data mirroring is that the potential decrease in application performance is significant. To achieve synchronous remote mirroring without affecting application performance, you need a high-speed, low-latency connection, such as dense wavelength division multiplexing (DWDM) over optical fiber.

Practicing for Disaster

One of the best ways to ensure a smooth recovery from a disaster is to provide staff with real-world training simulations. Allowing IT staff to practice different disaster scenarios greatly improves their ability to cope with actual disasters.

After a Disaster Occurs

Practice and planning are put to the test if a disaster strikes. To avoid confusion or worse (such as causing more damage), develop a checklist as part of the planning effort and follow it when the time comes. The checklist varies from business to business and situation to situation, but most should closely resemble this example:

1. Make sure that your people are safe. Are all personnel accounted for? Consider sending noncritical personnel home to avoid confusion.

2. Make sure the backup systems are online.

3. Assess the likelihood of additional or secondary disasters. An earthquake, for example, could spark fires or burst gas or water mains.

4. Monitor the network to ensure business continuation.

Restoring Primary Systems

Depending on the severity of damage and the duration of downtime for primary systems, restoring these systems might also disrupt business.

Consideration for backing up data stored on the backup systems, and the restoration of the primary systems, must be taken into account.

Disaster Recovery: Catastrophic Fail-Over

Normal Operation

During normal operation, data flows to and from the primary data center.

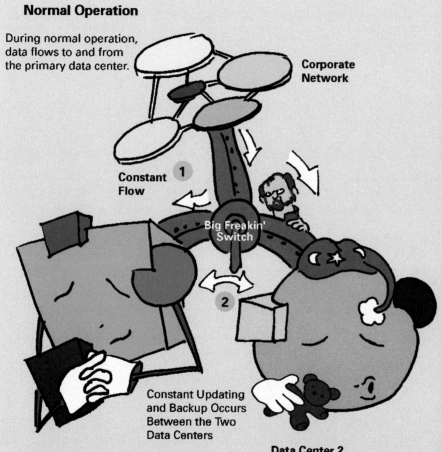

Corporate Network

Constant Flow

1

Big Freakin' Switch

2

Constant Updating and Backup Occurs Between the Two Data Centers

Data Center 1
- Credit Card Numbers
- Bank Transactions
- Expense Datatabase

Data Center 2
It can be idle during normal operation or help balance the work load. Data is backed up at regular intervals or constantly if performing load balancing.

Disaster Recovery

If the primary data center becomes unavailable, the backup data center *wakes up* and becomes the primary. Advanced data center networking technology allows this to occur automatically and without service disruption.

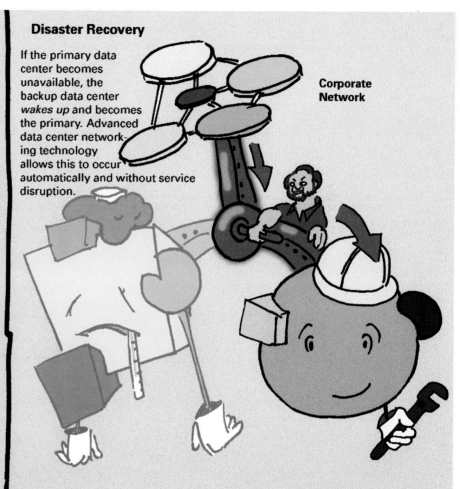

Corporate Network

Since Data Center 2 has been constantly backed up, little or no data is lost in the event of fire, flood, mouse attack or other disaster.

High Availability

Twenty-Four Seven

Network availability (commonly referred to as "high availability") is the design and measurement of a network in terms of the accessibility of the network services. The network must be available to access the services on it. *High availability* simply refers to the goal to keep the network available all of the time. Nonstop networking services is another term. *Network uptime* describes the availability of the network.

Designing networks for high availability

- Prevents financial loss
- Prevents productivity loss
- Reduces reactive support costs
- Improves customer satisfaction and loyalty

Businesses measure their network downtime in terms of average cost per hour. For example, if a portion of a credit-card transaction network goes down such that businesses are unable to swipe credit cards for sales, the credit-card company might end up losing millions of dollars per hour.

Devices such as ATM machines, web services, and automated check-in machines at airports require constant availability. If these machines are down, then they cannot conduct business and revenue is affected.

Common terms for discussing availability are "24x7x365" and "five 9s." The phrase *24x7x365* refers to keeping the network up 24 hours a day, 7 days a week, 365 days a year (366 in leap years). This demand reflects several trends:

- Businesses are international. While people in the US sleep, their coworkers in Australia and Japan conduct business, and they need access to network resources.
- Web presence lets companies keep their shops "open" 24 hours a day.

Five 9s refers to the measurement of availability in terms of a percentage: 99.999 percent. This measurement implies that the network is available 99.999 percent of the time (and not available for .001 percent of the time). This type of measurement made sense in the mainframe world (where its use began) in which it measured a set of hosts. However, today's networks are distributed and consist of hundreds and thousands of devices.

In terms of availability, the following table shows how the measurement translates into downtime per year.

Five 9s availability means the network is unavailable for a total of 5 minutes per year. Yeesh! How do you design a network such that devices are always working?

First, what contributes to the unavailability of the network?

- Human error
- Failed devices
- Bugs
- Power outages
- Service provider outages
- Natural disasters
- Backhoes
- Acts of war or terror
- Upgrades, scheduled maintenance, or hardware replacements

Notice that most of these examples are unplanned and thus generally outside the control of the network administrator. Human error tends to be the leading cause of network outages. It is the design of the network that allows (or prohibits) the network to be available during these planned and unplanned network outages.

Practices for Avoiding Downtime

Reaching any sort of constant uptime does not happen if the following factors exist:

- Single points of failure

- Outages resulting from hardware and software upgrades

- Long recovery times for reboots or switchovers

- Lack of tested spare hardware on site

- Long repair times due to a lack of troubleshooting guides or a lack of training

- Excessive environmental conditions

- Redundancy failure (failure not detected, redundancy not implemented)

- High probability of double failures

- Long convergence time for rerouting traffic around a failed trunk or router in the core

Because outages do occur, the goal of the network administrators is to reduce the outage to as short a time
as possible.

The following design practices increase network availability.

Concept	Example
Hardware redundancy	You achieve redundancy with redundant hardware, processors, and line cards; devices acting in parallel; and the ability to hot-swap cards without interrupting the device's operation (online insertion and removal, or OIR).
Software availability features	Availability features include Hot Standby Router Protocol (HSRP), nonstop forwarding, spanning trees, line-card switchovers, fast route processor switchovers, and nondisruptive upgrades.
Network and server redundancy	Redundant data centers mirror each other so if one data center (with its servers, databases, and networking gear) becomes unavailable, the network automatically reroutes to a redundant data center with minimal data loss.

Concept	Example
Link and carrier availability	Carrier availability comes from multihoming servers, multiple link connections between switches and routers, and subscriptions to several different service providers.
Clean implementation, cable management	You can take steps to minimize the chances of human error. Cleanly implementing a network (by labeling cables, tying cables down, using simple network designs and up-to-date network diagrams, etc.) helps prevent human error.
Backup power and temperature management	Using uninterruptible power supplies (UPSs) on primary network and server equipment ensures that when the power goes out, you have an alternative power source to keep the devices operational. UPSs vary in that they can provide enough power to keep devices running for days or weeks or just enough power for the devices to keep running during quick power surges. Keeping devices in temperature-controlled rooms (as opposed to hot boiler rooms or the cold outdoors) ensures that extreme temperature and moisture do not contribute to an outage.
Network monitoring	Monitoring the network, servers, and devices allows network administrators to detect problems or outages quickly, which minimizes network downtime. The goal is to detect problems before they affect the network's ability to pass traffic. Admins typically use network-management software to monitor the network as well detect trends.
Reduction of network complexity	Selecting a simple, logical, and repetitive network design over a complex one simplifies troubleshooting and network growth. It also reduces the chances of human errors. This step includes using standard released software, well-tested features (as opposed to bleeding-edge technology), and good design sense.
Change control management	Change-control management is the process of introducing changes to the network in a controlled and monitored way. This step includes testing changes before moving them onto the production network, researching software upgrades for known bugs, making a back-out plan in case a change causes a failure , and making one change at a time.
Training	Nothing is more important than a properly trained staff. This step significantly reduces human error by eliminating mistakes made out of ignorance.

At-A-Glance—High Availability

Why Should I Care About High Availability?

A *highly available* network means that a network and its applications are both operational and accessible at all times. As more businesses use networking to conduct day-to-day business, networking becomes a critical to business. To put this in perspective, look at the cost of a network outage. The following numbers reflect the cost of one hour of downtime for various business functions:

- ATM fees: $14,000
- Package shipping: $28,000
- Teleticket sales: $69,000
- Airline sales: $89,500
- Catalog sales: $90,000
- Credit-card authorization: $2.6 million
- Brokerage operations: $6.24 million

Designing a network for high availability does the following:

- Prevents financial loss
- Prevents productivity loss
- Reduces reactive support costs
- Improves customer satisfaction and loyalty

What Affects Network Availability?

The following three types of errors are the most common causes of network failures:

- Operational errors account for 40 percent of network failures; they are usually the result of poor change-management processes or a lack of training and documentation.

- Network failures account for 30 percent of network failures, and they include single points of failure.

- Software failures account for 30 percent of network failures. They can be caused by software crashes, unsuccessful switchovers, or latent-code failures.

How Do You Measure Availability?

The two most common methods for measuring availability are "number of 9s" and defects per million (DPM). Number of 9s refers to the measurement of availability in terms of a percentage. For example, five 9s implies that the network is available 99.999 percent of the time (and not available for .001 percent of the time). Although this measurement is still common, it is really a hold-over from the mainframe world, which measured only the availability of the mainframe hosts. Modern networks, however, are distributed and consist of hundreds and thousands of devices. In this case, DPM is a more realistic measurement. DPM is the number of defects per million hours of operations.

Availability	DPM	Downtime per Year
99.000%	10,000	3 days, 15 hours, 36 minutes
99.900%	1000	8 hours, 46 minutes
99.990%	100	53 minutes
99.999%	10	5 minutes

Best Practices

Hardware redundancy means redundant hardware, processors, line cards, and links. You should design the network such that critical hardware (e.g. core switches) has no single points of failure. Hardware availability also allows you to hot-swap cards or other devices without interrupting the device's operation (online insertion and removal).

At-A-Glance—High Availability, Continued

Reduction of Network Complexity

Although some redundancy is good (and necessary), overdoing it can cause more problems than it solves. Selecting a simple, logical, and repetitive network design over a complex one simplifies the availability to troubleshoot and grow the network. There is a trade-off between expenses and risk. A good design maintains the proper balance between the two extremes.

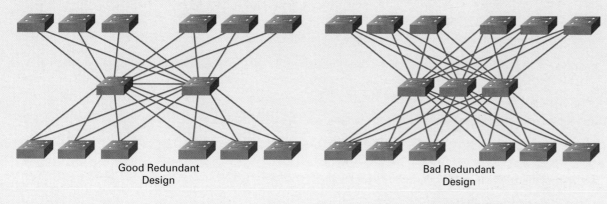

Good Redundant Design

Bad Redundant Design

The extra core switch adds much complexity with little additional benefit.

Software Availability

Software availability refers to both reliability-based protocols, such as Spanning Tree Protocol (STP) and Hot Standby Router Protocol (HSRP), and reliable code and nondisruptive upgrades.

STP, HSRP, and other protocols provide instructions to the network and to components of the network on how to behave in the event of a failure. Failure could be a power outage, a hardware failure, a disconnected cable, or any number of things. These protocols provide rules to reroute packets and reconfigure paths. *Convergence* is the process of applying these rules to the resolution of any such network errors. A converged network is one that, from a user standpoint, has recovered from a failure and can process instructions and requests.

You should thoroughly test and use software in a real (quarantined) or simulated real environment before putting it on the network. Avoid "bleeding-edge" or inadequately tested code. You should also follow procedures for introducing new or updated code. Shutting down the network, loading new code, and hoping it all works is usually a bad idea. You should first introduce new code on segmented, noncritical parts of the network. Plan for the worst case when loading new code.

Link and Carrier Availability

Another component in building highly available networks is understanding your service provider's plans and policies for network availability. For business-critical applications, it might be worthwhile to purchase a secondary service from an additional service provider. You can sometimes use this second link for load sharing.

Clean Implementation and Cable Management

This best practice might seem like a waste of time when first implementing a network, but disorganized cabling and poor implementation can increase the probability of network disasters and hinder their timely resolution.

You can save time, grief, and money by taking some simple steps, such as labeling cables, tying cables down, using simple network designs, and keeping up-to-date network diagrams.

At-A-Glance—High Availability, Continued

Network Monitoring

Monitoring the network servers and devices allows network administrators to detect problems or outages quickly, which contributes to minimizing network downtime. The goal is to detect problems before they affect the network's ability to pass traffic. You typically use network-management software to monitor the network.

Network and Server Redundancy

Redundant data centers mirror each other such that if one data center (with its servers, databases, and networking gear) becomes unavailable, the network automatically reroutes to a redundant data center with minimal data loss.

Training

Nothing is more important than a properly trained staff. Up-to-date, comprehensive training can significantly reduce failures. Human error will always exist, but you can limit that exposure through documentation, good design practices, and training. Human error can be forgiven; ignorance cannot.

Change-Control Management

Always expect the worst when first installing upgrades. It saves you time and trouble in the long run. Introduce all changes to the network in a controlled way. This method includes testing changes before moving them onto the production network, researching software upgrades for known bugs, and following a backup plan in case the change causes a failure or doesn't implement correctly.

Network Management

Keeping the Network Alive from Afar

Network management is the process of documenting, monitoring, troubleshooting, and configuring network devices. Network management gives visibility to the quality of the network's operation and identifies any problems that are about to occur or that have already occurred.

The routers and switches in a network have the same components as a regular PC. There are a CPU (or two), memory, storage, and network interfaces. The primary difference from a PC is that network equipment is highly optimized to perform certain functions such as passing packets quickly.

The nature of today's networks is that network equipment is distributed everywhere. Remote branches, data centers, locations around the world—all these places on the network have routers, switches, servers, and other networking gear.

A network administrator is responsible for the health and well-being of a company's network. Her goal generally is to provide uninterrupted network services. If a network outage or fault occurs, she wants to know about it as soon as possible and isolate the problem quickly.

When a problem occurs in the network, it can bring business to a grinding halt. The network administrators must find, isolate, and fix the fault as quickly as possible to restore business operations. The longer the fault persists, depending on the number of people and processes affected, the greater the monetary losses the company might experience.

For example, a manufacturing line might stop operating. Or a stock-trading firm might stop trading. A hospital might lose the ability to track patients. A theme park might be unable to collect tickets.

The purpose of network management is to provide methods to configure, monitor, and troubleshoot a network. After the fault occurs, a network administrator struggles to gain visibility to the network and any changes that might have occurred to determine the source of the problem.

Aside from dealing with faults, network management facilitates the orderly upgrade or maintenance of network devices. Remember, a company might have network devices installed all over the world, so it is not practical for a network administrator to physically travel to all of the various locations to upgrade code.

The current thinking defines network management in terms of five categories represented by the abbreviation FCAPS:

- **Fault**—Finding and correcting network problems.
- **Configuration**—Monitoring and controlling network devices and configuration.
- **Accounting**—Ensuring devices are distributed appropriately and providing an ability to account (and bill) for usage.
- **Performance**—Measuring the throughput in the network and looking for potential bottlenecks. This area is especially important when determining capacity for applications and users.
- **Security**—Protecting the network from inadvertent mistakes and intentional sabotage.

The elements that make up an effective network-management strategy include documentation, network-management protocols, and troubleshooting tools.

Network Documentation: A Must Have

A relatively simple yet often overlooked process of network management is documenting how all of the network devices connect to each other. Network documentation becomes indispensable during network problems.

Documentation takes all forms:

- Logical network diagrams show how all of the devices are connected.
- Cabling charts document where cable runs in a building. These charts are vital when you want to figure out where the other end of a cable terminates. (Is it an office or another floor?)
- A database correlates IP addresses and other network information with individual users and locations.
- Where more than a couple of people are responsible for a network, you need change-control documentation. Change control is the process of documenting any changes to the network *before* you make them so a group can review the changes and ensure that one set of changes doesn't overwrite another.
- You can reference logs from network devices when you want to determine the source of a problem. Cisco devices send *console messages* and Simple Network Management Protocol (SNMP) traps (to be discussed shortly) to a remote server for this purpose. By studying the log of messages, a network administrator might be able to determine the source of a problem.

Network-Management Protocols

Many tools and protocols help you effectively manage network devices. These tools and protocols assist with the configuration, backup, monitoring, and measurement of network devices. Network-management software makes efficient use of public domain protocols to discover and manage networks.

The first protocol is simply the Transmission Control Protocol/Internet Protocol (TCP/IP) ping tool. Network management-software, in its simplest form, uses ping as a heartbeat monitor. Ping sends a single request to a device, and the device is expected to send back a single response when it receives the request. Thus, if your system does not receive a response for a period of time (remember, packets might drop in the network occasionally, so ping needs to retry three or more times), you can assume the device is unreachable for some reason.

An unreachable device indicates that somewhere between the network-management workstation and the destination device, packets weren't able to pass. Commercial network-management software indicates this fault by coloring a graphical representation of a device red on a map of the network. (Green indicates that everything is okay.)

Whereas ping provides a heartbeat, SNMP lets you get and set information between a network-management station and a managed device such as a router or switch.

SNMP is a simple protocol that is similar to a database-retrieval program. The managed device maintains a database of information such as the health of its components (CPU, network interface, buffers, etc.) and throughput (how many packets are passing through an interface).

Using SNMP, a network administrator can send a new configuration file to a device, upgrade its software, check the status of its health, and measure how many packets are flowing through the device. You can store virtually anything about the device in the database in such a way that a network-management workstation can learn or configure any aspect of the network device.

SNMP also provides *traps*. Rather than a command-and-response like other SNMP commands, traps are unsolicited responses. Managed devices, such as a router, send a trap when something needs attention. For example, if an interface goes down, a router sends a trap, notifying the network-management workstation. The workstation then indicates there is a fault on the device.

Depending on the vendor, you might use other protocols to manage a device.

Troubleshooting Tools

The final component of network management is troubleshooting tools. These tools help the network administrator isolate and correct a network problem when it occurs.

These tools include cable testers, packet analyzers, and regular computers used to query information on location.

Cable testers and other physical-level devices let you determine whether a cable has a physical problem. For example, a cable might be too long and out of spec. Or something nearby might be causing interference and disrupting the flow of traffic.

Packet analyzers let a network administrator monitor traffic on a part of the network. The analyzer not only captures the traffic, but also decodes the contents of each packet into human-readable form. These tools are indispensable when you want to determine the source of a problem or the behavior of an application.

Because packet analyzers capture all traffic, a hacker can use the tool to not only observe data as it flows through the network, but also introduce lethal and disruptive traffic into the network.

The final tool is a regular laptop computer. A network administrator can install network-management, packet-analyzer, and database software and carry all the software tools he needs to troubleshoot and correct a problem on location.

At-A-Glance—Network Management

Why Should I Care About Network Management?

If you use a computer attached to a network at work, school, or elsewhere, chances are that the network manager knows about you and the types of programs you use. You are being watched!

Although user supervision is one management task (and the part most users tend to worry about), network management has more to it than that.

As networks get more complex and more intelligent, you must put tools in place to manage the network and ensure that it is operating efficiently and effectively.

What Are the Problems to Solve?

An ideal network-management system is everywhere all the time. With increased network intelligence and smart end devices, every point in the network can be part of an overall management-reporting system. Active network management can be difficult.

To manage a network, you usually perform tasks from one of five categories known as FCAPS (fault, configuration, accounting, performance, security).

Each category has its own methods, strategies, and protocols:

- **Fault detection and correction**—A good network-management scheme quickly finds and isolates problems.

- **Configuration**—As the network grows, manual configuration of devices becomes prohibitively difficult. Configuration also includes monitoring functions.

- **Accounting**—You track usage, distribution, and billing. In many cases, you use billing to justify departmental budgets.

- **Performance**—You measure performance to ensure the network is operating efficiently. If you find any bottlenecks, you can open alternate paths.

- **Security**—You take measures to protect the network. Although most people assume that hackers are the biggest threat, many attacks come from inside the network.

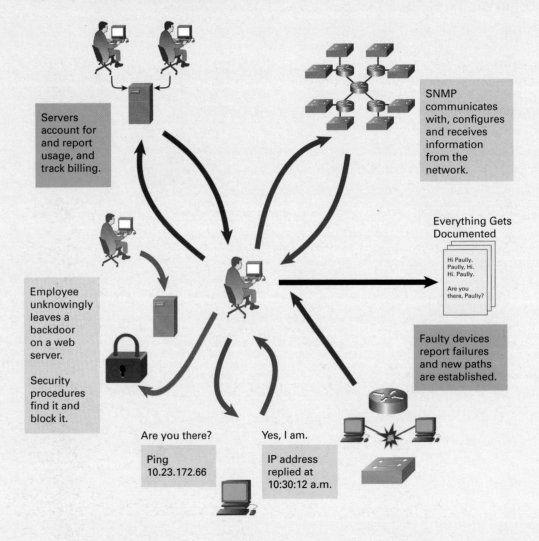

Servers account for and report usage, and track billing.

SNMP communicates with, configures and receives information from the network.

Everything Gets Documented

Hi Paully. Paully, Hi. Hi. Paully. Are you there, Paully?

Employee unknowingly leaves a backdoor on a web server.

Security procedures find it and block it.

Faulty devices report failures and new paths are established.

Are you there?

Ping 10.23.172.66

Yes, I am.

IP address replied at 10:30:12 a.m.

Network Management

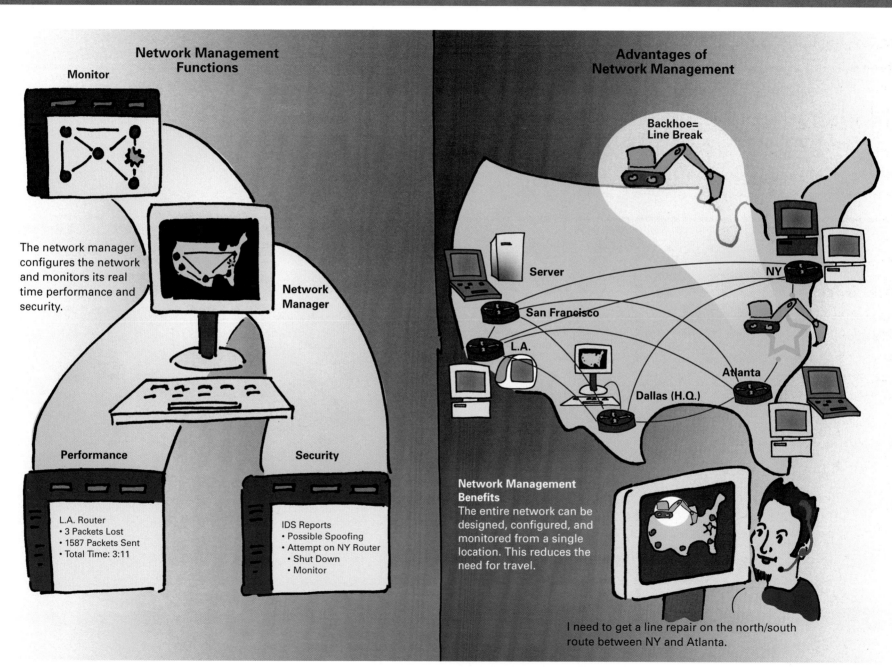

Network Management Functions

Monitor

The network manager configures the network and monitors its real time performance and security.

Network Manager

Performance

L.A. Router
• 3 Packets Lost
• 1587 Packets Sent
• Total Time: 3:11

Security

IDS Reports
• Possible Spoofing
• Attempt on NY Router
• Shut Down
• Monitor

Advantages of Network Management

Backhoe= Line Break

Server

NY

San Francisco

L.A.

Atlanta

Dallas (H.Q.)

Network Management Benefits
The entire network can be designed, configured, and monitored from a single location. This reduces the need for travel.

I need to get a line repair on the north/south route between NY and Atlanta.

QoS

QoS: Frequent Flyers and Air-Traffic Controllers

Quality of service (QoS) is the enabler of the Internet Protocol (IP) network convergence trend. The fundamental concept that enables IP network convergence is the conversion or tunneling of other network technologies into Transmission Control Protocol/Internet Protocol (TCP/IP) across traditional data networks. With voice, it's the conversion of traditional time-division multiplexing (TDM) voice streams into packetized voice packets. IP networks are built on shared bandwidth. Thus IP networks must have mechanisms that "simulate" the dedicated on-time delivery associated with traditional voice and video networks.

Moving voice, video, and other time-sensitive technologies onto traditional data networks requires that the streams be delivered on time with minimal loss and consistent delay. A delay or loss of packet in a voice stream, for example, causes a break or chop in the conversation. There is no need to retransmit a voice packet if it gets lost because that packet is only relevant at one point of time in the conversation.

Traditional data networks are less concerned with on-time delivery and loss. For example, although congestion slowing down a file download might be inconvenient and annoying, the file eventually downloads intact. The higher-layer protocols take care of making sure that all the bits transfer and that the bits end up as they were transmitted. Whether it takes 10 seconds or 10 hours for the file to transfer is irrelevant (although perhaps annoying) because the higher-layer protocols ensure the file arrives intact at the other end.

QoS is a collection of tools and practices that enable data networks to mark, prioritize, and schedule traffic. Each device on a network participates in QoS; otherwise, the quality of service varies throughout a network.

Elements of QoS include the following:

- **Network design**—You must design and build a network to handle the amount of data and time-sensitivity required for a company's network convergence. All of the devices in the network must support their roles in the QoS process. For example, if a company wants to enable voice across its wide-area data network, the WAN topology must have enough bandwidth to handle the calls and existing data traffic. Additionally, the routers and WAN service provider must be able to participate in the marking, prioritization, and scheduling necessary to deliver on-time reliable voice quality.

- **Packet marking**—The first step in the QoS process is indicating which packets have higher importance than others. When a packet comes into the network, it is assigned a number that indicates its importance. In TCP/IP networks, this number is called the *type of service (ToS)*, and it is a value from zero to seven (zero being the lowest and seven the highest priority).

- **Prioritization and queuing**—Traffic is prioritized according to the ToS setting in each packet or where the packet arrives from. *Queuing* is the mechanism in each device that enables the network to process higher-priority packets (such as important applications or voice traffic) before lower-priority packets. Just like the platinum frequent flyers at the airport, higher-priority packets get to jump ahead of lower-priority packets. Like a bouncer in a nightclub, if it sees too many low-priority packets in line, the router must throw out some of them to let the higher-priority packets through.

- **Scheduling**—After the packets are ordered by priority and processed by a network device (such as a router), they must be scheduled to go out a network interface. Interfaces with limited bandwidth (such as a WAN) might have more traffic waiting to be transmitted than there is bandwidth available. Traffic-shaping mechanisms act as air-traffic controllers at an airport in that they sort outbound traffic into priority order while also making sure the lower-priority traffic isn't starved.

- **Link fragmentation and interleaving**—Networks have big packets and small packets. Video and file transfer are examples of big packets, and voice is an example of small packets. Fifteen voice packets might be the same size as one file-transfer packet. If 15 voice packets must wait for one file-transfer packet to traverse a slow WAN, it might be too late for the voice traffic to be useful. This concept is called *delay*, and the variation in delay that occurs is called *jitter*. Delay and jitter are the enemies of voice and video over data networks. *Link fragmentation* is the process of slicing one large packet into many smaller packets. *Interleaving* is the process of placing important traffic in between the less-important traffic. Therefore, voice packets continue to make it to their destination on time in between the fragments of the original file-transfer packet.

- **Bandwidth reservation**—Also called *provisioning*, this process reserves certain portions of limited bandwidth for high-priority traffic. That bandwidth is always there. If the amount of low-priority traffic exceeds the bandwidth available, the network does not use the reserved bandwidth and instead discards low-priority traffic. Bandwidth reservation is a necessary component for handling time-sensitive traffic.

The combination of QoS mechanisms and effective network design ensure the success of converging voice, video, and data onto the same network.

At-A-Glance—Quality of Service

Why Should I Care About Quality of Service?

Quality of service (QoS) refers to the perceived and measured performance of a network, typically in terms of the sound quality of a voice call or the availability of critical data. If you don't implement a QoS strategy, applications for IP telephony, videoconferencing, and mission-critical data are subject to "best-effort" (nonguaranteed) transmission. This setup can result in choppy voice or video during times of network congestion or a loss of critical data.

This figure illustrates the differences between voice and (noncritical) data.

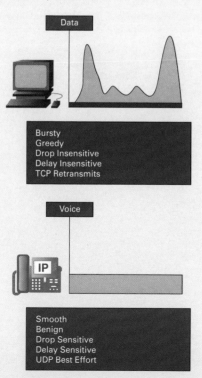

What Are the Problems to Solve?

The three parameters that define QoS are loss, delay, and delay variance (jitter). Controlling these three factors allows you to control the QoS:

- **Loss**—The percentage of packets dropped. In a highly available network, loss should be less than 1 percent. Voice networks should approach 0 percent loss.

- **Delay**—The time it takes for a packet to reach the target destination. Delay consists of fixed delay (serialization, quantization, etc.) and variable delay (network congestion). The total end-to-end delay should be less than 150 ms.

- **Delay variation (or jitter)**—The difference in the delay times of consecutive packets. A jitter buffer smoothes out arrival times, but the buffer's ability to smooth out arrival times has instantaneous and total limits. Voice networks cannot have more than 30 ms of jitter.

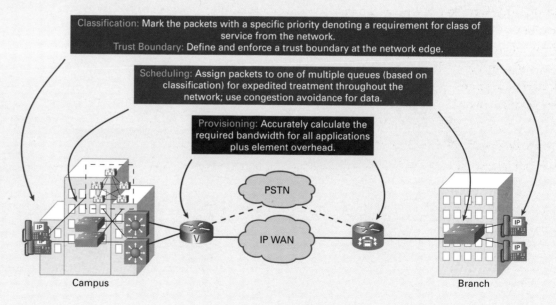

At-A-Glance—Ensuring Packets Arrive on Time and Intact

Three Steps to Quality

To mitigate the effects of loss, delay, and jitter, you must ensure that the network can properly handle time and not drop sensitive packets. To achieve QoS, you must first leave room (bandwidth) for certain packets, you must identify which packets require special treatment, and you must have rules for how to treat these packets. These three steps are also referred to as provisioning, classification, and scheduling:

• **Provisioning**—Ensuring that the required bandwidth is available for all applications as well as for overhead traffic.

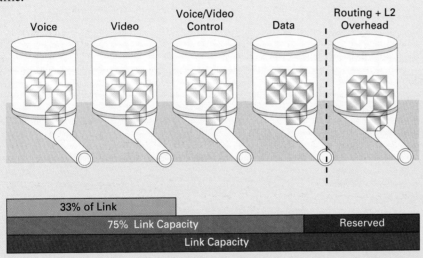

• **Classification**—Marking the packet with a specific priority denoting a requirement for special service from the network. Layer 2 or Layer 3 devices can do this marking at different places in the network. Typical classification schemes identify critical (voice and mission-critical data), high (video), normal (e-mail, Internet access), and low (fax, FTP) priorities.

• **Scheduling**—Assigning packets to one of multiple queues (based on classification) for priority treatment through the network. A good example is a commercial-airline boarding scheme. "Now boarding rows 40 through 50. First-class passengers and VIP members may board at any time."

At-A-Glance—Traffic Engineering and LFI

Low-Bandwidth Tools

In addition to the three main steps to ensure QoS, you also need some link-specific tools, such as traffic shaping and link fragmentation and interleaving (LFI), especially when routing traffic over low-bandwidth (768 Kbps or slower) links.

Traffic shaping is throttling back packet transmission rates. If there are line-speed mismatches between remote offices, the service provider connecting the offices might be forced to drop arbitrary packets going to the slower link. To prevent networks from dropping high-priority packets, an enterprise can engineer its traffic by provisioning its traffic on the slower link. Traffic engineering also allows the enterprise to decide which packets can be, or should be, dropped (low-priority packets) when instantaneous congestion occurs.

The three most common cases for traffic engineering occur in the following situations:

- Line-speed mismatches
- Remote-to-central-site oversubscription
- Traffic bursts above the committed rate

Link Fragmentation and Interleaving (LFI)

In addition to network congestion, one of the primary contributors to both delay and jitter is *serialization delay*. This delay often occurs when a time-sensitive packet gets "stuck in traffic" behind a large data packet (such as FTP data). *Link fragmentation* is the process of breaking up large packets to allow smaller, more time-sensitive packets to proceed through the network in a timely manner. Interleaving is the processes of "weaving" the time-sensitive packets into the train of fragmented data packets.

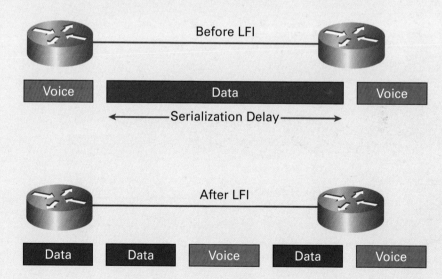

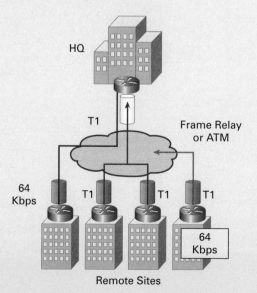

Low-Latency Queuing Logic: How Packet Traffic Flows Are Prioritized

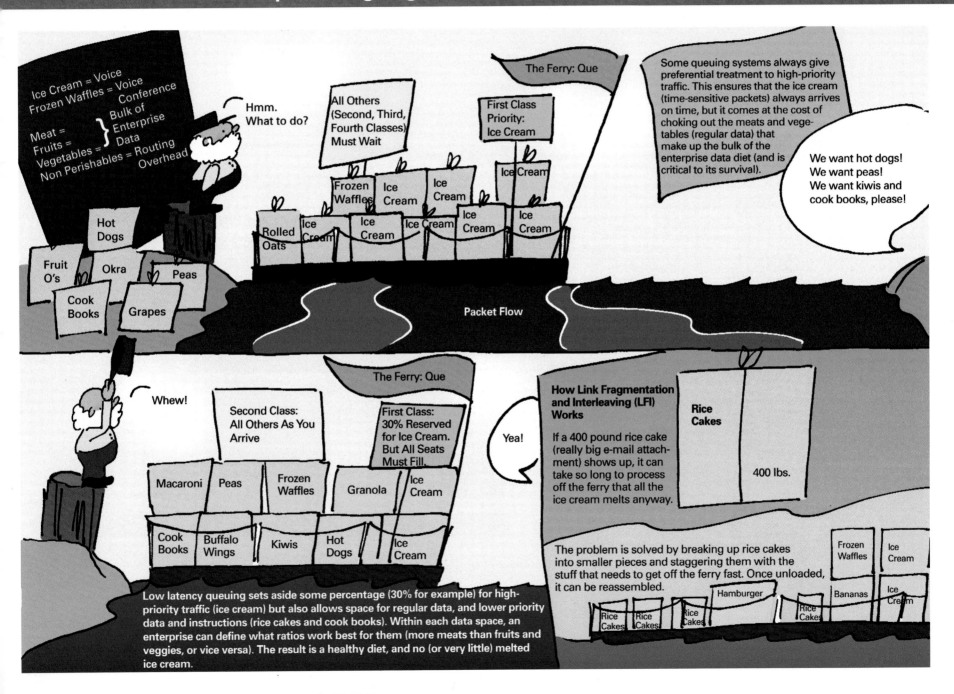

Routing Protocols

Moving Network Traffic Smartly

Routing is the process of moving traffic across an internetwork from one place to another. Intermediate devices called *routers* (or gateways) determine the traffic's path along the way. Routing is often confused with bridging in that both are responsible for making forwarding decisions. However, routing involves Layer 3 (network) decision-making, whereas bridging makes decisions based on Layer 2 (data link) information.

Routers perform two basic functions:

• Path determination

• Packet switching

Path Determination

Routers use *metrics* to determine optimal paths in a network. Metrics can range from the bandwidth of a particular path to the relative distance of one router from another. Routers maintain tables called *routing tables* that aid in the process of path determination.

Routing algorithms populate the routing tables with the information a router needs to make forwarding decisions. The primary piece of information stored in routing tables is the correlation of a destination with the nearest next-hop router. Destination/next-hop associations tell a router that it can reach a particular destination by forwarding the traffic to another router on the way to the packet's final destination. A router checks the destination address of an incoming packet and then attempts to associate the address with a possible next hop.

Routing tables can store other information that affect how a router makes a forwarding decision. For example, they can store the desirability of one route over another.

Routers communicate with one another by exchanging routing update messages. This way, all routers can synchronize their routing tables and agree on optimal paths. By analyzing the updates from other routers, a router can build a detailed view of the network. The router can also determine if a path changes or a router goes away.

Packet Switching

Aside from path determination, routers also provide packet-switching services. This process receives a packet on one interface and forwards the packet out the interface that gets the packet closer to its destination. The router uses the destination address in the packet as the indicator of where the packet is headed.

Upon inspecting the destination address in a packet, the router must determine whether it knows how to reach the destination. It makes this determination by consulting the routing table. If the destination is known, the routing table contains which interface the router should transmit the packet from. If the destination is unknown, the router typically throws the packet away.

The next hop on a packet's path to its destination is either the actual host the packet is destined to or another router. If the next hop is a router, that router performs the same analysis as the previous one.

As a packet traverses a network, the Layer 3 source and destination addresses remain the same. (They indicate the original sender and intended receiver.) However, the Layer 2 Media Access Control (MAC) addresses change from router to router and from router to destination host. This change is how a router indicates the intended next-hop device.

Determining a Good Path Through the Network

Routing-protocol algorithms vary in how they determine optimal paths in a network. A routing protocol typically has one or more of the following design goals:

- **Path optimality**—Ability to select the best path based on certain metrics.

- **Simplicity and low overhead**—Use of minimal router resources as possible and efficient operation.

- **Robustness and stability**—Algorithm performing correctly under undue circumstances, such as hardware failure, high load, or incorrect implementation.

- **Rapid convergence**—Process of all routers agreeing on the optimal paths. The time it takes for all routers to exchange routing updates and agree on routes must be fast. Slow convergence can result in routing loops or network outages.

- **Flexibility**—Algorithm adapting to network-circumstance changes quickly and accurately. Routing algorithms can adapt to changes in variables such as network bandwidth, router queue size, and network delay.

Routing algorithms determine path optimality according to some or all of the following metrics:

- **Path length**—Based on assignment of arbitrary cost to each network link.

- **Reliability**—Dependability of each network link.

- **Delay**—Time it takes to move a packet from one end of a network link to the other.

- **Bandwidth**—Available traffic capacity of a link.

- **Load**—How busy a router is.

- **Communication cost**—Monetary cost of a network link. Although one link might be slower than another, it might be cheaper to use the slower link.

Differences Among Routing Algorithms

Six types of routing-algorithm differentiators make each routing protocol unique.

The first type of differentiator is *static versus dynamic*. Static algorithms are simple in that the network administrator statically defines all routes, and the routes do not change unless the administrator changes them. Static routes make sense in simple network designs with predictable traffic. However, static routes cannot react to network changes automatically. Dynamic algorithms can adapt, and for that reason, they are more suitable for most networks. A router running a dynamic algorithm analyzes incoming routing-update messages and recalculates routes if a network change is detected.

The second type of differentiator is *single-path versus multipath*. Multipath algorithms support the multiplexing of traffic across multiple simultaneous paths to a destination, whereas single-path algorithms support only a single path. The advantage of multipath is that the algorithm offers substantially better throughput and reliability through load balancing.

The third type of differentiator is *flat versus hierarchical*. A flat routing structure means all routers communicate with each other. With a hierarchical structure, some routers form a routing backbone, and all messages outside a particular area must go through the backbone. This setup reduces the amount of routing information each router must maintain and exchange and therefore simplifies the routing algorithm on each router.

The fourth type of differentiator is *host-intelligent versus router-intelligent*. Some routing protocols require that the transmitting hosts be able to determine the route to the destination. The routers simply act as store-and-forward devices. This method is typically called source-routing. Router-intelligent routing assumes the hosts know little about routes, and the routers themselves contain the information necessary to route a packet through the network.

The fifth type of differentiator is *intradomain (interior) versus interdomain (exterior)*. Intradomain algorithms are tuned to most efficiently exchange routes with peer devices in a single routing domain. Interdomain algorithms exchange routes among different routing domains.

The final type of differentiator is *link state versus distance vector*. Link-state algorithms, also known as shortest path first, flood routing information to all nodes in the network. Each router only sends information concerning the state of its own links. Distance-vector algorithms instead have routers send all or part of their routing tables to only neighboring routers. In other words, link-state protocols send small updates everywhere, whereas distance-vector protocols send large updates only to neighbors.

Open Shortest Path First (OSPF), Enhanced Internet Gateway Routing Protocol (EIGRP), and Routing Information Protocol (RIP) are examples of intradomain IP routing protocols. OSPF is a link-state protocol, whereas RIP is a distance-vector protocol. EIGRP is Cisco's proprietary distance-vector protocol that incorporates some link-state characteristics. All three protocols (RIP v2 included) provide the ability to summarize routes. Border Gateway Protocol (BGP) and Intermediate System-to-Intermediate System (IS-IS) Protocol, which are examples of interdomain routing protocols, are the primary protocols used on the Internet.

AppleTalk and Novell Internetwork Packet Exchange (IPX), which each implement their own types of Layer 3 routing strategies, are examples of non-IP routing protocols.

Spanning Tree

Protecting the Flat Earth of Networking

The Spanning Tree Protocol (STP) is a Layer 2 protocol designed to run on bridges and switches. The main purpose of spanning tree is to prevent loops from forming in a bridged network. The de-facto implementation of STP is based on the Institute of Electrical and Electronic Engineers (IEEE) 802.1d standard.

Loops form when redundant connections between switches form a circular path; the same packet travels endlessly around the same path in a circle. Multicast and broadcast packets are the culprits for bringing down networks when loops form because the packet is not destined to a single device, and no device is responsible for removing the packet from the network.

Loops can be deadly, bringing whole networks to a halt. Because of this possibility, it is always a good practice to break up Layer 2 networks with Layer 3 routers. Implementing Layer 2 redundancy in networks is sometimes necessary, and spanning tree ensures that loops do not form. With redundant Layer 2 links, only one path is active at a time. When the single path goes down, another path becomes active.

As with most networking technologies, there is a pendulum effect in the popularity of Layer 2 bridged (flat) networks versus Layer 3 routed networks. Cisco's initial business convinced customers to insert routing devices to break up their predominately flat, bridged networks to more efficiently transmit traffic and reduce the number of users affected when broadcast storms and loops occurred. However, in the mid-1990s, LAN switches became wildly popular for replacing bridges and hubs. The "flat earth" craze went so far as to swing the pendulum back, with competitive sayings such as, "Switch if you can; route if you must."

Once again, network administrators learned the consequences of building massive Layer 2 networks: one loop in the network could kill an entire network. Today, the role for switching and bridging is more clearly defined, and experience has shown that networks are more resilient and recover from failures more quickly when they use Layer 3 redundancy (such as HSRP) instead of Layer 2 (spanning tree).

New Internet standards improve the efficiency of STP:

- **802.1w Rapid Spanning Tree Protocol (RSTP)**—By default, traditional 802.1d STP treated every port the same concerning the time it took to transition into an active state. It took switch ports anywhere from 30–180 seconds to transition into a forwarding state, which was an eternity in computer time. 802.1w defines shortcuts based on what is connected to the switch port that allow quicker transition times.

- **802.1s Multiple Spanning Tree (MST)**—Switches that implement virtual local-area networks (VLANs) traditionally needed to run one spanning tree process per VLAN. Networks with hundreds of VLANs required each switch to have enough spanning-tree instances running to match one instance per VLAN. This setup is CPU-intensive on the switches and complicates recovery after a network event. 802.1s MST reduces the overall number of spanning-tree instances by mapping multiple VLANs with similar topologies to a single spanning-tree instance. MST improves traffic load-balancing and network-recovery time.

Spanning-Tree Fundamentals

As previously mentioned, STP dynamically prevents loops in Layer 2 switched networks. STP defines a tree that spans all switches in a LAN by forcing certain redundant paths in the network into a blocked state. If a link that previously forwarded traffic becomes unavailable, STP dynamically reconfigures the network to redirect traffic flow by activating the appropriate standby path.

Switches dynamically determine the state of the spanning tree by exchanging information with others using bridge protocol data units (BPDUs). These packets contain information on each switch's view of the network. The absence of a regularly scheduled BPDU from a neighbor switch indicates that that switch has disappeared.

The first order of business with spanning tree is for all of the switches in the spanning tree to elect a root. The root serves as the focal point for the rest of the switched network. Once the root is elected, each switch's proximity to the root determines all forwarding and blocking decisions. Switches dynamically determine the root through the exchange of BPDUs containing root IDs. When determining the winner, smaller is better. If the root ID on Switch A is lower than that of Switch B, then Switch A becomes the root.

Traditionally, each VLAN on a switch had to have its own root, which could add considerable overhead to switches with a lot of VLANs. You can implement 802.1s MST to resolve this issue.

After a root is elected, switches implement the following rules for traditional 802.1d STP:

- All ports on the root switch must be in a forwarding state.
- After a switch determines that it is not root, it must identify the port that is closest to the root (called the root port) and put it in a forwarding state.
- When multiple nonroot switches occupy a common segment, they must determine which switch has the shortest path to the root (called the designated port) and put it in a forwarding state.
- All other ports connected to another switch or bridge must be in a blocking state. This arrangement is how STP prevents loops.

When a port first becomes active (for example, when a switch boots up), 802.1d STP requires that the port not forward traffic until the switch has had time to determine the state of the rest of the spanning tree. Specifically, a port must transition through the following states:

- **Listening/Blocking**—The port is blocked. However, the switch transmits and receives BPDUs to determine the state of the spanning tree. This state lasts 15 seconds by default.
- **Learning**—The port remains blocked and continues receiving and transmitting BPDUs. However, it also receives traffic and begins building a bridge table based on the source Media Access Control (MAC) addresses of the traffic it receives. This state lasts 15 seconds by default.
- **Forwarding**—If the switch determines that a port does not need to be blocked, it may begin forwarding traffic.

This process ensures that loops do not form when there is a topology change. However, if a failure occurs, all switches must go through the three states in the list. It takes at least 30 seconds for each switch to begin forwarding again. As far as network availability, this delay is generally too long for a recovery to occur.

Both proprietary and public-domain methods reduce the transition from blocking to forwarding. 802.1s, as mentioned earlier, enables specific types of switch ports to transition instantaneously, or near so. Basically, these shortcuts require careful planning: If a switch port is configured to expect a PC connected to it, and another switch is connected to the port instead, catastrophic temporary loops can form.

Spanning tree is an elegant solution for networks to automatically adjust to topology changes.

At-A-Glance—Spanning Tree

Why Should I Care About Spanning Tree?

Designing a redundant network is one of the key methods for keeping your network available at all times. Unfortunately, it can cause loops in a Layer 2 network, which often results in serious problems, including a complete network shutdown.

The Spanning Tree Protocol (STP) prevents looping traffic in a redundantly switched or bridged network by only allowing traffic through a single path to other parts of the network. Any redundant paths are shut off until they are needed (typically when the primary link goes down).

What Are the Problems to Solve?

To maintain the benefits of a redundant network, and simultaneously prevent the problems associated with loops, the network must perform the following functions:

1. First, recognize that a loop exists.
2. Designate one of the redundant links as primary and the others as backup.
3. Switch traffic only through the primary link.
4. Check the health of both links at regular intervals.
5. In the event of a primary link failure, switch traffic to one of the backup links.

The Problem with Loops

Although redundancy can prevent a single point of failure from causing the entire switched network to fail, it can also cause problems such as broadcast storms, multiple copies of frames, and Media Access Control (MAC) address table instability.

Broadcast Storms

A *broadcast storm* refers to the indefinite flooding of frames. Broadcast storms can quickly shut down a network.

An example of a broadcast storm appears in the figure below:

1. A broadcast frame is sent by another segment and is received by the top ports of Switches A and B.
2. Both switches check the destination and flood the frame out to the bottom segment.
3. Both switches now receive the frames on the bottom ports and flood copies to the top segment.
4. The switches have no way of knowing that the same frame is being sent over and over.

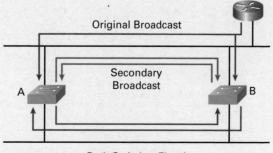

Both Switches Flood
the Broadcast

A large switched network can have multiple loops. In such networks, the number of broadcast frames generated can grow exponentially in a matter of seconds. When this happens, the network becomes overwhelmed and ceases to function.

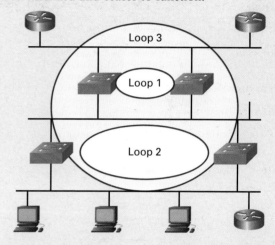

Multiple Copies of the Same Frame

Many protocols cannot correctly handle duplicate transmissions. In particular, protocols that use sequence numbering, such as Transmission Control Protocol/Internet Protocol (TCP/IP), assume the sequence has reached its maximum value and begin to recycle the sequence. Other protocols process the duplicate frame with unpredictable results.

At-A-Glance—Spanning Tree: How It Works

MAC Address Table Instability

A switch's MAC database becomes instable if it receives the same frame on different ports.

In this example, Host Q sends a frame to Router Y. Both switches also receive the frame on Port 0 and associate that port with Host Q. If the address of the router is unknown, both switches flood the frame out Port 1. The switches now receive the frame on Port 1 and incorrectly associate Host Q's MAC address with that port. This process repeats indefinitely.

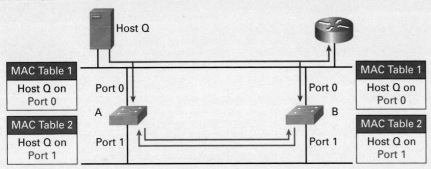

How Spanning Tree Works

Spanning tree works by assigning roles to switches and ports to ensure only one path through the switched network exists at any one time.

The roles assigned are root bridge, root ports, designated ports, and nondesignated ports.

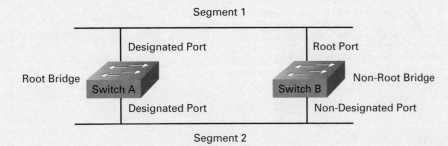

There is only one root bridge in any loop and only one designated port in any one segment. On the root bridge, all ports are designated. The selection of the root bridge is based on either an assigned number or a random number such as a MAC address, which is arbitrary.

Port States

When a link goes down, spanning tree activates a previously blocked redundant link. To avoid temporary loops while the network recalculates paths, the switches avoid sending traffic until the network converges on the new information. At any given time, all switch ports are in one of the states shown in blue.

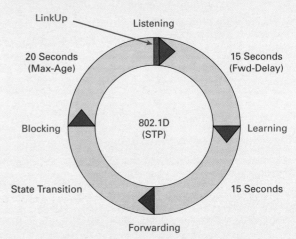

Every port must go through this sequence before it can be set to the forwarding (traffic-passing) state. This process can take up to 50 seconds (a very long period in switch time). In situations where it is critical to have instantaneous failovers, certain tools can allow the switch port to immediately go from the blocking state to the forwarding state.

On the root bridge, all ports are set to the forwarding state. For the nonroot bridge, only the root port is set to the forwarding state.

At-A-Glance—Links, Paths, and a Poem

Assessing the Health of Links

Switches running spanning tree exchange information with a frame called the bridge protocol data unit (BPDU), sent at regular intervals. This message is basically an "I'm alive" message informing the switches that the active path is still operational.

Recalculating Paths

When a link fails, the network topology must change. Spanning tree reestablishes connectivity by placing key blocked ports in the forwarding state. For example, if it does not receive the BPDU after a timer expires, spanning tree begins recalculating the network. In the example, Switch B is now the root bridge.

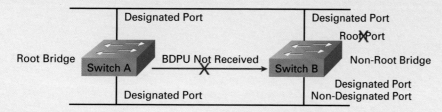

Rapid Spanning Tree

Looking again at the diagram in the port states section, spanning tree can take up to 50 seconds to converge. Emerging real-time applications such as voice and video cannot tolerate such a delay. Rapid Spanning Tree Protocol (RSTP) is the answer to this problem.

RSTP significantly speeds up the recalculation process after a topology change occurs in the network. RSTP works by designating an alternate port and a backup port. These ports are allowed to immediately enter the forwarding state rather than passively wait for the network to converge. Edge-port and link-type are new variables defined in RSTP.

Reflections on Spanning Tree

I think that I shall never see a graph more lovely than a tree.

A tree whose crucial property is loop-free connectivity.

A tree that must be sure to span so packets can reach every LAN.

First, the root must be selected; by ID, it is elected.

Least-cost paths from root are traced; in the tree these paths are placed.

A mesh is made by folks like me, then bridges find a spanning tree.

—Radia Perlman, Inventor of Spanning Tree

Part VI

Moving Traffic Across the Street and the World

Ever notice that computers seem to talk faster with each other when communicating across a local-area network (LAN) versus talking with a computer in another city, state, or country? The reason is cost: It costs a lot of money to transfer traffic across the country as opposed to transferring that same rate of traffic to a computer in the next room.

LANs are speedy and relatively low-cost. Want to transmit 100 Mbps of traffic between two computers in the same room? Connect an Ethernet cable between two computers with fast Ethernet cards at minimal cost.

However, it is impractical to do the same between two computers in two different states. Instead, companies known as service providers spend gobs of money building network infrastructures called wide-area networks (WANs). By combining traffic from multiple customers across their networks, they can sell network access. But this access can be expensive, and bandwidth is at a premium.

Moving traffic across the street has requirements far different than moving traffic across the world. In Part VI, you learn why different means deliver traffic for networks that cover different areas.

Campus Networks and Hierarchical Design

Building Networks for Ease of Use

Campus, as it applies to networking, typically describes the routers, switches, network appliances, and servers that make up the networking infrastructure for a set of buildings located in close proximity. A campus can be the manufacturing site of a large corporation, the headquarters for a bank, or a college campus.

Campus networks are characterized by high-speed connectivity. A design goal for campus networks is to separate buildings, floors, workgroups, and server farms into smaller Layer 3 groups to prevent network faults from affecting large populations of users. Layer 3 routers provide natural boundaries against debilitating network problems such as broadcast storms and loops.

Over time, the hierarchical approach to network design has proven the most effective. The three primary layers of a hierarchical campus follow:

- **Backbone or core**—The backbone is the central thoroughfare for corporate traffic. All other parts of the network eventually feed into the backbone. You should design the core to switch packets as quickly as possible. This level should not include operations that might slow the switching of the packet: the distribution layer should handle any packet manipulation or filtering that needs to occur.

- **Distribution**—The distribution layer provides policy-based connectivity and boundaries between the access layers and the core. For example, a building of 20 floors might have a distribution network that connects each of the floors with the backbone. It is at this layer that packets should be filtered or manipulated. Therefore, once packets are "prepped," the core simply needs to switch them quickly to the destination distribution location.

- **Access**—The access layer provides user access to the network. It is at this point that users are permitted (or denied) access into the corporate network. Typically, each person sitting at a desk has a cable that runs back to a wiring closet and connects to a switch; hence, this level is where the user "accesses" the network.

The distribution and core layers of the network provide vital services by aggregating groups of users and services. Therefore, if a distribution or core device dies, it can affect large communities of users. For this reason, reducing the chance of failure in these layers reduces and possibly prevents unnecessary and unplanned outages. Redundant network paths, redundant hardware, and fault-tolerant–related network protocols (such as Hot Standby Router Protocol) all aid in the ability of a network to recover quickly (and, you hope, transparently to the users) after a failure.

Companies prefer to reduce the number of routed protocols traversing the backbone or core layer. In the 1990s before the massive popularity of TCP/IP and the Internet, backbones carried the predominant protocols of the day: Novell, DECnet, AppleTalk, NetBIOS, and Banyan VINES. So many protocols complicated design issues. As TCP/IP became the de-facto networking protocol, companies worked to eliminate the non-IP traffic from the backbone.

At-A-Glance—Hierarchical Campus Design

Why Should I Care About Hierarchical Campus Design?

Campus networks represent a enormous investment for businesses. When correctly designed, a campus network can enhance business efficiency and lower operational cost. Additionally, a properly designed network can position a business for future growth.

A modular or hierarchical network consists of building blocks that are easier to replicate, redesign, and grow. Each time you add or remove a module, you don't need to redesign the whole network. You can put distinct blocks in service and out of service without impacting other blocks or the core of the network. This setup greatly enhances troubleshooting, aides fault isolation, and eases management.

The hierarchy consists of three functional divisions (or layers):

- **Access layer**—First level of access to the network. Layer 2 switching, security, and quality of service (QoS) happen at this layer.

- **Distribution layer**—Aggregates wiring closets and provides policy enforcement. When the network uses Layer 3 protocols at this layer, it realizes benefits such as load balancing, fast convergence, and scalability. This layer also provides first-hop default gateway redundancy to end stations.

- **Core layer**—Backbone of the network. This layer is designed to be fast converging, highly reliable, and stable. Also designed with Layer 3 protocols, the core provides load balancing, fast convergence, and scalability.

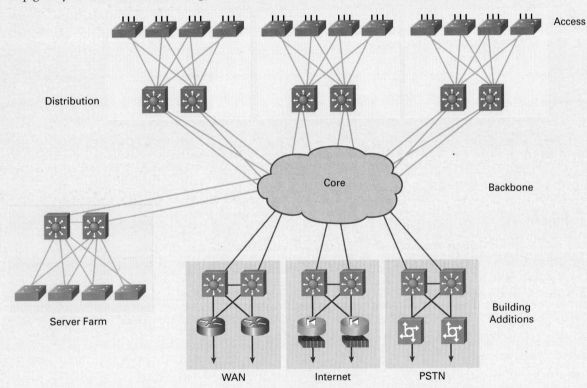

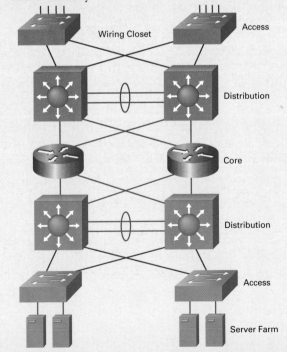

At-A-Glance—Campus Design Best Practices

Campus Design Best Practices

VLANs

The virtual local-area network (VLAN) organizes physically separate users into the same broadcast domain. The use of VLANs improves performance, security, and flexibility. VLANs also decrease the cost of arranging users because they require no extra cabling.

VLANs should each be on their own subnet. This arrangement is called *Layer 2 to Layer 3 VLAN mapping*. It allows for ease of route summarization and troubleshooting.

(You should avoid setting up campus-wide VLANs because they can slow convergence.)

High Availability

High availability refers to the network's ability to recover from different types of failures. A sound design easily achieves network stability. Troubleshooting is easier, and human error is reduced. You should design high availability at many layers:

- **Layer 1**—Redundant links and hardware provide alternate physical paths through the network.

- **Layers 2/3**—Protocols such as Spanning Tree Protocol (STP), Hot Standby Router Protocol (HSRP), and other routing protocols provide alternate path awareness and fast convergence.

- **Application availability**—The application server and client processes must support failover for maximum availability.

Redundancy

Redundancy is a key part of designing a highly available network. Although some redundancy is good, too much redundancy can actually be bad for a network. Issues with convergence (the network's ability to recover from a bad link) can result. Too much redundancy makes troubleshooting and management difficult. (This figure shows redundancy gone wrong.)

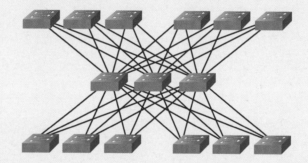

Oversubscription

Oversubscription occurs when the network has more traffic-generating endpoints than it can accommodate at a single time. Most networks are built with some amount of oversubscription. In the figure, the network has a 20:1 oversubscription rate from access to distribution and a 4:1 oversubscription rate from distribution to core. Networks should use QoS to ensure that they do not drop or delay real-time traffic such as voice and video or critical data such as SAP traffic.

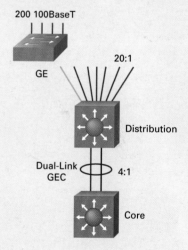

At-A-Glance—Small and Medium Campus Design

Campus Size Design Considerations

Size does matter. The following sections list some general rules of thumb for various campus sizes.

Small Campus

This figure shows the recommended design for a campus with fewer than 200 edge ports. This design has collapsed the distribution and core into a single layer, which limits scaling to a few access switches.

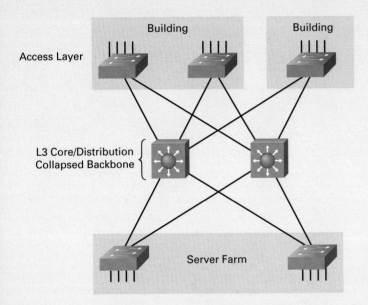

Medium Campus

This design is appropriate for campuses with 200–1000 ports. A separate distribution layer allows for future growth. A redundant core ensures high availability and allows equal-cost paths.

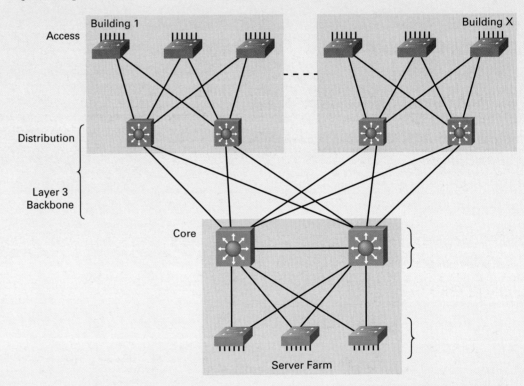

At-A-Glance—Large Campus Design

Large Campus

This high-performance design suits campuses with more than 1000 ports or those seeking cutting-edge design. A feature-rich core aggregates many distribution switches. You can easily add buildings and server farms anytime.

You must carefully consider services such as QoS, IP multicast, and security in any campus design strategy. Other chapters discuss these topics.

Optical Technologies

The Need for Speed

The explosive growth of the Internet and Internet Protocol (IP) applications such as voice, video, and storage area networks has boosted bandwidth demands for corporations. With LAN network speeds ranging from 10 Mbps to 10 Gbps, and quality of service (QoS) playing an important role in the delivery of this data, there must be an alternative to traditional WAN and LAN services for connecting metropolitan-area networks (MANs).

Network connections that traditionally carried T1 and T3 speeds of data now require fiber channel, Enterprise System Connection (ESCON), gigabit Ethernet, and 10 gigabit Ethernet to satisfy demand. The increased demand coupled with the advances in optical technology has dramatically increased capacity and reduced cost, making it attractive for service providers to offer fiber-based network services for the metro market.

Fiber-based metropolitan networks address business needs in three areas:

- **Data networking and migration**—Optical networking technologies offer many data speeds and connections that allow the support of a variety of networking technologies, such as IP, synchronous optical network (SONET), Asynchronous Transfer Mode (ATM), and time-division multiplexing (TDM). Networks can consolidate multiple wavelengths of traffic onto a single fiber to provide multiservice transport and facilitate the migration from traditional electrical networking technologies onto a common optical transport.

- **Disaster recovery and business continuance**—Having a backup data center with backup storage is a primary consideration for most large businesses today. Metro optical networks provide fast, campus-to-campus transport with redundancy. Real-time disaster-recovery solutions, such as synchronous mirroring, guarantee that mission-critical data is securely and remotely mirrored to avoid any data loss in the event of a disaster.

- **Storage consolidation**—Network attached storage (NAS), when integrated with storage area networking (SAN) applications, provides IP-based storage consolidation and file sharing. You can use multiple file storage access methods (such as Network File System [NFS] and CIFS) against the same storage farm to share unique data with multiple users and applications. Metro optical networks facilitate not only the implementation of storage, but also the extension of storage beyond a single data center.

SONET, DWDM, and DPT

The three primary optical technologies employed today are

- SONET and synchronous digital hierarchy (SDH)
- Dense wavelength division multiplexing (DWDM)
- Dynamic packet transport (DPT)

All three technologies provide the conversion of electrical signals into light and back again. Fiber Optic Transmission Systems (FOTS) do the conversion. Fiber-optic signals are not susceptible to electrical interference. The signals can transmit over long distances and send more information than traditional electrical transports. The combination of these benefits provides lower costs than traditional data electrical transport mechanisms.

Service providers have offered SONET services for some time. Benefits of SONET networks include high-speed network services that meet voice-transport requirements as well as survivability and availability needs. SONET network speeds currently range from 51.84 Mbps to 9953.28 Mbps.

You can connect SONET nodes in the following ways:

- **Point to point**
- **Linear**—Each device connects to the device before and after it, with up to 16 devices total.
- **Unidirectional path-switched ring (UPSR)**—All traffic is homed to a central location.
- **Two fiber bidirectional line-switched ring (2F BLSR)**—Traffic is local to each set of neighbors, and bandwidth is reusable.
- **Four fiber bidirectional line-switched ring (4F BLSR)**—Same as 2F BLSR except with multiple rings for diversity.

DWDM is based on the premise that optical signals of differing wavelengths do not interfere with each other. Wavelength-division multiplexing (WDM) differs from time-division multiplexing technologies (such as SONET) in the following way:

- TDM employs a single wavelength across a fiber. Data is divided into channels so that multiple channels can travel across a single fiber.
- WDM employs multiple wavelengths (lambdas) per fiber, which allows multiple channels per fiber (up to 160). Each lambda can include multiple TDM channels.

DWDM offers scalability over traditional TDM technologies. Because data can travel considerably farther across DWDM than traditional TDM (120 km versus 40 km), you need fewer repeaters. DWDM also allows for higher capacity across long-haul fibers as well as quick provisioning in metro networks.

Metro DWDM needs to be cheap and simple to install and manage. It must also be independent of bit rate and protocol as a transport and provide 16–32 channels per fiber. DWDM nodes attach to each other in a ring pattern using optical add-drop multiplexers, which add and drop traffic at each remote site, and all traffic is homed to a central site.

DPT uses SONET/SDH framing and employs intelligent protection switching in the event of fiber facility or node failure or signal degradation. DPT uses a bidirectional, counter-rotating ring structure for metro applications and a star structure with a central switching device for service PoP backbones.

DPT facilitates the bridging of dark fiber, WDM, and SONET networks. On a campus-ring application, DPT interconnects buildings, data centers, and WAN services. It allows the extension of real-time applications as well as multisite distributed virtual private networks (VPNs).

DPT metro loop rings allow the delivery of voice, video, and Internet connectivity to businesses and high-rise residential buildings.

At-A-Glance—Metro Optical

Why Should I Care About Metro Optical?

Companies, universities, and government organizations often have several campuses in proximity to one another. In addition to the high bandwidth requirements for application sharing and communication between campuses, networks also need to support applications such as the following:

- Business resilience (disaster recovery)
- Storage consolidation (centralized data)
- Distributed workplace (resources throughout the network)

Fiber-optic networks can carry large amounts of multiple types of services simultaneously. They can also provide connectivity between LANs, access to WANs, and consolidation of storage area networking/network attached storage (SAN/NAS) applications.

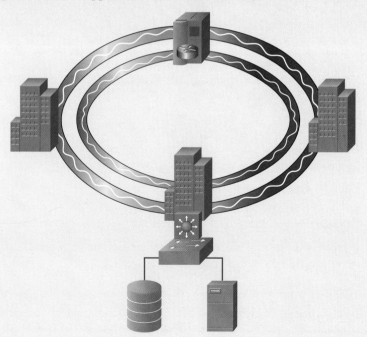

What Are the Problems to Solve?

Optical networking uses pulses of light to transmit data over fiber-optic cables. These pulses of light are subject to degradation as they travel down the fiber, but in general, the deterioration is less than that of copper, so fiber signals can travel much further.

Metro fiber optics networks have a range of 20 to 250 km. You can deploy them as point-to-point, ring, and mesh topologies. The four main protocols are Optical Ethernet, course wavelength division multiplexing (CWDM), dense wavelength division multiplexing (DWDM), and synchronous optical network (SONET).

Optical Ethernet

Gigabit Ethernet is the simplest and least expensive form of optical transport. Optical Ethernet uses a device called a Gigabit Interface Converter (GBIC), which plugs into a switch port and converts an Ethernet stream to an optical signal. Ethernet can leverage the growing service-provider metro Ethernet infrastructure or dark fiber.

At-A-Glance—CWDM, DWDM, and SONET

CWDM

CWDM uses wavelength-specific pairs of GBICs to combine up to eight optical signals onto a single fiber.

Each switch pair is fitted with one or more pairs of GBICs. Each GBIC pair is tuned to a specific frequency, which allows the switch to add in (multiplex) or pluck out (demultiplex) a single beam of light (data stream).

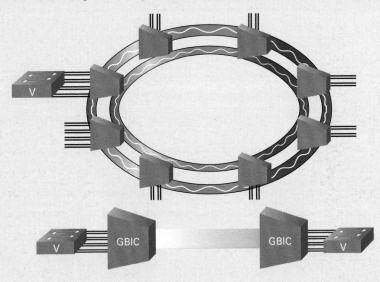

You can deploy CWDM as ring or point to point. One major drawback to CWDM is that it cannot be amplified, which limits the distance. The rule-of-thumb maximum distance is 80 km for point to point or a ring circumference of 30 km.

DWDM

DWDM uses the same multiplexing scheme as CWDM. DWDM signals, however, are spaced more closely together, allowing DWDM systems to multiplex up to 32 signals on a single fiber.

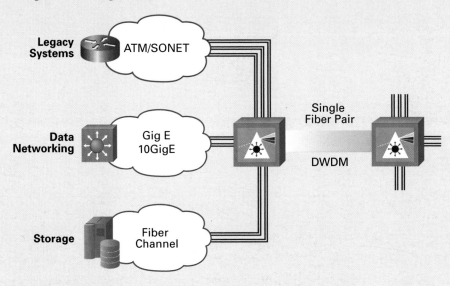

DWDM signals can be amplified, making the system ideal for backup data centers or larger (more geographically dispersed) campuses. With amplification, DWDM signals can transmit up to 250 km.

SONET

SONET is a Layer 1 technology that supports the high transmission rates (155 Mps to 10 Gps) needed in metro applications.

SONET serves as a transport for other technologies such as Ethernet and Asynchronous Transfer Mode (ATM). Service providers commonly use it for transport (metro and long haul). SONET also has extensive operation, administrative, maintenance, and provisioning (OAMP) capabilities, allowing precise fault detection and rapid (50 ms) failover.

At-A-Glance—Fiber, Design, and Multiplexing

Fiber Basics

The two types of optic fiber are multimode and single-mode.

With *multimode fiber*, light propagates in the form of multiple wavelengths, each taking a slightly "different" path. Multimode fiber appears primarily in systems with short transmission distances (under 2 km).

In *single-mode fiber*, light can propagate in only one mode. Single-mode fiber usually appears in long-distance and high-bandwidth applications.

Multimode Fiber

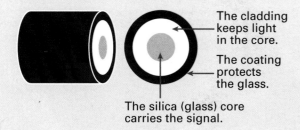

The cladding keeps light in the core.

The coating protects the glass.

The silica (glass) core carries the signal.

Key Design Criteria

Optical signals are subject to deterioration as they travel down fibers in the form of attenuation, dispersion and nonlinearities, chromatic distortion, and polarization mode distortion. These factors limit the distance and bandwidth of optic signals:

- **Attenuation**—Loss of power over distance. In some cases, amplifiers can boost power.

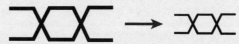

- **Dispersion and nonlinearities**—Distance and speed erode signal clarity.

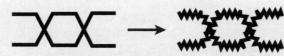

- **Chromatic distortion**—Spreading of the signal over distance. This spreading can cause signals to interfere with each other.

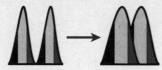

- **Polarization mode distortion**—At 10 Gb rates and higher, signals tend to broaden as they travel down the fiber, causing intersignal interference.

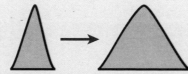

Multiplexing

Multiplexing is the process of combining multiple signals over a single wire, fiber, or link. Time-division multiplexing (TDM) brings in lower-speed signals assigns them time slots, and places them into a higher-speed serial output. The receiving end reconstructs the signals.

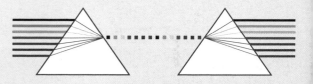

One of the properties of light is that light waves of different wavelengths do not interfere with one another within a medium. Because of this property, each individual wavelength of light can represent a different channel of information. Combining light pulses of different wavelengths, many channels can transmit across a single fiber simultaneously. This process is *wave-division multiplexing (WDM)*.

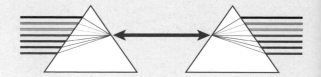

Broadband Technologies

Always-On Access

Until recent times, people connected remotely to their offices or the Internet using dialup connections. An "always on" remote network connection was not possible for a reasonable price. To connect to the remote network, the user ran a program that dialed a phone number. Unless he had a second phone line, being online prohibited incoming or outgoing phone calls.

The user entered a user ID and password to gain access to the system. The fastest speed available over phone lines was 56 kbps, which was fine until the web became popular in the 1990s. Downloading large pictures, documents, applications, or audio files took what seemed like forever.

Then, along came broadband. Broadband networking offered a reasonable high-speed alternative to traditional dialup networking. Using existing cabling to houses (either phone or cable TV), service providers offered Internet services at 5 to 15 times the speed of dialup. Downloading a 100 MB file became palatable with broadband.

Broadband technologies allow service providers to offer "always on" connectivity similar to what people use in a corporate network. Computers on the broadband network always have access to the network; there is no intermediate dialup step. Sit down, load the browser, and off you go.

High-speed Internet access to homes offers new levels of productivity and entertainment not possible before the commercialization of the Internet and the web. Aside from apparent uses such as online shopping and video streaming, corporations can accommodate road warriors and work-from-home folks in a way not previously possible. Using encryption technologies, an employee with a laptop computer can securely access her corporate network from any Internet access point in the world. Additionally, employees can attach IP phones, allowing them to work on their computers and make calls from their office-phone extensions as if they were sitting at their desks.

Broadband Technology Evolution

Integrated Services Digital Network (ISDN) was the first commercially viable broadband option available. Using existing phone lines, home users commonly subscribed to a Basic Rate Interface (BRI), which had a throughput maximum of 128 kbps. In the US, ISDN was eclipsed by more cost-effective broadband technologies before it had a chance to become commonplace.

Cable modem and digital subscriber line (DSL) services became the premier broadband technologies. Although other broadband technologies existed, the primary determination of a technology's viability was access to "last mile" wiring to houses. Anything that required new wiring probably wouldn't make it. Other technologies that take advantage of other media exist, such as satellite television dishes, but for quality issues did not become as popular.

Cable Modem

Cable modems provide high-speed data communication using existing cable-television coax cabling. Current implementations of cable-modem technologies offer speeds as fast as Ethernet (10 Mbps), which means a file that takes two minutes to transfer over ISDN takes two seconds over cable modem. Cable modem can provide higher speeds than traditional leased lines, with lower cost and easier installation.

Because a cable-modem connection is permanently established, it cannot dial multiple locations directly. As a result, cable-modem access must be to the Internet. This restriction means that employees can connect to their company's network only if the company provides access through the Internet.

DSL

Like cable modem, DSL provides high-speed Internet access for reasonable cost using existing cabling to houses and businesses. DSL carves off a portion of the telephone line to use for data transmission without interfering with existing phone service.

Because of the multiple flavors of DSL services, DSL is generically referred to as xDSL. The two popular forms of xDSL service currently available are Asymmetrical DSL (ADSL) and Symmetrical DSL (SDSL). ADSL provides faster download speeds because traffic toward the user is given more bandwidth than traffic from the user. SDSL assigns equal bandwidth in both directions.

Which One Is Better?

Both DSL and cable modems provide high-speed Internet access at a relatively low cost. Both provide "always on" connectivity. Both have technical advantages and disadvantages over each other. Either technology makes a good to-the-home or small-office solution for Internet connectivity. Because both technologies are "always on," a firewall must protect the local network from Internet-based attacks.

Some practical issues affect how widespread the technologies become. Virtually all businesses and homes have telephone lines, which means DSL is possible, but fewer homes and businesses have cable television lines.

At-A-Glance—Broadband Technologies

Why Should I Care About Broadband Technologies?

The availability of high-speed Internet or business-class access from the home has dramatically changed the way people work, seek entertainment, and connect to the rest of the world.

Whether working from home with a high-speed Internet Protocol (IP) telephony connection, downloading movies online, or sending pictures to friends and family, broadband has made the promise of true multimedia-capable home connections a reality.

What Are the Problems to Solve?

The key to broadband access to the home was finding a way to offer the service at a price acceptable to the majority of users while still making a profit for the service providers. With the decreasing cost of high-speed routers and switches, the major cost component of the service was connecting local high-speed aggregation points with the homes in the area. This part of the network is called "the last mile."

The whole business case boiled down to this: The only way to make broadband access profitable was to use the last mile infrastructure already in place, and the only businesses with in-place infrastructures were local phone and cable companies. Both industries then figured out innovative ways to solve the technical issues of making broadband work.

The Need for Speed

The availability of high-speed Internet connections begs the question, "Why does anyone need a high-speed connection in the first place?"

With all forms of multimedia in demand on the Internet, the following graph might offer some perspective. As a point of reference, a high-quality digital recording of a song is about 9 Mb.

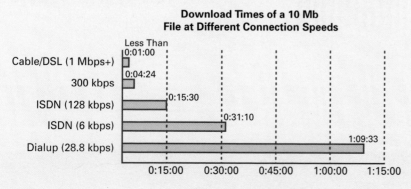

Download Times of a 10 Mb File at Different Connection Speeds

Digital Subscriber Line

Digital subscriber line (DSL) service uses the existing phone wires connected to virtually every home in most countries. The twisted-pair wires that provide phone service are ideal because the available frequency ranges on the wires far exceed those required to carry a voice conversation. Human speech occupies frequencies of roughly 4000 hertz (4 kHz) or less. The copper wires that provide phone service can carry in the range of 1–2 million hertz (MHz). DSL provides more downstream data (from the Internet to you) than upstream data (from you to the Internet) based on user profiles, but this can change for businesses or those running web servers.

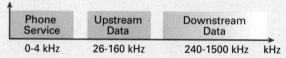

DSL Equipment

DSL requires some specialized equipment to ensure that the voice and data are kept separate and routed to the right place.

All phone jacks not used by a computer have low-pass filters (LPFs) to prevent interference from the high-frequency data signals.

At-A-Glance—Broadband Technologies, Continued

A DSL modem is the interface from the phone line to the computer.

DSL access multiplexers (DSLAMs) aggregate hundreds of signals from homes and are the access points to the Internet.

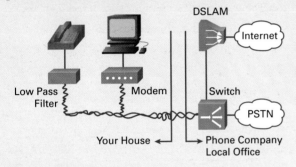

Limitations and Advantages

DSL signals are distance sensitive, which means that the available throughput decreases the farther away from the local office your house is. The maximum distance is about 18,000 feet. DSL signals cannot be amplified, nor can they be converted from one medium to another between the DSL modem and the DSLAM. (For example, optical fiber extensions are not possible.) The good news for DSL is that throughput is not affected by the number of users as long as the phone company continues to add DSLAMs to support new users.

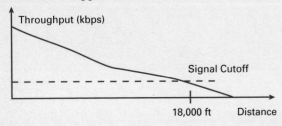

Cable

Cable uses the same basic principal as DSL in that the bandwidth needed to accomplish the primary function is only a fraction of the available bandwidth on the wire, or in this case, cable. Cable access is slightly different, however, in the way it divvies up the available frequencies.

The cable spectrum was already divided into several hundred 6 MHz blocks to account for the various cable channels. Your cable-ready TV simply tunes its receiver to the frequency that corresponds to the channel you choose. For Internet capabilities, each user is assigned one or more blocks for downstream data. (Each 6 MHz block is good for about 30 Mbps of data.) For the upstream piece, the lower end of the spectrum is divided into 2 MHz blocks because most people pull down more information than they upload. Each subscriber is assigned one or more 2 MHz blocks.

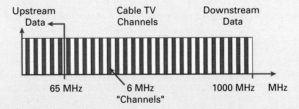

Cable Equipment

Cable requires that each home user have a cable modem because cable-ready televisions provide their own filtering. Interference between data and TV signals is not an issue.

The cable company must have a cable modem termination system (CMTS) to aggregate upstream and downstream.

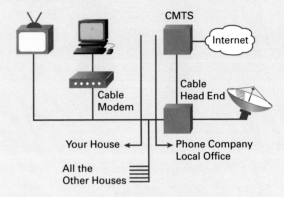

Limitations and Advantages

A CMTS has a fixed number of slots (1000) meaning that there is a limit to the number of subscribers who can access the service. With relatively few subscribers, each user enjoys greater throughput than when the number of subscribers reaches its maximum and each user is assigned a single pair of "channels." Cable is not distance sensitive, however, and the signal can be amplified if needed.

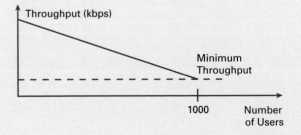

At-A-Glance—ISDN

Why Should I Care About Integrated Services Digital Network?

Today, data traffic dominates voice traffic, and data networks are moving toward transporting voice. Prior to the technology explosion of the late 1990s, however, voice networks were more prevalent than data networks, and engineers focused on sending data over voice networks. Integrated Services Digital Network (ISDN) is a collection of standards that define how to integrate a data architecture into the public switched telephone network (PSTN). ISDN standards define both the hardware and call setup schemes.

In addition to data communications, ISDN provides the following additional benefits:

- **Multiple traffic feeds**—Voice, video, telex, and packet-switched data are all available over ISDN.

- **Fast call setup**—ISDN uses out-of-band signaling (D or delta channel) for call setup. ISDN calls can often be completely set up in less than a second.

- **The ability to combine data channels for increased bandwidth**—With multiple channels, one form of ISDN is capable of 128 Kbps, whereas leased lines usually only provide 56 Kbps in North America.

- **The ability to purchase digital services directly from the local phone company**—You can avoid the expense and hassle of purchasing a dedicated leased line.

Although the benefits of ISDN have largely been eclipsed by standard routers and cable Internet access, ISDN still appears in areas where cable is unavailable or as a dialup backup in case of private WAN failure.

What Are the Problems to Solve?

ISDN is not compatible with many other protocols and requires special equipment to operate.

ISDN must run over multiple wires and must have mechanisms for breaking up and reassembling signals.

ISDN and Internet Access

ISDN has been around for many years. Although the business applications were well used, ISDN struggled for many years to fulfill its original promise to home users. Often referred to as "It Still Does Nothing," ISDN was for years a solution in search of a problem. That changed with the advent of the Internet and the ever-increasing need for bandwidth at every house on the block.

ISDN solves two of the major issues with the rising need for broadband connectivity:

- It's already there. ISDN runs over standard phone lines, which means nearly every household is a potential ISDN customer.

- It's relatively fast. ISDN offers more than twice the available bandwidth over the same phone lines not running ISDN.

ISDN Standard Access Methods

ISDN has two types of interfaces: Basic Rate Interface (BRI) and Primary Rate Interface (PRI). Both types have bearer channels (B), which carry data, and delta (D) channels, which carry signal and call control information. The D channel can also carry low-rate packet data (e.g. alarms).

BRI has two bearer (B) channels (64 kbps each) and one delta (D) channel (16 kpbs). BRI is sometimes written as 2B+D.

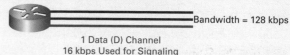

BRI (2B+D) 2 Bearer (B) Channels
64 kbps Each Used for Data

Bandwidth = 128 kbps

1 Data (D) Channel
16 kbps Used for Signaling

In North America and Japan, PRI has 23 B channels and one D channel (all channels are 64 kbps). In Europe, PRI has 30 B channels and one D channel. PRI is noted as 23B+D.

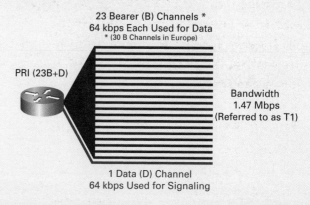

23 Bearer (B) Channels *
64 kbps Each Used for Data
* (30 B Channels in Europe)

PRI (23B+D)

Bandwidth
1.47 Mbps
(Referred to as T1)

1 Data (D) Channel
64 kbps Used for Signaling

Making an ISDN Call

Prior to sending any data or voice traffic over the B channels, ISDN must make a connection using the D channel. The D channel initiates the call by establishing a path between switches and passing information about the source and called numbers. When the destination receives the setup information, it uses the D channel to signal the ISDN switch that it is available. After this connection is complete, the B channels can begin exchanging data and voice.

ISDN Device Types and Reference Points

ISDN specifies both the equipment and the connection points between equipment to ensure compatibility with the PSTN and among ISDN vendors:

- **Terminal endpoint 1 (TE1)**—Devices that have a native ISDN interface.
- **Network termination 2 (NT2)**—Aggregates and switches all ISDN lines at customer-service sites using a customer-switching device.

- **Network termination 1 (NT1)**—Converts signals into a form used by the ISDN line. An NT1 plugs into a standard phone jack.
- **Terminal endpoint 2 (TE2)**—A non-ISDN terminal. TE2s require a terminal adapter.
- **Terminal adapter (TA)**—Performs protocol conversion from non-ISDN (such as Electronic Industries Association/Telecommunications Industry Association (EIA/TIA)-232, V.35, and other signals) into ISDN signals.
- **R**—A connection point between a non-ISDN compatible device and a terminal adapter.
- **S**—The connection point into the customer-switching device (NT2). It enables calls between customer equipment.
- **T**—The outbound connection from the NT2 to the ISDN network. This reference point is electrically identical to the S interface.
- **U**—The connection point between NT1 and the ISDN network.

Service Provider Identifiers

Your service provider assigns service-provider identifiers (SPIDs) to identify your switch at the central office. A company's SPID is linked to the services that the phone company ordered. When the central office makes a connection, the SPID tells the switch which services the company is entitled to.

Each channel of the BRI can have a separate SPID configured. SPID requirements depend on both the software revision and the switch type. SPIDs are required only in the U.S.

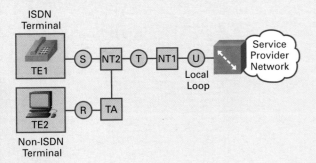

WAN Technologies

Moving Information Across Vast Areas

How does a company connect the network in its New York office to the network in its Los Angeles office? It doesn't make sense to run a cable across the United States. Instead, the company subscribes to wide area services.

A *wide-area network (WAN)* is a network that covers a broad geographic area and often uses transmission facilities provided by common carriers. WAN functionality occurs at Layers 1–3 in the Open System Interconnection (OSI) reference model. The bicoastal company in the example would contact its service provider to purchase WAN connectivity between the offices. WAN services are leased from service providers with either a monthly flat fee or a per-usage charge. More bandwidth attracts more costly charges.

WAN Services

The three types of transports used for WANs are the following:

- **Point-to-point**—Also known as leased line, a point-to-point connection is a pre-established link from one site, across a carrier's network, to a remote site. The carrier establishes the point-to-point link for the private use of the customer.

- **Circuit switching**—A service provider establishes a dedicated physical circuit into a carrier network for two or more connections. Unlike point-to-point, which has exactly two sites connected to a single connection, multiple sites privately connect into a carrier's switched network to communicate with each other. Circuit switching operates like a normal telephone call. ISDN is an example of circuit-switched WAN technology.

- **Packet switching**—This type of transport is similar to circuit switching in that multiple sites privately connect into a carrier-switched network. However, packet switching involves the statistical multiplexing of packets across shared circuits. Frame Relay is an example of packet switching.

Some WAN technologies, such as Frame Relay and Asynchronous Transfer Mode (ATM), use *virtual* circuits to ensure reliable communication between two network devices. The two types of virtual circuits are *switched virtual circuits (SVCs)* and *permanent virtual circuits (PVCs)*. A SVC is dynamically established on demand and torn down when transmission is complete. A connection uses SVCs when data transmission between devices is sporadic. A PVC is a permanently established logical circuit and is useful for connections between two devices in which data transfer is constant.

WAN dialup services are available as alternative backup technologies for traditional WAN services. As the name implies, dialup services use plain old telephone service (POTS) and are inexpensive alternatives when the main WAN service goes down. Cisco routers offer two popular types of dialup services: *dial-on-demand routing* (DDR) and *dial backup*. DDR works like this: A router has an interface connected to a modem. If an interesting frame of traffic arrives, the router dials up another router over the phone line. The router transmits the packet and, after a period of inactivity, hangs up the phone line. Dial backup initiates a dial connection to another router after it determines that the primary WAN service is unavailable. The dial connection remains active until the WAN service returns.

High-Speed Serial Interface

High-Speed Serial Interface (HSSI) is a standard for high-speed, point-to-point data communications over serial WAN links. HSSI operates at speeds up to 52 Mbps.

Frame Relay

Frame Relay is a packet-switched WAN service that operates at the physical and logical layers of the OSI reference model. Frame Relay was originally designed to operate over ISDN but today operates over a variety of network interfaces. Typical communication speeds for Frame Relay are between 56 kbps and 2 Mbps (although lower and higher speeds are supported).

Frame Relay provides connection-oriented services using virtual circuits. A Frame Relay virtual circuit is a logical connection between two data terminal equipment (DTE) devices across a Frame Relay packet-switched network. A data-link connection identifier (DLCI) uniquely identifies each virtual circuit. You can multiplex multiple virtual circuits on a single physical circuit.

Frame Relay switched networks provide simple congestion-notification mechanisms. Frame Relay switching equipment can mark a Frame Relay packet with a front-end congestion notification (FECN) or back-end congestion notification (BECN). The equipment marks the packets with a FECN or BECN if congestion occurs during the transmission of the packet. The DTE equipment at the other end of a circuit notices whether a packet has experienced congestion and notifies a higher layer that congestion has occurred.

Additionally, the equipment can mark a packet as Discard Eligible (DE) to indicate that it is less important, which means it can be dropped if congestion occurs.

ATM

ATM is a standard for cell-based relay that carries voice, video, and data in small, fixed-size cells. ATM networks are connection-oriented networks that combine the benefits of circuit switching (guaranteed capacity and constant transmission delay) with those of packet switching (flexibility and efficiency for intermittent traffic). ATM transmits at speeds from a few Mbps to many Gbps.

Traditional circuit-based networks use time-division multiplexing (TDM), in which users are assigned a predetermined time slot; no other device can transmit during this time slot. If a station has a lot of data to send, it can only transmit during its time slot, even if the other time slots are empty. Conversely, if the station has nothing to transmit, the time slot is sent empty and is wasted. This arrangement is called *synchronous transmission.*

ATM is asynchronous, meaning time slots are available on demand. This allows for a more efficient use of available bandwidth. ATM uses single-sized cells (as opposed to variable-sized frames in Frame Relay), which are 53 bytes in size. A size of 53 bytes is asize for anything involving computers (which usually define things in powers of 2 or 8). The cell size represents a compromise between the phone-standards folks and the data-standards folks.

ATM networks have two devices: ATM switches and ATM endpoints. ATM switches accept cells from an endpoint or another switch, evaluate the cell header, and quickly forward the cell out another interface toward the destination. An ATM endpoint contains an ATM network interface adapter and is responsible for converting digital data into cells and back again. Examples of ATM endpoints include workstations, LAN switches, routers, and video coder-decoders (codecs).

ATM networks can mark traffic, after it is converted from its original data format, to require different types of handling. Some traffic, such as voice and video, must be transferred through the network in regular intervals with little variation of delay. Otherwise, the destination receives low-quality voice or video transmission. Data traffic is less sensitive to network delays and can be handled differently.

To ensure the appropriate delivery for each of these traffic types, ATM devices employ quality of service (QoS) mechanisms that involve the reservation of bandwidth, the shaping of traffic to meet the reserved bandwidth, and the policing of traffic that exceeds the reservation.

WAN Devices

Numerous types of devices are associated with WAN service delivery.

The first is a WAN switch. Usually located in a carrier's network, a WAN switch is a multiport internetworking device whose job is moving traffic from the source to destination. Routers at the customer sites attach to the edges of the carrier's switched network. Examples of switched traffic include Frame Relay and ATM. WAN switches operate at Layer 2, the data link layer, in the OSI model.

A modem is a device that converts between digital and analog signals, enabling data to be transmitted across phone lines. At the source, a modem converts computer data from digital to analog and transmits the signal across a phone line. At the other end, a modem receives the analog signal, converts it back to digital, and forwards the information onto a computer. The word "modem" is a contraction of the terms that describe this conversion: MOdulation and DEModulation.

An access server is a device that acts as a concentration point for dial-in and dial-out services. An example of an access server is dialing into an Internet service provider from home: a computer at home dials through a modem across a phone line. The modem at the service provider answers the call and establishes a network connection across the phone line. Multiple modems are connected to the access server.

A channel service unit/digital service unit (CSU/DSU) is similar to a modem in that it adapts the physical interface on a DTE device, such as a router, to the interface of a data circuit-terminating device (DCE), such as a carrier switch. The CSU/DSU provides signal timing between the DTE and DCE.

At-A-Glance—Frame Relay

Why Should I Care About Frame Relay?

Frame Relay is one of the predominate WAN transport methods for connecting remote sites because its cost is lower and its scaling more effective than those of leased lines. Whenever two or more locations must have data connectivity, Frame Relay is an option.

Frame Relay offers known performance and manageability. It is the most common mode of private network connectivity.

What Are the Problems to Solve?

Frame Relay is a connection-oriented Layer 2 protocol that lets you multiplex several data connections (referred to as virtual circuits) onto a single physical link. The higher-layer protocols often perform error correction and flow control, so the primary consideration for Frame Relay is establishing connections between customer equipment.

A connection identifier maps packets to outbound ports on the service provider's switch. When the switch receives a frame, it uses a lookup table to map the frame to the correct outbound port. The switch determines the entire path to the destination before it sends the frame.

Frame Relay only specifies the connection between a router and a service provider's local access switching equipment. It does not specify the data transmission within the provider's Frame Relay cloud.

Frame Relay Equipment

The two general categories of Frame Relay equipment are data terminal equipment (DTE) and data communications equipment (DCE).

DTE is the terminating equipment used by companies or organizations using Frame Relay connections. Typically located on the customer's premises, DTE can be owned by the customer or rented by the Frame Relay provider. Examples of DTE devices are terminals, personal computers, routers, and bridges.

DCEs are carrier-owned internetworking devices. DCEs provide clocking and switching services in a network.

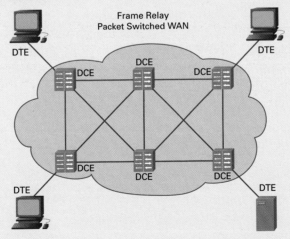

Frame Relay
Packet Switched WAN

Virtual Circuits

Logical connections called *virtual circuits* establish Frame Relay connections. Virtual circuits can pass through several DCE devices throughout the Frame Relay packet-switched network (PSN). You can multiplex several virtual circuits into a single physical circuit for transmission across the network. The two types of virtual circuits are switched virtual circuits (SVCs) and permanent virtual circuits (PVCs).

Switched Virtual Circuit

A *switched virtual circuit* (SVC) is a temporary connection for sporadic data transfer between DTE devices across the Frame Relay network.

SVC sessions have four distinct operational states: call setup, data transfer, idle, and call termination.

If the connection is idle for some predetermined amount of time, the network terminates the connection. After the connection is terminated, the network must establish a new call for data to flow again.

At-A-Glance—Frame Relay, Continued

PVC

A *permanent virtual circuit (PVC)* is an established connection that remains up at all times. You should use PVCs for frequent and consistent data transfer between DTE devices.

PVCs require no call setups or termination procedures. The operational states are data transfer and idle.

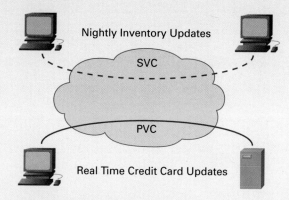

Local Management Interface

Local Management Interface (LMI) is a signaling standard for managing a connection between a router and a Frame Relay switch. LMIs track and manage keepalive mechanisms, multicast messages, and status.

Data-Link Connection Identifier

Frame Relay virtual circuits are identified by data-link connection identifiers (DLCIs). Typically, the Frame Relay service provider assigns DLCI values.

Frame Relay DLCIs are of local significance only. In other words, the DLCI values are only unique at the endpoints, not over the WAN. Therefore, two DTE devices connected by a virtual circuit might use different DLCI values to refer to the same connection.

In addition, two DTEs can connect on the same virtual circuit but still have different DLCIs. This figure shows how a single virtual circuit might be assigned a different DLCI value on each end of the connection.

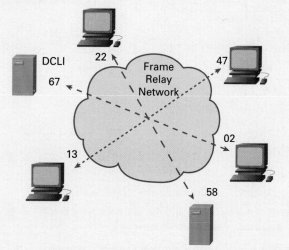

Congestion Notification

Frame Relay reduces network overhead by implementing simple congestion-notification mechanisms.

Frame Relay uses two methods of congestion notification, forward explicit congestion notification (FECN) and backward explicit congestion notification (BECN).

FECN sends a message to the destination device when a Frame Relay switch senses congestion in the network. A DTE device receiving this message can relay this information to a higher-layer protocol for processing, which in turn can initiate flow control or simply ignore the message.

BECN sends a message to the source router when a Frame Relay switch senses congestion in the network. A BECN message requests a reduced data-transmission rate. BECN messages are also relayed to the higher-layer protocols, which can initiate some form of flow control or traffic shaping. In some cases, the higher-layer protocols ignore BECN messages.

At-A-Glance—ATM

Why Should I Care About ATM?

Asynchronous Transfer Mode (ATM) is one of the primary Layer 2 WAN transport protocols. Originally developed as high-speed public WAN transport for voice, video, and data, ATM was later modified to include transport over private networks by the ATM Forum.

What Are the Problems to Solve?

ATM faces the same problems as the other Layer 2 transport protocols, namely the establishing connections and the formatting information.

ATM was developed before the availability of quality of service (QoS) and traffic engineering. At the time of its development, ATM was one of the only protocols capable of providing differentiated service for customers or traffic types.

ATM Devices

ATM networks consist of ATM switches and ATM endpoints. ATM switches are responsible for moving cells through the ATM network. ATM endpoints—including workstations, routers, data service units (DSUs), LAN switches, and video coder-decoders (codecs)—all require an ATM interface adapter to access the ATM network.

ATM Network Interfaces

ATM networks consist of ATM switches interconnected by point-to-point ATM links. The links connecting the switches come in two forms,

user-network interfaces (UNIs), which connect ATM endpoints to ATM switches, and network-node interfaces (NNIs), which connect ATM switches.

UNIs and NNIs are further classified by the type of network that the switch resides in (public or private). This figure shows examples of several interfaces.

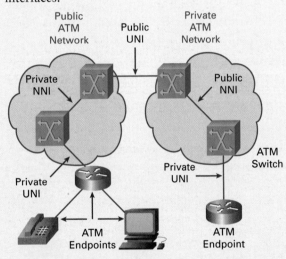

ATM Features

ATM implements two features that make it both useful and interesting (well, interesting in a network-geek kind of way). Anyway, the two features are asynchronous transmission and fixed cell size.

Asynchronous Transmission

The asynchronous part of ATM refers to the ability of the protocol to use a more efficient version of time-division multiplexing (TDM). *Multiplexing* is combining multiple data streams onto a single

physical or logical connection. *Time-division* means that each data stream has an assigned slot in a repeating sequence. Although this process is more efficient than giving each data stream its own physical connection, it still has some inefficiencies, as shown in this figure.

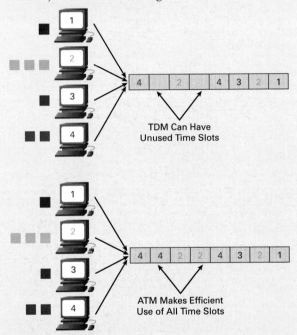

With standard TDM, each end station essentially owns a time slot, preventing any other end station from using it, even when it is idle.

With asynchronous TDM, each end station has a primary time slot where it has priority when it has data to send; however, other end stations can use it when the time slot is idle.

At-A-Glance—ATM, Continued

With standard TDM, each end station essentially owns a time slot, preventing any other end station from using it, even when it is idle.

With asynchronous TDM, each end station has a primary time slot where it has priority when it has data to send; however, other end stations can use it when the time slot is idle.

Fixed Cell Size

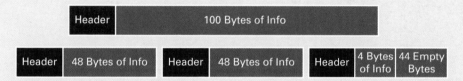

ATM delivers information in fixed-size units called cells. Every ATM cell, regardless of the type of information (voice, video, data), is exactly 53 bytes (or octets) with 48 bytes of information and 5 bytes of header (overhead) information. This arrangement is different from that of other protocols that can increase the cell size and actually increase the header or overhead traffic on a network. However, two distinct advantages in using fixed cell sizes outweigh the cost of the additional overhead.

The main advantage is that the serialization delay or the delay of processing cells is deterministic (regular and predictable), which aids in the management of the network. This feature also makes ATM better suited for voice and video traffic, which is time sensitive. With fixed-length cells, there is no danger of a voice cell getting "stuck in traffic" behind a large data cell.

ATM Connections

ATM is a connection-based service that uses two primary types of circuits, permanent virtual circuits (PVCs) and switched virtual circuits (SVCs). ATM is also capable of using a connectionless service, but it is relatively rare.

A connection-based service means that the network must request, establish, and confirm a connection before it sends any user information (such as voice, video, or data).

PVCs typically make direct connections between sites. Similar to a leased line, the connection remains open even when idle. PVCs guarantee availability, but you must configure them manually.

SVCs are set up and torn down dynamically. The connection is only open while the network actively sends information. SVCs use a signaling protocol between the ATM endpoint and the ATM switch to establish a dynamic connection. SVCs are more flexible than PVCs but require additional overhead. An SVC is similar to a phone call.

Virtual Connection

As previously mentioned, ATM is a connection-based protocol. The network establishes ATM connections using a combination of virtual paths and virtual channels.

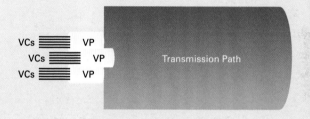

An ATM connection actually consists of a number of *virtual channels*, which can take different physical paths through the network. ATM then bundles virtual channels into logical groups called *virtual paths*. Several virtual paths can also be bundled into a larger logical grouping called a *transmission path*. All of this bundling is transparent to the user. This figure illustrates this concept.

LAN Emulation

LAN emulation (LANE) is a standard that allows end stations connected via an ATM network to communicate as if they were connected across an Ethernet or Token Ring LAN, but at a much faster speed.

LANE uses LAN emulation clients (LEC) and LAN

Traffic Engineering with MPLS

Bagging and Tagging

Multiprotocol Label Switching (MPLS) is a Layer 2 WAN backbone technology that delivers virtual private network (VPN) services over Internet Protocol (IP), traffic engineering capabilities, and a converged network infrastructure that replaces traditional Frame Relay and ATM networks. Originally developed by Cisco Systems in the form of tag switching, MPLS was adopted as an Internet standard by the Internet Engineering Task Force (IETF). Service providers are the primary implementers of the technology.

Service providers offer MPLS services as an alternative to traditional Frame Relay, leased line, and ATM services. With MPLS, service providers can offer similar services to traditional WAN technologies at lower costs and provide additional IP-based services previously not available.

At the heart of MPLS is an encapsulation scheme that serves as an alternative to traditional IP routing. When a packet comes into the service-provider edge, a router assigns a tag to the packet based on the destination IP network. The tag is a type of shorthand for a traditional IP-based route. After the tag is applied, the router forwards the packet into the MPLS core. The core routers read the label, apply the appropriate services, and forward the packet based on the label. After the packet reaches the destination edge of the service-provider network, the MPLS label is removed and the IP packet forwarded onto the IP network.

Traffic engineering is a core component that allows service providers to deliver services predictably for each of their customers. MPLS traffic engineering expands on the capabilities offered by ATM and Frame Relay. Tagged IP packets are routed through the MPLS core based on the resources required by the packet and available network resources. The MPLS network chooses the shortest path for a traffic flow based on its resource requirements. It determines resource requirements by the size and priority for a traffic flow. MPLS networks honor IP quality of service (QoS) by delivering both best-effort delivery as well as time- and bandwidth-sensitive guarantees.

Service providers offer MPLS-based services in the form of VPNs. Using MPLS labels, service providers can deliver IP-based services to many customers without the complexity of traditional Frame Relay or ATM circuit management. Customers can use private or public IP addressing without concern for overlapping other customer addressing.

MPLS VPN services are as secure as Frame Relay in that one customer cannot see the traffic from another customer even though they traverse the same MPLS network. For additional security, customers can place firewalls between their private network and the service provider, as well as encrypt the traffic as it goes into the MPLS network. As long as the packets have standard IP headers, the MPLS network can ship the packet to its destination.

Because MPLS networks look like a private intranet to the connected IP networks, service providers can provide additional IP-based services, such as QoS and telephony support within the VPN, and centralized services, such as web hosting.

At-A-Glance—MPLS

Why Should I Care About MPLS?

Multiprotocol Label Switching (MPLS) was originally developed to speed up the routing of packets through the WAN network. Since its development, the speed of traditional routing has increased considerably, but MPLS still has many benefits.

MPLS enables service providers to offer additional services to its enterprise customers, including virtual private networks (VPNs), improved traffic engineering, quality of service (QoS), Layer 2 tunneling, and multiprotocol support.

You can deploy MPLS as a multiservice-based network, providing an Internet Protocol (IP) alternative to Frame Relay, ATM, and leased line. This feature presents a cost savings to service providers. Rather than build out separate networks for IP, Frame Relay, and ATM users, the provider can build a single MPLS network and support them all.

What Are the Problems to Solve?

An MPLS network must differentiate all the packets from each other. It does so by labeling each packet. To add a label to a packet, the network must first determine all the normal information that a typical router does. In other words, the first router a packet encounters must fully analyze the header, from which the label is made.

After the packet has a label, the rest of the routers in the network must have a way to act upon the information contained in the label.

Equipment and Stuff

The three primary equipment types in an MPLS networks are the following:

- **Customer premise equipment (CPE)**—Equipment on the customer site. All traffic leaving the local site is routed through this point. Often referred to as customer equipment (CE).

- **Edge label switch routers (ELSR)**—Located at the ingress point of the service-provider network, this equipment assigns (and removes) labels. ELSR can either be routers or high-end stitches. Often referred to as provider equipment (PE).

- **Label switch routers (LSR)**—Located in the core of the service-provider network, LSRs forward packets or cells based on their labels.

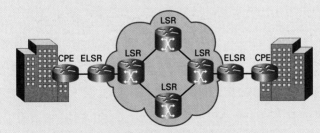

The Label Distribution Protocol (LDP) distributes label information throughout the network.

MPLS Labels

The forwarding mechanism in MPLS uses a label to make decisions where and how to send packets or cells through the network. The label is applied at the ingress to the service-provider network and removed at the network egress point. The router responsible for adding the label is the only network router that needs to process the entire packet header. The network uses the information contained in the header, along with the preconfigured instructions, to generate the label. Routers can base labels on IP destinations (this is what traditional routing uses) and other parameters, such as IP sources, QoS, VPN membership, or specific routes for traffic-engineering purposes. MPLS also supports forwarding mechanisms from other protocols.

Types of Labels
IP destination address
IP source address
QoS parameters
Specific routes
VPN membership
Other protocols

MPLS Security

An additional benefit of MPLS is its inherent security. As illustrated in the next diagram, after the packet or cell from a company enters the service-provider network, the label essentially keeps that packet segregated from all other customers' packets and cells. Because there is no place where one customer

At-A-Glance—MPLS, Continued

can view another customer's packet and cells, there is no danger of someone outside the network snooping for packets. Obviously, this limitation does not stop someone bent on illegally accessing a company's information, but it does remove the possibility of someone claiming that he "accidentally" received the information.

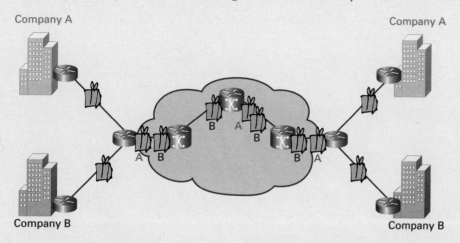

Note: MPLS is no more or less secure than Frame Relay or ATM. Also, there is a common misconception that MPLS is encrypted. Although it is possible to encrypt MPLS, it is not encrypted by default.

MPLS Architecture

MPLS has two layers, or planes, each with an area of specific function in the network. The layers are the control plane and the data plane. The *control plane* is responsible for the exchange of routing information (including labels) between adjacent devices. The *data plane* handles forwarding operations.

How Does the Router Know Where to Send Stuff?

The routers in an MPLS network forward packets based on labels, but the router must know the relationship between a label and a path through the network. This relationship is established and communicated throughout the network using forwarding equivalence classes (FECs). A FEC is a specific path through the network of LSRs; it is equal to the destination network stored in an IP routing table. The LSRs simply look at the label and forward the packet based on the contents of the FEC. This process is simpler, faster, and more flexible than traditional IP routing.

Other MPLS Features

Traffic engineering is the ability to dynamically define routes based on known demand or alternate available routes. Traffic engineering can also optimize network usage.

Intelligent rerouting refers to MPLS's ability to reroute based on network congestion. Rather than change the route on a packet-by-packet basis, MPLS can reroute on a flow-by-flow basis.

MPLS is particularly well-suited to support VPNs. With a VPN, the packets from one enterprise are transparent to all other enterprise VPNs. The labels and the FECs effectively segregate VPN traffic from other packets on the Internet.

MPLS Layer 2 tunneling, also known as Any Transport over MPLS (AToM), allows a service provider to transport Frame Relay and ATM over an MPLS-based network. This feature increases the range of services that the service provider can offer.

MPLS Traffic Separation

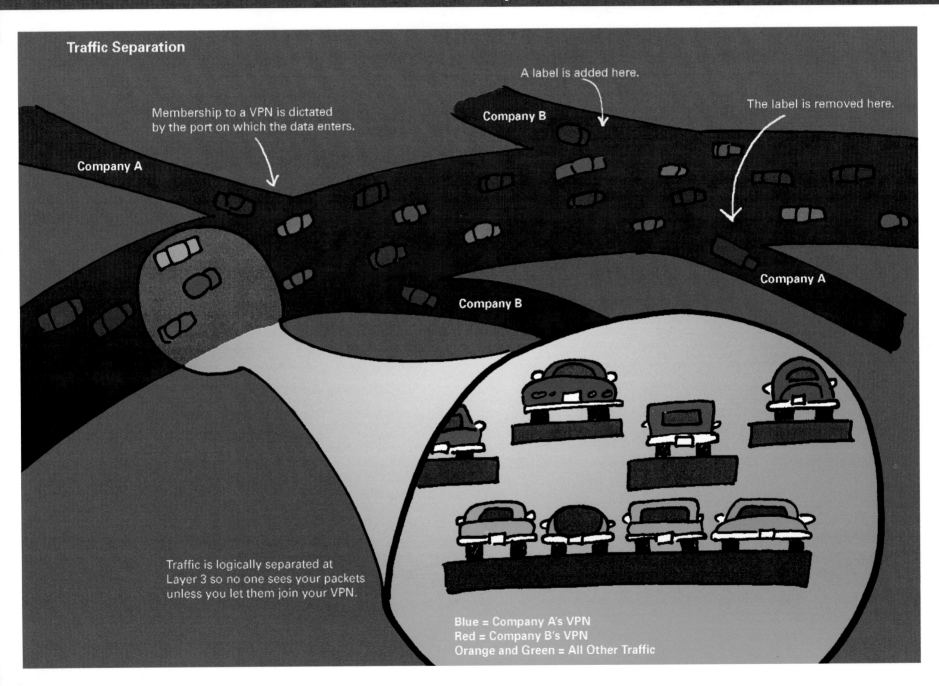

Traffic Separation

A label is added here.

The label is removed here.

Membership to a VPN is dictated by the port on which the data enters.

Company A

Company B

Company A

Company B

Traffic is logically separated at Layer 3 so no one sees your packets unless you let them join your VPN.

Blue = Company A's VPN
Red = Company B's VPN
Orange and Green = All Other Traffic

Part VII

How Businesses Share Data

Remember the talk of bricks and mortar versus clicks and portals? During the 1990s, prognosticators and financial "experts" predicted the demise of traditional brick-and-mortar businesses. Web-based commerce and information exchange would replace traditional physical forms of business such as malls and banks.

Although this scenario never quite developed, web-based commerce and business-to-business information exchange has. Large businesses today rely on their computer networks for critical functions such as trading stock, transferring money, manufacturing, providing security, administering critical medical care, and controlling air traffic. The network is a key asset to a company, and a network outage can cripple its earnings.

As a result, companies have invested considerable money and expertise in designing networks that facilitate the interchange of data among their employees, customers, and partners.

Additionally, companies are finding new ways to deliver services across the Internet. As discussed earlier in the book, you can transmit voice, music, and video over the Internet. Unfortunately, video traffic is a resource hog. Video packets are fat and can saturate a slow line. Technologies such as content routing and caching work to localize the traffic to the person requesting it.

Most companies today could not function without networks and the Internet. Part VII shows you different ways in which businesses use networks and the Internet to make it all work.

Data Center

Store Once, Use Often

Data centers are centralized locations where companies house their business-critical network and server resources. Data centers provide secure centralization of corporate computing resources. Mainframes, application and web servers, data storage, secure printers, WAN aggregation, Internet connectivity, and network core switches are examples of devices that are commonly located in the data center. IT functions, such as network and server operations and support, generally sit near the data center. Satellite data centers provide regional services as well as disaster recovery for the primary data center.

Having these resources centrally located provides administrative benefits but also presents network-design challenges. Whether accessing a server in the data center, exchanging files with a remote office worker, or accessing the Internet, most network activity passes through the data center at some point. Additionally, the data center houses much of the company's critical data and computing resources. High-bandwidth networking and business-resiliency measures become critical design factors in providing smooth and reliable services.

The primary components of a data center network include some or all of the following:

- Campus
- Private WAN
- Remote access
- Internet server farm
- Extranet server farm
- Intranet server farm

Located in the data center are applications that support business-critical functions as well as network operations and network-based applications, such as IP telephony, video streaming, and IP videoconferencing.

n-Tier Model

Mainframes and server farms represent the heart of the corporate computing resources. Today's data-center server-farm design incorporates what's called an *n*-tier model. This model describes a method for separating application services into manageable and secure tiers. The *n* indicates that there can be any number of distinct tiers in the data center, typically three. The purpose for separating these functions into separate tiers is to break the dependence of all functions residing on a single server. Separating the customer-facing applications from the backend servers increases the scalability of the services and eases the management of large-scale server farms.

The first or front tier is the actual application a user might run, such as customer resource management (CRM), enterprise resource planning (ERP), e-commerce, or order processing. The application might or might not be web-based, although newer applications are migrating towards the web. This tier provides the client-facing services.

The next tier, the middle tier, provides the glue between the client-facing application and the backend database and storage servers. Typically, these middle-ware applications provide the business logic that maps corporate data to how a company operates.

The final tier, the back end, contains all the databases, storage, and raw data to be shared with the various applications.

Functions and Requirements

These server farms need a network infrastructure that supports them. Although the growth and design of data centers tend to happen gradually over time, what evolves is a layered approach in which the data-center network is divided into distinct functions. These layered functions include the following:

- **Aggregation**—Connects the data center to the corporate backbone network.
- **Front end**—The servers that users interact with.
- **Application**—The servers running code that glues the front-end applications to the back-end data and reflects the business processes in how the data is used. Also referred to as middleware or business-logic software.
- **Back end**—Where data is stored, typically in relational database systems.
- **Storage**—The actual storage devices in which data is stored.
- **Data-center network transport**—High-speed optical networking that facilitates the sharing of data between distributed data centers. Larger companies implement distributed data centers to provide redundancy in case a server farm or entire data center goes offline.

In each case, the network must provide the infrastructure, security, and management to accommodate the requirements for each particular layer:

- **High availability**—Access to data center applications, data, and networking services must continue in the event of a device or network failure.
- **Scalability**—Because servers are centralized in the data center, the network must be able to handle the sheer amount of traffic from corporate users to the central location, as well as server-to-server traffic. Additionally, data center services must be able to scale to multiple locations when distributed data centers are needed.
- **Security**—Data center devices must be physically secure, and the data and applications must be protected from internal and external threats.
- **Management**—The IT staff monitors, configures, and troubleshoots network and server resources.

At-A-Glance—Data Center

Why Should I Care About Data Centers?

Data centers house computing resources used to support business-critical applications and accompanying computing resources such as mainframes, servers, and server farms. The applications housed in business centers vary but typically include those related to financial, human resources, e-commerce, and business-to-business. Server farms within the data center also support many network-operation applications such as Telnet, FTP, e-mail, Internet Protocol (IP) telephony, Media on Demand (MoD), and IP videoconferencing.

By consolidating critical computing resources under a controlled, centralized management, data centers enable enterprises to operate around the clock or according to their business needs. With fully redundant backup data centers, enterprises can reduce the risk of massive data loss in the event of natural disaster or malicious attack.

What Are the Problems to Solve?

Building a data center requires extensive planning; Think of it as building a network within a network. The specifics of each data center are personalized to the company deploying it, but it must solve the following problems:

- **Facility planning**—Location and supporting equipment
- **Storage methods**—Format and technologies
- **Distribution**—Retrieval, and fast and reliable transport of data
- **Backing up**—Connection methods and frequency
- **Management**—Making the whole thing work
- **Security**—Protecting from inside misuse and external theft

Types of Data Centers

Data centers are defined by what type of network they support. The three basic classes are Internet, intranet, and extranet. Each type of data center has specific infrastructure, security, and management requirements for its supporting server farms.

Internet server farms are accessed from the Internet and are typically available to a large community. Web interfaces and web browsers are widely available, which makes them pervasive.

Intranet server farms should have the same ease of access as Internet server farms but should only be available to internal enterprise users.

Extranet server farms fall somewhere between Internet and intranet server farms. Extranet server farms use web-based applications, but unlike the Internet or intranets, only a select group of users (business partners, customers, or trusted external user) accesses it.

At-A-Glance—Data Center Layers and Distribution

Data Center Layers

Data centers have six logical layers. The layers are based on logical functions:

- **Aggregation layer**—Consists of network-infra-structure components that connect all data center service devices, such as firewalls, content switches, call managers, and content distribution managers.
- **Front-end layer**—Contains FTP, Telnet, e-mail, web servers, and other business-application servers.
- **Application layer**— Performs translations between users requests and the back-end database systems.

- **Back-end layer**—Houses security infrastructure, management infrastructure, and the database systems that interface directly with the business data.
- **Storage layer**—Consists of the infrastructure, such as fiber-channel switches, as well as the storage devices. A data center should always have a secondary (backup) storage facility that is updated regularly. In cases where the data center backs up its data synchronously (in real time), the storage layer can load-balance for increased efficiency.
- **Metro optical layer**—Consists of the optical devices used to communicate between distributed server farms across multiple data centers.

Distribution (The N-Tier Model)

As the importance and size of server farms have increased, the limitations of a traditional client/server model of data storage and retrieval have become more evident. A new model, the *n*-tier model, separates the server-farm functions into distinct tiers, which improves both efficiency and ease of management. The model typically has three tiers. The first tier runs the user-facing applications, the second tier maps users requests to the data, and the third tier actually stores the data.

The traditional client/server model requires heavy management. With that model, the application runs on the client, but the server stores all the data and then presents it.

The *n*-tier model needs little client management because it only presents information. All the computing and processing is performed on the server side.

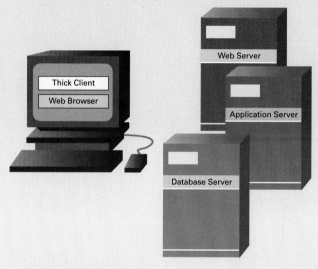

Data Center Facilities

The housing of critical computing resources, such as those in a data center, typically require specialized facilities and trained personnel to run a 24-by-7 operation. The efficient, protected, and secure operations of these business-critical systems require consideration and planning for the following:

- Power capacity
- Cooling capacity
- Cabling (raised flooring or overhead tracks)
- Temperature and humidity controls
- Fire and smoke systems
- Restricted access and surveillance systems
- Space planning for future scaling

Although including some of these items might seem like overkill, the loss of data can actually cause a business to fail, so you should never underestimate the importance of protecting the data and the equipment that stores and transports it.

Storage Methods

Storage services include both the consolidation of information and the methods of connectivity. A separate sheet explains the details of storage services, but this section lists the basics.

Storage methods include network attached storage (NAS), which uses a specialized file server to connect storage devices to a network, and storage area network (SAN), which is an independent network designed specifically for connecting storage devices.

NAS is optimized for file-based access to shared storage over an IP network. SANs are optimized for the efficient collection, storage, and retrieval of raw data.

The primary connection method is a small computer systems interface (SCSI, pronounced "skuzzy"), which uses a parallel-bus interface to connect to storage devices. SCSI commands can travel over fiber (optical) or IP (referred to as ISCSI).

Data Center Management

Management services typically cover all other services. Every layer of the data center model requires its own set of management considerations but must be supported by different organizational entities or even by distinct functional groups within the enterprise. Specific management categories include configuration management, fault management, performance management, security management, and accounting management.

The management-services plan must include each one of these categories.

Security Services

Given the importance of the data center, security plans should encompass all services and all devices supporting those services. The security features include access control lists (ACLs), firewalls, intrusion-detection systems (IDSs), and authentication, authorization, and accounting (AAA).

Putting a security plan in place for all services and into the data center.

Data Center Application—Corporate Expense System

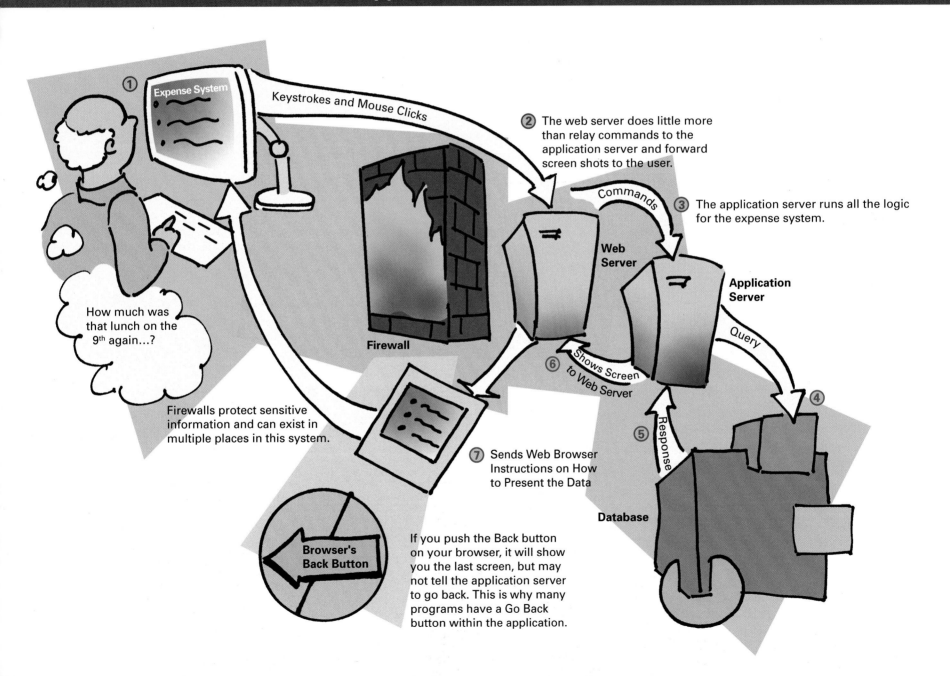

① Expense System

Keystrokes and Mouse Clicks

② The web server does little more than relay commands to the application server and forward screen shots to the user.

Commands

③ The application server runs all the logic for the expense system.

Web Server

Application Server

Query

How much was that lunch on the 9th again...?

Firewall

Firewalls protect sensitive information and can exist in multiple places in this system.

⑥ Shows Screen to Web Server

⑤ Response

④

Database

⑦ Sends Web Browser Instructions on How to Present the Data

Browser's Back Button

If you push the Back button on your browser, it will show you the last screen, but may not tell the application server to go back. This is why many programs have a Go Back button within the application.

Storage Area Networks

Efficient Deployment of Critical Data

In an effort to improve business productivity, corporations are implementing web and Internet applications such as customer relationship management (CRM), enterprise resource planning (ERP), and e-mail. This move has resulted in the accumulation of large amounts of corporate data, and these voluminous stores of data are critical to a company's operation.

Large amounts of data require large amounts of storage. *Storage area networks (SANs)* have emerged as the premiere technology for advanced storage requirements. SANs address an IT manager's needs by providing a scalable, manageable, and efficient deployment of mission-critical data.

Aside from offering advanced technology for storage needs, SANs also reduce costs when deploying highly scalable storage versus traditional direct-attached storage (DAS). Hence, SAN reduces cost and offers new levels of performance and scalability previously unavailable. It's a popular technology that is still being defined and explored.

SAN addresses the following issues currently experienced with DAS:

- Difficulty of managing large, distributed islands of storage from multiple locations
- Complexity of scheduled backups for multiple systems
- Difficulty of preparing for unscheduled outages
- Inability to share storage among multiple systems
- Sheer expense of distributed disk farms

SAN addresses these issues by doing the following:

- Reducing management costs through centralized control for monitoring, backup, replication, and provisioning.
- Reducing subsystem costs through any-to-any connectivity between storage and servers. This setup allows networks to match servers with underutilized storage subsystems.
- Reducing backup costs through the centralization and consolidation of backup functionality.
- Offering highly available disk services by providing redundant, multiple paths between servers and storage devices. This provision allows for automated failover across all storage in an easily scalable manner.
- Offering highly scalable and location-independent disaster recovery. You can replicate entire data centers to multiple locations, allowing quick and efficient switchover if the primary data center becomes unavailable. DAS networks are unable to provide this level of disaster recovery.

Traditional JBOD (just a bunch of disks) DAS networks are file-system– and platform-dependant. The disks are associated with a single set of servers, and only the attached host can access them. Examples include small computer systems interface (SCSI), fiber channel, and enterprise system connection (ESCON). Redundant Array of Inexpensive Disks (RAID) addresses fault tolerance.

Because SAN removes the device, operating-system, and location dependencies of traditional DAS, new capabilities emerge. Storage expansion no longer has an impact on servers and vice versa. Bandwidth is available on demand, and load-balancing can occur across multiple active paths.

Fiber Channel and IP

The two access methods available for SANs are fiber channel and Internet Protocol (IP).

Dedicated fiber-channel networks attach servers to storage devices. The fiber-channel network passes data blocks around (blocks are used by disk access), which the servers access through host-bus adapters. The servers then attach to LANs to provide the information to the rest of the network. SAN components include host-bus adapters, storage systems (RAID, JBOD, tape, and optical disk), hubs, switches, and SAN-management software.

Fiber channel is an American National Standards Institute (ANSI) standard that combines both channel and network technologies. SCSI and IP are the primary upper-layer protocols available on fiber channel. Fiber channel operates at gigabit speeds.

You can use several topologies for fiber-channel deployment:

- **Point to point**—Dedicated connections between a server and storage device. This method is suitable when storage devices are dedicated to a single file server.
- **Arbitrated loop**—Storage and file servers connect to each other in a closed loop with up to 126 nodes. Maximum bandwidth is 100 MB shared between all the nodes. Therefore, the number of attached nodes directly affects the performance of the loop.
- **Switch fabric**—As with Ethernet, performance and reliability vastly improve when moving from shared media (such as an arbitrated loop) to switched fabrics. A fiber-channel switch offers up to 100 MB to each switched port. You can trunk switches together to attach up to a theoretical 16 million nodes.

The other access method to fiber channel is IP.

Because SANs connect to IP networks, the storage can be accessed across LANs, WANs, metropolitan-area networks (MANs), and the Internet. You can manage the devices using Simple Network Management Protocol (SNMP) and operate in a secure mode with the use of Internet Protocol Security (IPSec), firewalls, and virtual local-area networks (VLANs). Storage devices can connect to Ethernet devices.

Whereas fiber channel separates disk-block–based traffic from the rest of the network, IP-based SAN tunnels block traffic through the IP network using the Internet Protocol SCSI (ISCSI) protocol. ISCSI uses Transmission Control Protocol (TCP) as its transport.

Fiber channel over IP (FCIP) is another technology that allows fiber-channel networks to connect to each other over LANs, MANs, and WANs. FCIP uses TCP to tunnel fiber-channel block traffic across the IP network.

At-A-Glance—Storage Area Networks

Why Should I Care About Storage Area Networks?

Most companies use online storage to house business-related information. As more information from business functions—such as sales, inventory, payroll, engineering, marketing, and human resources—is stored online, the efficient acceptance, management, and retrieval of this information becomes more critical to the success of the business. By storing data in common devices, companies can also leverage economies of scale, reducing the total cost of data storage.

What Are the Problems to Solve?

For many years, information was stored in server-centric architectures. As businesses grew and encountered greater storage needs, they added servers when and where they needed them.

However, this direct-attached storage (DAS) approach is limited in its ability to scale because it is expensive to manage and it uses resources inefficiently. Each server that you add (in each department, for example) is associated with a specific CPU. Additionally, standard activities such as backing up data or adding capacity are difficult and inefficient.

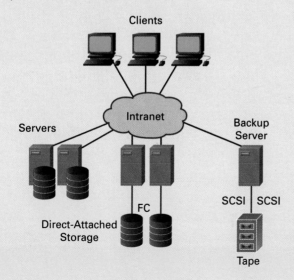

What Is Storage Networking?

Overcoming the drawbacks of server-centric storage is a network-centric model called *storage networking*. Storage networking is the software and hardware that enable you to consolidate, share, access, replicate, and manage storage over a shared network infrastructure.

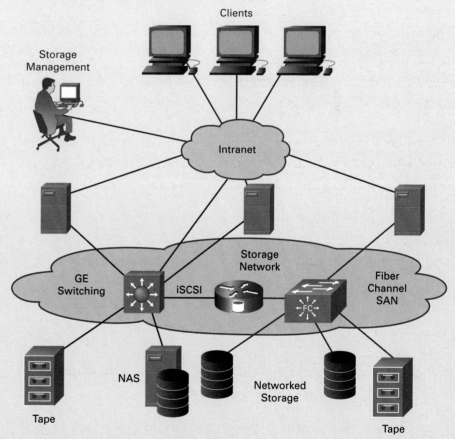

To understand how storage networking works, you must understand the different storage methods and technologies.

At-A-Glance—Storage Area Networks, Continued

Traditional Server-Centric Storage Methods

Redundant Array of Inexpensive Disks

Redundant Array of Inexpensive Disks (RAID) is a fault-tolerant grouping of two or more disks that a server views as a single disk volume. It is a self-contained, manageable unit of storage.

Just a Bunch of Disks

Aside from being one of our favorite acronyms, just a bunch of disks (JBOD) is a simple and efficient method for raw storage. Each drive is independently attached to an input/output (I/O) channel.

This method has limited scalability because it requires separate servers to manage multiple volumes of disks. Drives share common power supplies and physical chassis.

Storage Networking Technologies

Small Computer Systems Interface

Small Computer Systems Interface (SCSI, pronounced "skuzzy") is a parallel-bus interface port used to connect peripheral devices such as RAID, tape devices, and servers. SCSI is a low-cost method of directly connecting devices but is limited in scalability and distance.

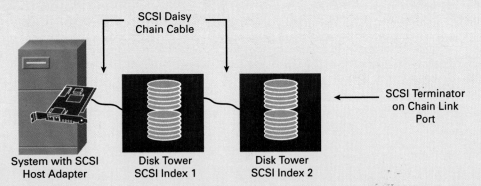

SCSI Daisy Chain Cable

SCSI Terminator on Chain Link Port

System with SCSI Host Adapter

Disk Tower SCSI Index 1

Disk Tower SCSI Index 2

Fiber Channel

A fiber channel is both a physical connection and a Layer 2 protocol used by storage area networks (SANs). Fiber channel is the most common method of transporting SCSI commands and data between servers.

Fiber-channel capabilities have kept up well with companies' ever-increasing need for bandwidth. Using fiber channel, application servers can access data on a SAN without impacting the company IP network.

Internet Small Computer Systems Interface (ISCSI)

ISCSI (pronounced "i-scuzzy") is a method of encapsulating SCSI data and command frames into IP packets, enabling universal access to storage devices and SANs over standard TCP/IP networks.

Retrieval Methods

The two main methods for retrieving stored data are block retrieval and file retrieval. A *block* refers to the largest amount of data that a single operation can access. Blocks are the most elemental units of storage. SANs access blocks directly.

A *file* consists of several blocks. In network attached storage (NAS) systems, the server organizes blocks into files.

At-A-Glance—Network Attached Storage Versus Storage Area Networks

Storage Networks

Network Attached Storage

NAS uses specialized file servers to connect storage devices to a network. NAS is well suited for collecting, storing, retrieving, and sharing data over IP networks. NAS also supports multiple operating systems, file system, and protocols. NAS is optimized for file-based access to shared storage over an IP network.

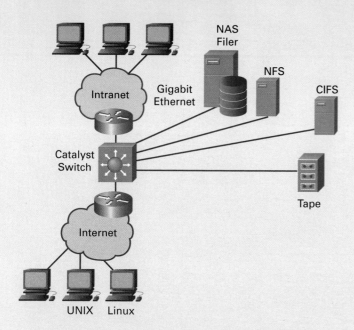

Storage Area Network

A SAN is an independent network designed specifically for connecting storage devices. SANs are optimized for the efficient collection, storage, and retrieval of raw block data. Most SANs use fiber-channel interconnections and require a media converter to connect to an IP network.

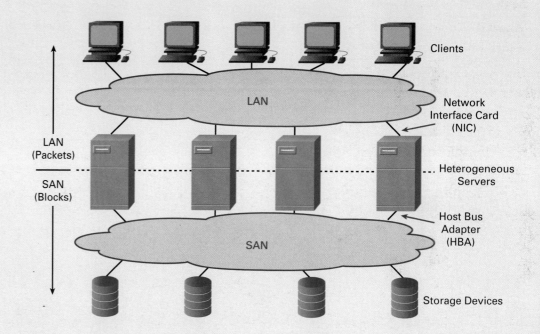

Server-Centric Storage

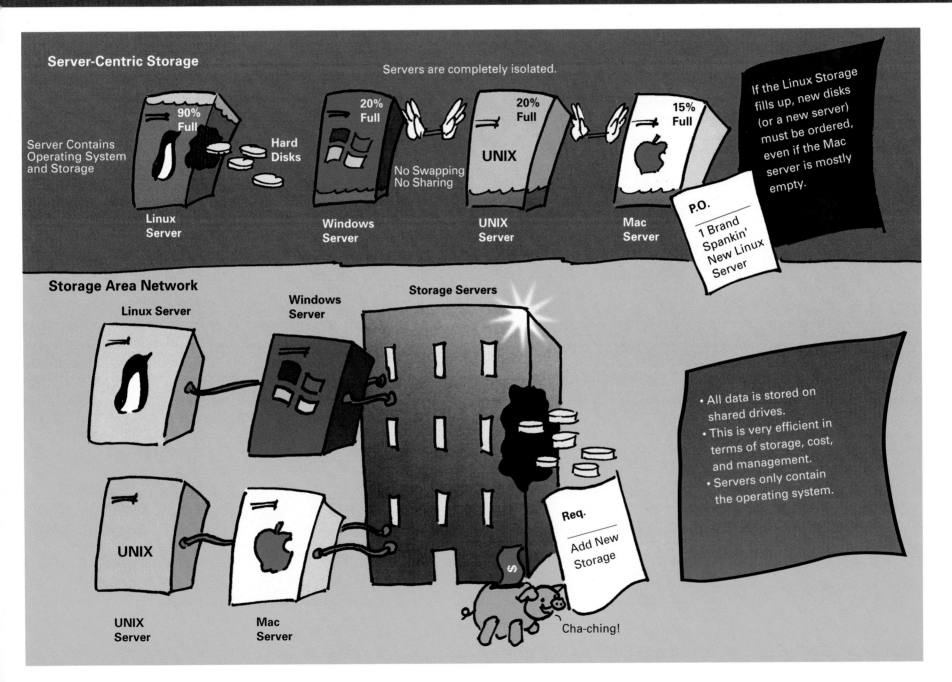

Content Networking

Coordinating Access to Limited Resources

Air-traffic controllers coordinate access to runways. Busy airports have more planes wanting to take off and land than runways available. Runways can only facilitate one plane at a time. In generic terms, the air-traffic controllers coordinate access to a limited resource (the runway).

Such is the purpose of content switches: coordinating access to limited resources, in this case, through load balancing. The primary example for content switching is the load balancing of HTML and XML traffic among multiple web servers.

The number of users needing to access a particular website might exceed the capacity of a single server. You could implement multiple servers to handle the increased load. However, because every device on a network requires a unique IP address, how does the user select which server to access? Some server farms (such as large Internet-based retailers) might require hundreds of servers to accommodate their online customers.

Content switches resolve this problem by transparently intercepting all traffic destined to a website and distributing each request to an available server. For example, when a user visits http://www.cisco.com, a load-balancing content switch can ensure that a server that is not overloaded handles the request. The user sees a single web server, www.cisco.com. But in reality, there might be tens or hundreds of servers.

Content switches can provide relief in the following situations:

- **Server load balancing**—As described earlier, a content switch can ensure proper load balancing across a group of servers transparently to the user.

- **Firewall load balancing**—As server farms increase in size, companies want to protect the systems from unauthorized access. They do so with firewalls. Content switches can enable load balancing across multiple firewalls.

- **Distributed data centers**—As the ultimate show of redundancy, some companies might choose to duplicate all network and computing services in a data center on an alternate site. Thus, if the original data center becomes unavailable, all services can continue on the alternate site. Although the implementation of distributed data centers requires careful planning and integration, content switches become the traffic cop during an accident. Any traffic destined to a data center transparently meets the content switch first. The content switch then redirects the traffic to the original data center, as usual, or to the alternate site if the original site disappears.

At-A-Glance—Content Networking

Why Should I Care About Content Networking?

The near instantaneous availability of data from internal and external network sources has helped transform networking from a high-tech tool with narrow appeal to a broad method of delivering business tools, educational resources, and entertainment to a worldwide audience.

Although the massive decrease in the cost of bandwidth (dollars/kilobits/seconds) has been a big part of the increased use and availability of the Internet, the network still has far too many bottlenecks that you must overcome to make networks and data distribution work efficiently.

Content networking solves this problem by mitigating the effects of network bottlenecks by providing an efficient (and transparent) means for distributing all forms of downloadable media (content) across networks and balancing traffic loads over multiple devices.

What Are the Problems to Solve?

The two keys to content networking are overcoming bottlenecks and maintaining relevant data across multiple sites.

A bottleneck is the slowest point in the network, which forces other faster parts of the network to perform at slower speeds than they are capable of. Although you can easily address bottlenecks by adding more bandwidth, it is not always a viable solution. In such cases, you can still address them by getting data as close to the user as possible prior to a user request. This process is known as *caching*.

Assuming that multiple sites are prepopulated, the issue becomes one of updating and synchronizing remote sites because many types of data have a "shelf life."

The Brains of the Operation

Two key pieces of equipment are responsible for the intelligence behind content networking:

- **Content manager**—Responsible for the distribution (caching) and update of material. Whenever possible, it delivers content prior to a request and then, based on administrative input, performs caching updates prior to shelf-life expiration.

- **Content switches**— The traffic cops of the network. Whether you are accessing a website, data server, or remote network, a content switch directs you to the device that provides the shortest delay possible.

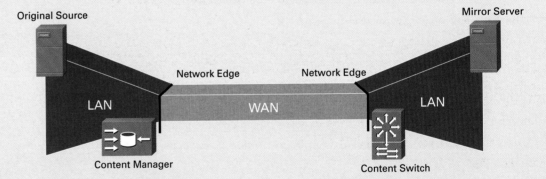

Content Distribution and Management

In many cases, an original source of data or information is not local to all users and must traverse a wide-area network (WAN) to reach a user. The point where a LAN ends and WAN begins is the *network edge*. The network edge is almost always a choke point, meaning that the available bandwidth on the LAN side of the edge is larger than that on the WAN side. To avoid annoying delays in responsiveness for the content requested, as well as for other competing traffic such as voice or video, a content manager can prepopulate a remote location with content, update a local server with real-time updates, and perform complete backups during nonpeak hours.

Remote servers populated with content from another source are often called *mirror sites*.

At-A-Glance—Content Availability

Content Manager

The content manager requires some intelligence so that it can make decisions about where to prepopulate, what to prepopulate, and how to bill and provision services.

Content Routing

When a user requests content, a router receives the request and determines the best possible site to route the request based on the location of the user, the availability of content among different sites, and network status. Other rules defined by a network administrator might apply as well.

Content Availability

One of the main advantages of content switching is the ability to transparently deal with network or hardware and software errors. If a server (or a device such as a firewall) goes down, a content switch simply removes it from the list of available endpoints, and user requests are directed elsewhere. This process happens without the user realizing it. For retail websites, this transparency is especially important because users are less likely to shop on a site if availability is questionable.

Content Switching

The purpose of content switching is to provide intelligent load balancing for servers and other devices such as firewalls.

The need for load balancing stems from the fact that a single device cannot always adequately serve all requests at any given moment in time. Therefore, the information must reside among several devices.

Content switching prevents users from knowing the name or location of every device. Users simply request the access (typing a single URL, for example), and a content switch chooses the best device to access based on the type of request, the priority of the request, and other defined rules.

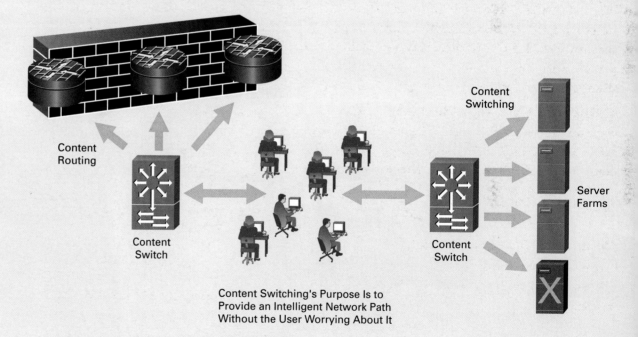

Content Routing

Content Switch

Content Switch

Content Switching

Server Farms

Content Switching's Purpose Is to Provide an Intelligent Network Path Without the User Worrying About It

Caching

Moving Content Close to the User

Since the 1990s, the World Wide Web has taken off as fast as air conditioning. The Internet boom has created challenges for network engineers, including congestion, inconsistent quality and reliability, and cost-efficient scalability. Examples of these problems include the following:

- Not being able to access a news website during a huge news event because the web servers are unable to handle more users
- Trying to view web pages located in another country
- A company with international presence trying to localize its web pages for each country

Network caching has emerged as the primary tool for localizing network content close to the requester. Caching addresses the preceding problems by accelerating content delivery and optimizing WAN link utilization. In other words, it moves the content closer to the user. Examples of cacheable content include web pages, audio files, and streaming video.

How Caching Works

Caching works in cooperation with specific choke points in a network. You can localize traffic by strategically placing caching devices in a network. Network caches transparently store frequently accessed content on hard drives, intercept requests for that stored content, and present the page back to the user. Thus, the request never makes it to the intended destination, saving bandwidth and server resources.

An example follows:

1. A user enters a URL in her browser.
2. A network device (such as a switch) analyzes the request, and if it meets certain criteria, the network transparently redirects the request to a local network caching device.
3. The caching device, upon receipt of the request, determines whether it has the requested content stored locally. If not, the caching device makes its own request to the original web server.
4. After the original web server returns the content, the cache server stores the content on its hard disk and returns the content to the original requester. The material is now cached locally.
5. Later, if another user requests the same web page, the cache intercepts the request and responds by returning the locally stored copy, never communicating with the original web server.
6. Because the request was fulfilled locally, the user perceives fast response time (which is good), and the request never leaves the local network, thereby saving WAN and Internet costs and reducing the load on the destination web server.

A cache server can provide its effectiveness to multiple locations. One place is at a company's main access point to the Internet. You can reroute all outbound requests to the local cache, thereby saving Internet access fees and providing quicker responses for frequently requested pages.

Another location is at branch sites, such as at a chain store, remote sales office, or bank branch. By caching content locally, the network can conserve WAN bandwidth for more mission-critical applications.

Caching More than Web Pages

The initial benefits of caching were realized with static web content. However, video and audio files are also appropriate candidates for caching. One example is a CEO's address to the company. You can broadcast the address live and then store it as video on demand for people to watch when they have time. You can push the broadcast to local caching servers so that an employee in another country can watch the video without having it stream from the location of the original video.

To the overseas employee, the performance is fast because the content is local. Additionally, as other employees overseas watch the video, the WAN link back to the origin is not affected.

Issues Affecting Caching

During a sudden surge of web traffic, a caching device can become overloaded, no longer able to handle additional web requests. To solve this problem, cache engines determine when they reach a particular load limit. At the point of overload, the cache device refuses additional requests and forwards subsequent requests directly to the destination web server to handle directly. After the cache device can process the backlog of requests, it then intercepts requests again.

Another issue is keeping the cached content current. The cache device becomes less effective if it can't show the same content as if the user visited the web server directly. An example might be a stock-tracking page: What good is the caching device if the stock price is an hour or day old compared to the actual website?

You have three different ways to indicate whether content can be cached and how long it can be cached. The first method is in the actual HTTP document. HTTP can specify whether a document is cacheable. Additionally, with HTTP 1.1, the web page author can specify the expiration time for a particular page. HTTP 1.1 also allows a caching device to send small requests to the source web server so it can determine whether content has changed.

The second method for ensuring content freshness is through the configuration of the caching device. You can configure the cache device to "expire" pages at a certain rate, at which the cache device makes requests to the source web servers for updates to the pages.

The final method to ensure content freshness is through the user's configuration of his browser. A user can ensure fresh content by clicking on his Reload/Refresh button. Browsers by default cache web content locally, and you can configure them to do no caching either explicitly or using the Shift-Reload/Shift-Refresh method.

Desktop Protocols

From Thin to Fat

During the 1980s and 1990s, companies were interested in migrating from "thin" clients, such as mainframe terminal sessions, to "fat" clients. The idea was that instead of concentrating all the computing power onto central mainframes, they could distribute the power among all the PCs on people's desks. Centralized server resources no longer provided central processing as mainframes previously did and instead simply provided file- and print-sharing services.

This pendulum change from thin to fat clients was considered revolutionary, which would only swing back with the introduction of the World Wide Web. Corporate computer users were newly empowered: They had the freedom to run whichever software they wanted and to purchase fast desktop computers. The central servers were relegated to the lowly roll of file and print sharing. PC hardware and software business flourished while mainframe business slowed.

The irony of this migration was that although corporate users got what they wanted, IT groups lost the ability to effectively troubleshoot and support their users. PC operating systems allowed users to install and run any application, game, or gadget they wanted. Any person could buy a PC and turn it into a file server on the corporate network. Computer viruses could quickly snake through corporate computers due to a lack of security or reduced security. And when things stopped working, these users turned to their IT group for rescue. The IT groups had to troubleshoot mysterious problems, of which the origin could be any piece of software or user mistake.

Eventually, the WWW and the popularity of IP as the de-facto networking protocol swung the pendulum back toward thin, easier-to-maintain clients and centralized server resources. Today's networks still have a place for file and print services, but they are much less diminished from the user perspective. The web browser is the terminal emulator of the new millennium.

The fat-client phenomenon of the 80s and 90s centered on network operating systems (NOSs), the central component that fueled the ability to convert a PC into a file and print server. The protocols that these servers used to communicate with clients and other services across a network were collectively called *desktop protocols*.

Network Operating Systems

NOSs provide file sharing, print sharing, security, directory services, and application interfaces. With the exception of IP-based protocols such as Network File System (NFS), the rest of the NOSs implement their own network protocols. To discuss the NOSs, we also include some of the predecessor protocols, which led to the eventual development of NOSs.

Xerox Network Systems

Xerox developed the Xerox Network Systems (XNS) protocols in the late 1970s and early 1980s. As the first to reach popularity and hit the market, XNS became the model adopted by other NOS vendors, such as 3Com Banyan and Novell. Eventually, the other NOS vendor's software became more popular and replaced XNS.

XNS was defined on a five-layer model that generally followed the same principles of OSI's seven-layer reference model. Layer 1, the network layer, is called the Internet Datagram Protocol (IDP). A unique host and network number identified each host and each network in an XNS network. XNS used the Routing Information Protocol (RIP) for routing XNS packets through an internetwork.

DECnet

DECnet was originally developed in 1975 by Digital Equipment Corporation (DEC) as a series of protocols used to connect two PDP-11 minicomputers directly to each other. Subsequent releases of DECnet added support for other proprietary and standard protocols while still maintaining backward compatibility. DECnet Phase IV and V were the last most popular versions of DECnet.

DECnet implemented an eight-layer network model, as opposed to OSI's seven-layer model; it was one of the few protocols to incorporate network management into its network protocol definition.

Unique to DECnet Phase IV's implementation was its network addressing. DECnet addresses were not associated with the physical networks to which the nodes were connected. Instead, DECnet located hosts using area/node address pairs. When implementing routers in a DECnet network, this design meant that each interface on the router had the same logical *and* physical Media Access Control (MAC) layer address. Phase V opened the door for migration to TCP/IP by implementing DECnet's upper four layers on a regular TCP/IP stack.

Routing Phase IV traffic involved implementing the DECnet Routing Protocol (DRP). Phase V combined DRP with the OSI routing protocol—hence, Phase V's other name, DECnet OSI.

AppleTalk

Apple Computers developed a protocol suite called AppleTalk in the mid 1980s in conjunction with its Macintosh computer. AppleTalk's purpose was to let multiple users share resources such as printers and files. Clients were the computers that access the resources, and servers were the computers that make the resources available for sharing. AppleTalk was one of the early protocols developed explicitly for distributed client/server networking.

AppleTalk was designed with a transparent network interface. Users needed little interaction to get their computers talking to other computers, and the network protocols were invisible to the user.

AppleTalk had two phases before eventually being replaced by TCP/IP. Strictly for workgroup use, Phase 1 was limited to 127 hosts and 127 servers on a network. Phase 2 was developed to operate on larger internetworks and included features that made it more extensible and appropriate for quickly growing user networks.

An AppleTalk node was a device connected to an AppleTalk network. An AppleTalk network consisted of a single logical cable with multiple nodes attached. AppleTalk zones were logical groups of nodes or networks that were defined when the network administrator configured the network. Zones did not need to be physically contiguous.

One of the unique aspects of AppleTalk was how nodes automatically retrieve their network addresses. It was not necessary to statically define an AppleTalk address; instead a node was automatically assigned an address when it connected to the network.

The routing of AppleTalk traffic was more complex than other routing protocols. Routers had to maintain and transport not only network routing information, but also other information such as name lookup and zone information.

The Routing Table Maintenance Protocol (RTMP) was the primary routing protocol, based on the RIP. RTMP advertisements contained information from each router on the networks it could reach.

Routers also had to be aware of other protocols such as the Name Binding Protocol, Zone Information Protocol, Printer Access Protocol, and AppleTalk Filing Protocol. This awareness was necessary so that when a user opened a chooser menu, he would be able to see the other Apple resources on the network.

Banyan VINES

Banyan VINES was ahead of its time. Banyan was a company (no longer in business) who created a distributed network operating system on a proprietary set of protocols based loosely on the XNS protocols. The network operated similarly to XNS but included the first implementation of directory services that truly set the trend for future directory services. With a single logon, a user could access any network resource, file server, or printer by name. It was fast and efficient when implemented correctly. In this author's opinion, Banyan suffered from ineffective marketing and failed to keep up with the growth and scaling demands of its customers.

The Novell juggernaut at the time overwhelmed Banyan with its sheer marketing muscle and managed to finally release a scalable and working directory services 10 years after Banyan. Banyan quietly went out of business, leaving Microsoft and Novell to duke it out. Microsoft eventually won.

Novell NetWare

Novell developed NetWare in the early 1980s. NetWare, like VINES, was based on the XNS networking protocols.

The NetWare Layer 3 protocol is called Internetwork Packet Exchange (IPX) and is connectionless similar to IP's User Datagram Protocol (UDP). A network number assigned by a network administrator identifies each network. Initially, routers exchanged routing information using a RIP protocol, but with NetWare 4.x, Novell added support for an OSPF-like link-state protocol called Network Layer Security Protocol (NLSP). Later, Novell added support for NetWare/IP, in which IPX datagrams were encapsulated in standard IP UDP packets.

As with AppleTalk and VINES, users did not need to statically configure node addresses for their machines. Instead, when a NetWare PC attached to the network, it looked for the nearest server and automatically received a network and node number.

In addition to exchanging routing information, NetWare servers also exchanged Service Advertising Protocol (SAP) packets. SAPs contained information about available network resources such as printers and file servers. Therefore, if a client wanted a network resource available from a distant server, the local server gave the address of the resource to the client, and the client then contacted the distant server directly.

At-A-Glance—Desktop Protocols

Why Should I Care About Desktop Protocols?

The emergence of desktop protocols was one of the key pieces of both the PC and Internet booms in the 80s and 90s. Prior to their emergence, connected terminals were "dumb," and smart PCs were unable to connect and effectively communicate.

It can be argued that the Internet revolution was fuelled by desktop protocols in much the same way that the Industrial Revolution was fuelled by the development of a mass-production model.

What Are the Problems to Solve?

Desktop protocols concern themselves with allowing desktop devices (usually PCs) to communicate efficiently and effectively. Several companies developed novel solutions to this problem.

Although many companies offered good solutions, it was not until the market "voted" on a clear winner before many vendors put their thought and muscle behind making the model work on a large scale.

Protocol Wars

Throughout the 1970s and 1980s, a number of desktop protocols emerged and competed for user acceptance (and market dominance). These protocols included Xerox Network Systems (XNS), DECnet, Banyan VINES, AppleTalk, Novell NetWare, and Transmission Control Protocol/Internet Protocol (TCP/IP). Although some of the other protocols are still in use, TCP/IP is dominant. Along the way, TCP/IP picked up and incorporated pieces from other protocols. One interesting thing is that all the desktop protocols that eventually fell to TCP/IP were all proprietary (owned by some corporation), whereas TCP/IP is an open standard.

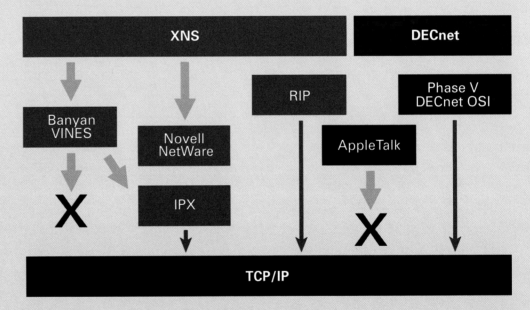

At-A-Glance—Thin Clients and PCs

Thin Clients

Most companies first started using computers with a "thin client" model, which put virtually all the computing power in a central processor or mainframe. The terminals were typically regarded as dumb. The user was prompted for data or commands, and the mainframe sent an updated picture of the screen.

Personal Computers

The advent of inexpensive, relatively powerful personal computers meant that the computing power moved to the desktop. Now all the programs resided in each computer, which was great for the user, but PCs quickly ran out of storage, they did not talk to each other, and each PC needed a dedicated printer. These limitations were very hard on the network administrators who had to keep up with software licenses and other management issues.

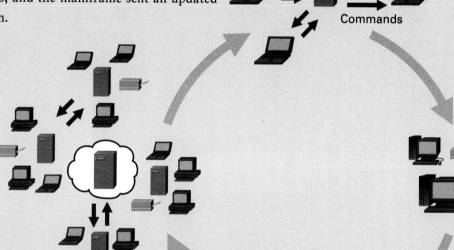

Screen Shots

Commands

Web Servers and the Return of Thin

Today's PCs are blazing fast and have gigs of storage, but with the emergence of the web and Internet as a business tool, many PCs behave as thin clients in common situations. Whether using a browser or running a Java applet or Flash application, the user enters information and receives screen shots, with most of the intelligence residing in the web servers.

Desktop Protocols

The advent of desktop protocols meant that PCs could talk efficiently and effectively with other devices. This advent also coincided with added power and more storage in PCs, so centralized servers functioned as just another drive on any given PC. Not only did this mean PCs could run more programs and more powerful programs, but also it was easier to manage software licenses. You could purchase fewer licenses because not everyone used any given program at the same time. Oddly, one of the biggest benefits of desktop protocols was shared printers. Now an entire floor can share a single printer through a print server. Despite many advances and cheaper printers, this aspect of desktop protocols is still here and likely to stick around.

SNA Infrastructure

Systems Network Architecture

Believe it or not, most of the networking concepts in this book are not new. Most networking issues were resolved in concept long ago when the same types of problems cropped up in the mainframe world. In fact, it is ironic that the trend towards web-based applications revives technologies similar to mainframe 3270 terminal applications.

IBM's mainframe-network infrastructure is referred to as Systems Network Architecture (SNA, pronounced "snah"). SNA was the prevailing enterprise network infrastructure. It was developed in the 1970s at IBM with an overall architecture similar to the Open System Interconnection (OSI) reference model. A mainframe running Advanced Communication Facility/Virtual Telecommunication Access Method (ACF/VTAM) serves as the center of an SNA network. ACF/VTAM is responsible for establishing all network sessions and for activating and deactivating network resources. SNA explicitly defines all resources, which eliminates the need for broadcast traffic and reduces header size.

As Transmission Control Protocol/Internet Protocol (TCP/IP) (and other desktop protocols such as the Novell Internetwork Packet Exchange (IPX)) gained acceptance in enterprise networks, companies faced having to support multiple network infrastructures. The desire for a common set of protocols grew. TCP/IP eventually became the protocol of choice for convergence mainly due to certain technical benefits and the open nature of the protocols, which facilitated support from multiple vendors. Additionally, with the wide acceptance of the Internet and corporate intranets, companies wanted their traditional non-IP infrastructure devices to communicate with the new IP devices.

Larger companies had, and continue to have, large investments in SNA equipment. Although the maintenance and annual upkeep for these devices is relatively more expensive as they grow older, companies want to bridge the two worlds of SNA and TCP/IP together.

It is the convergence of these two worlds that is relevant to Cisco networking. The three components of interest are the following:

- **Line consolidation**—With a single network infrastructure based on TCP/IP, you can collapse multiple single-protocol lines to remote locations into a single line.

- **Front-end processor (FEP) replacement**—Channel-attached routers can replace considerably more expensive FEPs (and other special-purpose mainframe channel-attached equipment).

- **Desktop consolidation**—Desktop computers required multiple protocol stacks (one for 3270 mainframe connectivity, one for TCP/IP, and one for a file- and print-sharing service such as Novell's NetWare). Multiple protocol stacks are expensive and difficult to support. Instead, TCP/IP can serve as the single transport for terminal emulation as well as the other services.

Why Are Companies Migrating Their SNA Networks?

Until recently, all midsize and large corporations, government institutions, and educational organizations ran their applications on IBM (and compatible) mainframes and midrange systems that ran primarily on SNA networks. SNA networks provided the following benefits:

- **High availability**—Well-designed SNA networks provided services around the clock and experienced little disruption in service: 99.99 percent or better availability.

- **Predictable response times**—Built around high transaction rates, SNA networks could provide predictable and consistent response times.

- **Secure**—SNA networks, by design, were difficult to hack into, thus providing secure access to mission-critical applications.

Despite these benefits, TCP/IP, which was considerably weaker in the preceding SNA characteristics, became popular because it addressed the following SNA weaknesses:

- **Lack of dynamic definition and configuration of resources**—You had to predefine everything in an SNA network. Although IBM addressed these issues later with its Advanced Peer-to-Peer Networking (APPN), TCP/IP had already taken hold with its more flexible and dynamic nature.

- **Proprietary protocols**—IBM defined, owned, and managed SNA. At the end of the 1980s, IBM customers began demanding support for protocols based on open standards. Rather than adopt an existing open standard, IBM attempted to introduce its own protocols into the public domain (APPN). However, APPN was more expensive and available on fewer platforms than TCP/IP.

Eventually, IBM's attempt to provide its own standards lost out to TCP/IP.

SNA to IP Migration Paths

Corporations could not migrate to IP in one sitting. Instead, they needed to take a methodical multistep approach to making the switch.

The first step to migration was the tunneling of existing SNA protocols across IP networks. As corporations began considering their migration, they discovered that they were managing at least two network infrastructures: TCP/IP and SNA. Companies had a choice: Run the IP traffic across an SNA backbone or vice versa.

For reasons stated earlier, SNA as a backbone didn't make sense. As a result, routers, which formed the core of IP internetworks, began supporting the encapsulation (tunneling) of SNA-related protocols. Some advantages realized with SNA encapsulation include the following:

- **Dynamic rerouting**—You can route IP-encapsulated SNA traffic around a failure using the inherently dynamic IP routing protocols.

- **Flexible encapsulation schemes**—SNA encapsulation allows for more flexible SNA device configurations and reduced polling across the backbone.

Cisco Systems introduced remote source-route bridging (RSRB) as a proprietary solution for SNA encapsulation. The industry has since adopted the data-link switching (DLSw) standard, which is widely accepted and implemented. Routers also provide the capability to encapsulate other types of legacy traffic, such as async and bisync.

The final step in the migration is a complete conversion to IP-based mainframe connectivity. You achieve this step through IP-based client applications and IP connectivity direct to the mainframe.

Index

About the Authors

Paul L. Della Maggiora

Paul currently runs his own consulting business in the areas of computer networking and education. Previously, he worked at Cisco Systems, Inc., from 1994–2003. At Cisco, Paul was involved with technical training and Cisco certification development. Originally starting out in the Cisco Technical Assistance Center, supporting routers, switches, and network management, he has moved on to perform product marketing, technical marketing engineering, and development in various capacities. Paul is CCIE No. 1522 in LAN switching and network management. He holds a Computer Science B.S. from the University of South Carolina. He has developed multiple boot camps, training courses, and labs over the years to help initiate college students, high school students, and interns into the world of networking. Prior to joining Cisco, he held network-related jobs in information systems at Lexmark, Duke Power, and the University of South Carolina Medical School. Paul is the coauthor of *Performance and Fault Management*, published by Cisco Press.

Jim Doherty

Jim Doherty is currently employed with Cisco Systems as a solutions marketing manager, with responsibility for Routing and Switching and Security. He also served as project manager on IP Telephony and Call Center Solutions. Over the past several years, he has taught professionals in both academic and industry settings on a broad range of topics, including electric circuits, statistics, economics, and wireless communication methods. Jim authored the Study Notes section of the *Cisco CCNA Exam #640-607 Flash Card Practice Kit*, published by Cisco Press. Jim holds a B.S. in Electrical Engineering from N.C. State University and an MBA from Duke University. Prior to joining Cisco, Jim worked for Ericsson Mobile Phones. Jim also served in the United States Marine Corps, where he earned the rank of Sergeant, before leaving to pursue an education.

Jim and Paul during one of their first collaborations.